In the Time before Steamships

IN THE TIME
BEFORE STEAMSHIPS

BILLY BUDD,
THE LIMITS OF POLITICS,
AND MODERNITY

THOMAS J. SCORZA

Northern Illinois University Press

DeKalb / 1979

*Publication of this book was made possible
by a grant from the Earhart Foundation.*

Excerpts taken from *Billy Budd, Sailor: An Inside Narrative* by
Herman Melville, edited from the manuscript with introduction
and notes by Harrison Hayford and Merton M. Sealts, Jr. (copyright
© 1962 by The University of Chicago) are reprinted with the
permission of the editors and The University of Chicago Press.
Excerpts taken from *Billy Budd, Sailor: An Inside Narrative* by
Herman Melville, edited, with an introduction and annotation,
by Milton R. Stern (copyright © 1975 by Milton R. Stern) are
reprinted with the permission of the editor and
The Bobbs-Merrill Company, Inc.

Library of Congress Cataloging in Publication Data
Scorza, Thomas J   1948–
   In the time before steamships.
   Bibliography: p.
   Includes index.
   1.   Melville, Herman, 1819–1891.   Billy Budd.
I.   Title.
PS2384.B7S35   813'.3   78-54746
ISBN 0-87580-071-8

In Memory of Jean Gutmann Meyer

ἔγνων οὖν καὶ περὶ τῶν ποιητῶν ἐν ὀλίγῳ τοῦτο, ὅτι
οὐ σοφίᾳ ποιοῖεν ἃ ποιοῖεν, ἀλλὰ φύσει τινὶ καὶ
ἐνθουσιάζοντες, ὥσπερ οἱ θεομάντεις καὶ οἱ χρησμῳδοί.

CONTENTS

PREFACE

AN EDITOR'S CRITICAL FOOTNOTE to a passage in Shakespeare led Herman Melville to note in the margin, "Peace, peace! Thou ass of a commentator!"[1] Considering Melville's famous frustrations with his own critics, his marginal note may well have been fairly representative of his considered views on the worth of literary criticism in general, and if so, there is no little irony in the fact that his own works have attracted such an incredibly large number of literary "commentators." However much Melville may have wished his books to "speak for themselves,"[2] the fact is that the serious student of Melville's works is confronted by a virtually insurmountable mass of criticism, much of which is contradictory, and all of which attempts to "speak for" the author. If the student turns to the literary critics to clear up his perplexity about Melville's intended meaning, he will not only find no easy answers, but he will also have difficulty taking in the very number of answers offered. While it may be true, as Henry James once observed, that the individual literary critic often manages to present a "strangely simplified" silhouette of his complex and full-bodied subject, the multiplicity of such simple outlines of Herman Melville has reintroduced the robust "confusion of life" into the attempt to understand him and his work.

There is the added apparent irony that Melville's works, and *Billy Budd* in particular, have attracted the attention of many nonliterary critics and commentators as well. *Billy Budd* has been the subject of comments by political scientists, psychologists, legal and religious scholars, historians, and other social theorists.[3] Since Melville questioned the wisdom of professional literary critics, one might assume that he would be positively contemptuous of the efforts made by literary amateurs to "speak for" him. Moreover, the critical offerings from outside the field of literary expertise have only added to the controversies generated within that field. As one now surveys this mass of conflicting expert and amateur criticism, one might indeed be led to the conclusion that Melville's wishes would have been better fulfilled had *all* his own "commentators" kept their "peace" too.

No one who writes books, however, seeks to remain anonymous or to be ignored. In particular, Herman Melville would not have labored on *Billy Budd* during the last years of his life unless he had something to say and unless he wanted to be heard.[4] Whatever may have been Melville's sentiments about contemporary literary criticism (whether it be of Shakespeare or of his own work), he tried virtually up to the moment of his death to write something that would endure and rescue his name from the critical obscurity of his last quarter-century. With this observation in mind, one might consider the fact that Melville's works have attracted so many serious critics not as an ironic counter to his openly expressed scorn for literary criticism and literary success, but as the fulfillment of a hope which he must have held deeper in his heart. Indeed, the controversies among his literary critics are but added insurance that his fame will endure, and the interest of his nonliterary critics is a certain guarantee that his fame will be widespread. In all, notwithstanding his caustic remarks about critics, Herman Melville would, I think, be well pleased not only by the variety and abundance of, but also by the disputes among, his "commentators." It is through these many and varied critics that Melville has captured the continuing audience of readers which eluded him during his lifetime.

It is, of course, a conveniently happy thought for one presenting yet another study of *Billy Budd* that Melville would welcome all additions to the secondary sources. And it is an especially happy thought for a political scientist that Melville would welcome even nonliterary "commentators" upon his books! Yet there is a very real and uncontrived sense in which *Billy Budd* explicitly invites nonliterary critics to reflect upon and learn from it. Indeed, even the literary criticism of the novel testifies constantly to its political, psychological, legal, religious, historical, and sociological implications. While there is, of course, the danger that the outside commentator might reduce what is a literary masterpiece to a mere tract from another discipline, it would be impossible to argue that *Billy Budd* is simply irrelevant to such nonliterary concerns as those mentioned above. It is in this spirit that I offer this political commentary upon *Billy Budd*.

I use the word "political" in the broadest sense of the term; therefore I do not deal with such matters as Melville's views on the partisan issues of his day. Rather, I see as the "political dimension" of *Billy Budd* the fact that it compels the reader to reflect upon a wide variety of the fundamental problems of political science and political philosophy. Among these problems are such matters as the contrasts between nature and convention, and between the demands of justice and the limits of law; the conflicts between authority and egalitarianism, and between conservatism and revolution; the contest between pious politics and secular ideology; and the question of the prerogatives and limitations of statesmanship. Moreover, I have adopted the hypothesis that Melville sought not only to induce reflection on these problems but also to teach his readers about them. *Billy Budd*, in my view, presents the reader with Melville's own thoughts on the nature of the best political regime,

the causes of political tragedy, and the limits of political life.
I have assumed that while, in the end, one may disagree with
Melville's teaching on these and other points, understanding
his teaching on its own terms is a necessary prior task, and
seeking his teaching is the only procedure that does justice to
the intention of his work.[5]

Admittedly, any conclusions reached in the kind of enterprise attempted here must be regarded as tentative. In the
first place, there is a sense in which no prose commentary can
do justice to the poetic power of a novel like *Billy Budd*. I do
not imply by this remark that I have romantic notions about
the works of poets or artists. In short, I certainly do not believe
that all creative literature is radically subjective or idiosyncratic
and grounded only in an author's own sentiments and passions,
so that the meaning of a work is beyond rational comprehension by a reader. On the contrary, as previously noted, I have
operated on the hypothesis that while writing *Billy Budd*,
Melville had a conscious and comprehensible teaching in mind
which he meant to convey to his readers. Rather, the tentative
character of my conclusions derives first from a respect for the
inherent limitations upon the attempt to translate a teaching
conveyed through poetic images and dramatic action into an
argumentative commentary. A dramatic novel like *Billy Budd*
causes a kind of interchange between the text and the reader
in which both become participants in a serious dialogue, and
as Socrates tells us at the end of Plato's *Phaedrus*, no written
discourse can measure up to the actual discourse between two
interlocutors.

My comments are also admittedly tentative because I have
adopted other hypotheses which are as open to debate as my
hypothesis about Melville's intention to teach through *Billy
Budd*. For instance, I have assumed that the only way to discern
Melville's teaching is to give full play to the text of *Billy Budd*,
and I therefore quote the text frequently, hoping that atten-

tion to detail will lead to the core of Melville's book. This procedural assumption in turn involves two other hypotheses. First, I have assumed that, despite the technically "unfinished" state of the *Billy Budd* manuscript, there is now a text of the novel with which one can confidently work. Secondly, I have assumed that this text takes precedence over any purported "historical sources" for the story of a young sailor's execution at sea. (I present further remarks on the first of these hypotheses in the Appendix, on the second in Chapter 1, and on both in footnotes throughout this study.) With hypotheses such as these, I can ask only for a tolerant hearing of my observations and conclusions.

I would summarize those conclusions, abstracting from the details and intricacies in my full text, as follows. Throughout, *Billy Budd* advances the pessimistic teaching that nature imposes insurmountable limitations upon human life and therefore that politics is marked by ineradicable strife, inevitable frustrations, and unavoidable calamity. At the same time, *Billy Budd* suggests that nature, the ultimate source of the limits of politics, is also the true author of political grandeur: nature's own noblemen are endowed with the heroic capacity to face nature's hostility and to reveal the natural glory of man in their fronting the admittedly unconquerable limits of political life. Furthermore, *Billy Budd* teaches that the modern age completes a critical and disastrous decline in the possibility of man's actually earning glory in the face of the perennial limits of politics. I argue that, for Melville, modernity—in its politics, its philosophy, and its science—represented the culmination of a fundamentally flawed project in which man attempted to deny both the supremacy of nature and the force of the limits it imposes upon man. Modern man finds tragedy and not the possibility of glory in the limits of politics because he attempts to conquer nature (as in modern science and enlightened messianism), or to strip nature of its fixed limits upon human potentiality (as in romanticism), or to turn his back upon nature as the definer of right (as in modern conservatism). The attempts to conquer, to level, or to ignore nature deprive man of the truth about his condition, leaving him either with a false optimism, which denies the limits which it is man's glory to front, or with a tragic inability to defend the natural character of the only true stature of which man is capable. Finally, I argue that Melville's analysis of the tragic character of modernity led him to understand the modern age as the full flowering of the original prideful project of rational philosophy, that project in which man first demonstrated the hubris that has become rampant in modern times. Thus, I argue that Melville should ultimately be understood as a poet like the Aristophanes of the *Clouds*, whose conservatism issued in an attempt to defend a poetic vision of political and moral virtue against the destructiveness of philosophy and pure reason. In other, here enticingly enigmatic words, I believe that in *Billy Budd*, Melville re-presented Socrates in the person of John Claggart, and he thereby gave us another episode in the "old quarrel between philosophy and poetry."[6]

I should acknowledge my indebtedness to my teachers, many of whom contributed greatly to the formal education that preceded this study and which will always direct my lifetime education. I would especially like to note my gratitude to my teachers at the University of Notre Dame and Claremont Graduate School, where I received my undergraduate and graduate degrees, respectively. As a student should, I hope that this book will cause my teachers a good deal of pleasure and as little embarrassment as possible.

At various stages in the process of writing and publishing this book, I received advice, help, and criticism from Sacvan Bercovitch, Robert Cantwell, Martin Diamond, Robert Horwitz, Irving Kristol, Herbert Storing, Stephen Tonsor, and

Preface

two anonymous manuscript reviewers. My debt weighs especially heavily in the cases of Professors Diamond and Storing, whose untimely deaths have deprived me of the opportunity of indicating to them my gratitude. Also, I am especially indebted to Milton R. Stern, who graciously consented to read, comment upon, and boost a stranger's strange study of a novel upon which he is the leading expert.

For the timely publication of this book, I gladly acknowledge my debts to the personal effort of Irving Kristol and the financial support of the Earhart Foundation.

I had intended to dedicate my first book to my wife, Judy, upon whose typing and love I am totally dependent. We have decided, however, to dedicate the book to the memory of Judy's mother, Jean Gutmann Meyer, whose understanding and love at a critical juncture was an important ingredient in our beginning a happy life together and whose death has left us with a sorrow that we cannot express.

Thomas J. Scorza
Gambier, Ohio
January 1978

Notes

[1] The editor's footnote attempted to explain a line in *Timon of Athens*. See Jay Leyda, *The Melville Log: A Documentary Life of Herman Melville, 1819–1891*, 2 vols. (New York: Harcourt, Brace, 1951), 1:290.

[2] Cited by John Mason Brown, "Hanged from the Yardarm," in *As They Appear* (New York: McGraw-Hill, 1952), p. 192.

[3] See, for example, Hannah Arendt, *On Revolution* (New York: Viking, 1965), pp. 74–83, 96; Rollo May, *Power and Innocence: A Search for the Sources of Violence* (New York: Norton, 1972), pp. 205–11; Jack W. Ledbetter, "The Trial of Billy Budd, Foretopman," *American Bar Association Journal* 58 (June 1972): 614–19; James H. Smylie, "Billy Budd: The Work of Christ in Melville," *Religion in Life: A Christian Quarterly* 33 (Spring 1964): 286–96; R. R. Palmer, "Herman Melville et la Révolution Française," *Annales Historiques de la Révolution Française* 26 (1954): 254–56; and Charles A. Reich, "The Tragedy of Justice in *Billy Budd*," *Yale Review* 56, New Series (Spring 1967): 368–89.

[4] According to Leon Howard, in *Herman Melville: A Biography* (Berkeley: University of California Press, 1951), p. 342, "Careless as [Melville] professed to be about literary fame in his later years, he could hardly have continued to strive so diligently with *Billy Budd* and with his poems had he not possessed a natural longing for such immortality as may be found in remembrance."

[5] Milton R. Stern, in *The Fine Hammered Steel of Herman Melville* (Urbana, Ill.: University of Illinois Press, 1957), p. 27, supports this point: "If any writer can be said to be prescriptive, Melville was. Necessarily so, because he was trying to tell America what the correct and incorrect courses of behavior and belief are."

[6] Plato *Republic* 607b; on Aristophanes' *Clouds*, see especially Leo Strauss, *Socrates and Aristophanes* (New York: Basic Books,

1966), pp. 11–53. And for a recent indication that the issues raised in the "old quarrel" are still with us, see Iris Murdoch, *The Fire and the Sun; Why Plato Banished the Artists* (Oxford: Clarendon Press, 1977).

INTRODUCTION

WHEN HARRISON HAYFORD and Merton M. Sealts, Jr., published what was intended to be a definitive edition of *Billy Budd* in 1962, they expressed the hope that "a comprehensive scholarly edition of the work will narrow the ground of disagreement and widen that of understanding" between the two major camps of criticism of the novel.[1] As it turned out, however, the distance between those critics who, in one way or another, interpreted *Billy Budd* as a conservative novel and those who saw it as a literary statement of radical rebellion was too great to be narrowed even by the monumental textual scholarship of Hayford and Sealts. The debate among the different critical parties survives to the present and continues to call the artistic integrity of *Billy Budd* into question. Indeed, the diametrical opposition between the various conservative and the various radical interpretations of the novel has led neutral critics to wonder whether *Billy Budd* has any real form or definite meaning beyond its very "ambiguity" or beyond a thematic inclination towards "nothingness."[2]

The earliest of the "conservative" critics interpreted *Billy Budd* in quasi-Christian terms and saw the novel as "the last will and spiritual testament of a man of genius . . . telling the story of the inevitable and utter disaster of the good and trying to convey to us that this must be so and ought to be so."[3] In like manner, other early critics saw the novel as Melville's "everlasting yea" or his "final affirmation."[4] *Billy Budd* was Melville's "testament of acceptance," a final novel in which the cosmic revolutionary who wrote *Moby-Dick* "is no longer a rebel." This loss of Melville's early rebelliousness was shown in the character of Billy Budd, who "has not, even under the severest provocation, any element of rebellion in him. . . . His nature spontaneously accepts whatever may befall." Captain Vere also embodied "this supreme quality of acceptance . . . with full consciousness, and weighted with the responsibility of understanding the natural naturalness of man's volition and the unnatural naturalness of the law."[5] Like his two final heroes, Melville supposedly had come to accept the universe as it is and with all its imperfections.

While the strictly political implications of these first literary views were somewhat subdued, the foundations of the corresponding political interpretations were present from the beginning. Melville supposedly had shown his acceptance of evil and the inevitable tragedy of the good in *Billy Budd*. Acceptance rose out of tragedy, in the view of most of the early critics, through the redemption implied in the death of Christ-like Billy Budd.[6] Billy's temporal tragedy is thus actually a signal of the way to spiritual salvation, the tragedy of innocence serving only to highlight the redemptive strength of innocence. The message of *Billy Budd* was more or less that of orthodox Christianity: whatever may be the success of evil in the temporal world, the final spiritual reckoning reconciles all imbalances and injustices, and real salvation is to be found only in the world of the spirit. The political stand appropriate for this world is then certainly not one of rebellion against whatever injustice or oppression may happen to afflict one during his brief life on earth. Since, for the early critics, Melville had come to see salvation and justice only in eternity, his temporal politics could be understood only in conservative terms: the redemptive sacrifice of Billy Budd both indicated and justified

Melville's tragic acceptance of convention, law, expediency, and authority. While the earliest critics concentrated upon Melville's Christian resignation, they thus also prepared the way for a secular picture of Melville's politics. In their presentation of Melville's Christian view of the battle between good and evil, they had also laid the foundation for the later claim that the Melville of *Billy Budd* was a Whig.[7]

It was precisely this political dimension of the first criticism of *Billy Budd* that led to a political reaction by later critics. In 1943, one critic raised the question of the story's concern for "social repercussions" rather than "personal ethics,"[8] and the question apparently brought to the forefront the political conservatism which had been implicit in the first critics' emphasis upon the matter of personal salvation. Now other critics arrived on the scene and found that they could overcome the problem posed by the superficially conservative tone of the novel by reading the narrative which is *Billy Budd* as an ironic creation of the author and by suggesting that the novel thus might best be understood as a work of irony.[9] By the end of the 1950s, one critic could summarize the later critics' argument with the earlier "acceptance" and "conservative" critics by calling *Billy Budd* a "testament of resistance."[10]

The "resistance" critics presented *Billy Budd* as an ironic statement that was consistent with the earlier, "rebellious" Melville. Rather than having indicated his own resignation to evil (and implicitly asking for ours), Melville had asked us once again in *Billy Budd* to follow him in his cosmic rebellion against evil. The novel showed "that it is wrong to submit to unjust law. Those in power, such as Vere, should do all they can to resist the evil inherent in any institution or government. . . . In a larger context, man should not resign himself to the presence of evil but must always strive against it." By "demonstrating the consequences of unresisting acquiescence" in Captain Vere's tyrannical condemnation of Billy Budd, Melville had once again called for a rebellion against worldly evil.[11] Thus, a novel which had previously been read as a Christian "testament of acceptance" or as a conservative manifesto now came to be read as a call for resistance to institutionalized evil in the name of justice, equality, nature, and the rights of man. Billy Budd was no longer to be seen as a sacrificial and redemptive hero but as a victim whose execution indicated the horror of acquiescence to the status quo. Alternately, Captain Vere was not a tragic hero of the law, but a villainous instrument of repression. The author of *Billy Budd* accepted neither Christ nor Burke: he was a poetic follower of Thomas Paine.[12]

Even a brief survey of the unresolved critical controversy over *Billy Budd* is sufficient to indicate that the division between the critics is essentially a *political* one. Nor is this surprising since, as Milton R. Stern recently pointed out, *Billy Budd* is in essence "political fiction." Like "almost all serious literature," *Billy Budd* is "political" not, of course, in the sense that it is concerned with the mere "*trappings* of human politics" (like parties, voting, and so forth), but in the sense that it forces us to think about "deep attitudes and visions . . . concerning the nature of human possibility and, therefore, . . . the nature and function of the state, the very concept of government."[13] Precisely because *Billy Budd* is so emphatically *political* in this way, critics have differed *politically* over its message. The story of the controversy over *Billy Budd* thus has as much to do with the political ideologies of the novel's many critics as it has to do with changing schools of literary criticism. "To put the matter most crudely, a critic will not be disposed to find that a writer he admires . . . is in the political 'enemy's' camp."[14] As Stern points out too, the change from the conservative to radical interpretations of *Billy Budd* clearly paralleled complex attitudinal changes among professors in departments of English in the United States, and this fact further emphasizes the difficulty of achieving nonpartisan scholarly objectivity in the criticism of political literature.

Stern's own critical evaluation of *Billy Budd* is noteworthy in this regard. Not only does he strongly imply that the "radical" critics of the novel have told us more about their own political views than about Melville's, but he also argues forcefully that *"Billy Budd* is a politically conservative tale" despite his own admitted "wish that Melville had developed an anti- or non-conservative orientation in the profundity of his ideas."[15] While Stern understands the difficulty of achieving objectivity, he does not deny that the achievement is possible, and he implicitly offers his own work as an example of just such an achievement. The implicit claim to objectivity here is in fact essential if presenting one's own views is to be something other than an exercise in futility. If the substance of *all* literary criticism were fully and simply determined by each critic's ideology, there would be no such thing as a true or right critical view and thus no real point to literary criticism, unless literary critics are willing to understand their project as the mere accumulation of an infinite number of equally acceptable perspectives.

A closer look at Stern's substantive remarks on *Billy Budd* can serve as an introduction to my own position. Stern argues that Melville's final novel must be understood in the context of the poetry which occupied Melville "during his last, retrospective years" and out of which the story of young Billy Budd gradually evolved. Stern finds Melville's late poetry to be of an "essentially conservative nature"; somewhere in his late "prose years," Melville's "rebellious attitudes [had] diminished—although his anger [had not]—and his doubts about human progress and the nobility of the common man had increased considerably." While *Billy Budd* is "made complex by all the bitterness Melville feels about fallen man, the doom of prelapsarian Billy, and historical necessity," nevertheless "the conservative tone of the tale is to be taken not ironically but at face value." In sum, in *Billy Budd*, the balance between Melville's earlier radical (or iconoclastic) and conservative sides had tipped decisively in favor of the latter.[16]

For Stern, Melville's conservatism consists in his "sense of history and of historical necessity . . . coupled with an insistence on human limitation and the consequent need for control and for guidance from the experience of the past—an insistence on law and precedence, together with a suspicion of change." According to Stern, however, the terms "conservative" and "radical" are too susceptible to changes in meaning as they are applied to "particular people and particular issues at particular times." More "useful" for defining "the continuing dialectic between left and right, between radical and conservative" are T. E. Hulme's terms "romantic" and "classicist." For Hulme and Stern, the romantic adheres to "a belief in inexhaustible human potential and, therefore, in individual liberty and in endless perfectibilitarian change." On the other hand, the classicist adheres to "a belief in the limited nature of human potential and the fallen nature of man, and therefore, in control and decorum and in the illusory quality of change and perfectibility." Relying on these definitions, then, Stern argues that the "conservative tale" of *Billy Budd* evidences the "classicism of [Melville's] old age."[17] Thus, while Stern's Melville is too angry to be a resigned Christian, he most certainly is a conservative or classicist believer in unconquerable human limitation and imperfection.

Now, I should indicate at the outset that I am in broad agreement with Stern's analysis, as far as it goes. My own final position is also that the Melville of *Billy Budd* is conservative in the sense that he stands in opposition to the belief that man is perfectible or capable of infinite progress. I am more interested, however, in delineating the precise character of Melville's conservatism and the foundations upon which that conservatism is based. I am interested thus in differentiating Melville's particular brand of conservatism from other brands, including those brands that might be represented by any of his characters. These interests ultimately lead me to make distinctions which Stern's method and terminology do not allow.

In the first place, I believe that Stern is too ready to see the "conservative tone" of the *Billy Budd* narrative as indicative of Melville's own final position and therefore, by implication, of Melville's own kind of conservatism. His inclination in this regard is no doubt prompted by his general argument with the position of the "radical" critics of the novel, who began by arguing that Melville spoke ironically in *Billy Budd*, and who later came to present the novel as one narrated by a conservative speaker to whom Melville was simply and always opposed.[18] While I agree with Stern that neither of these ironist approaches is supported by the text of *Billy Budd*, I do believe that the text supports the claim that Melville deliberately created *some* distance between his narrator and himself. While the one ironist position far too facilely presents the narrator and the author of *Billy Budd* as nearly absolute poles, Stern far too easily presents them as identical.

Quite simply, as *Billy Budd* first strikes the reader's eye, it presents the "true story" of a series of events which have been incorrectly recorded by "official" history. Alternately, the narrator of the novel purports to tell the historical truth about the execution of Billy Budd, a truth which has previously been concealed. Both the "true" and the "false" stories of Billy Budd, however, are parts of the fictional universe created by Herman Melville when he wrote his final novel. The speaker of the novel, who apparently understands the difference between true and false only within the context of this fictional universe, is as much a created part of that universe as the characters of whom he speaks. In the end, we cannot prejudge Melville's attitude towards his narrator any more than we can prejudge Melville's attitudes towards Billy, Vere, or Claggart, and we must at least begin with the notion that it is possible that Melville may agree *or* disagree with the conservatism, or the particular *kind* of conservatism, represented by his narrator's various judgments or prejudices. While this notion is certainly far more complex than the notions that the narrator and the author of *Billy Budd* are either simply identical or completely opposed, it at least correctly locates the standard for judging *how* the narrator and the author are related. The text of the novel carefully read, and not any preconceived assumptions, is the only proper guide for the critic.

My second disagreement with Stern will also serve to illustrate what I mean by "some" distance existing between the narrator and the author of *Billy Budd*. Stern argues that the novel is "classicist" and therefore that the conservative hero, Captain Vere, whom I see as clearly a Burkean figure, is a "sympathetic character."[19] While I would agree that Melville intends for us to sympathize with his Captain Vere, I would argue that, for this very reason, questions are raised about the adequacy of finally seeing Melville as conservative in the same sense as Captain Vere is conservative. There is no doubt that Vere is the narrator's hero and that the narrator can adequately be described as a Burkean conservative. But Melville has given his narrator a tale which, when closely read, shows that the tragedy aboard H.M.S. *Bellipotent* presupposes and grows with the decisions and the principled arguments of Captain Vere. (Most obviously, of course, it is Captain Vere's fateful decision to have Billy face John Claggart that first sets the story's tragic series of events into fast motion.) This observation does not mean, certainly, that Vere is a villain, but it most certainly implies that the conservative Vere's procedures and principles are not meant simply to be applauded. (I also do not imply that Melville's *true* hero would be fully perfect, but I do imply that such a true hero's imperfections would not be those of Captain Vere.) In any case, it is precisely this implication, that Vere's heroism is, in a particular way, imperfect, that alerts us to the possibility that Melville is attempting to show the reader things which are muted in the narrator's account of the events of the novel. I would argue that the most important of those things are the *limitations* of the kind of conservatism or classicism embodied by Captain Vere and the narrator. If *Melville* could be adequately understood as a conservative in the Burkean sense, his Burkean hero would win as much of our awe and respect as is won by the transcendent character of Lord Nelson. As it is, Captain Vere receives, as Stern himself sees, our sympathy, and this is the measure of the extent to which, in Melville's eyes, Vere is certainly preferable to the available alternatives and yet, more importantly, fatally flawed.

Thus, I believe that Stern's undifferentiated use of the terms "conservative" and "classicist" contributes to a blurring of the distinction which I see between the narrator and the author of *Billy Budd* and invites what I see as a questionable identification of the conservatism of Melville and the conservatism of Captain Vere. But going beyond these particular difficulties, I think that Stern's terminology is more generally inadequate for interpreting the ultimate implications of *Billy Budd*. More positively, I believe that the term "classicist" is simply too imprecise, that Stern's denial that Melville is a "romantic" is undermined by his own further views on Melville's role as artist, and finally that the antithesis between classicist and romantic conceals a deeper antithesis which is a more adequate context for the comprehension of *Billy Budd*. As will be explained, these three points are interrelated.

Generally, Stern associates the term "classicist" with a belief in human limitation or imperfection, a reliance upon tradition or history, a suspicion of change, and an advocacy of the need for legal restraint. While it is true, however, that these elements typically are joined together in one consistent complex of conservative political opinions, it is also true that these same general opinions can be held upon radically different philosophical grounds and therefore that any apparent agreement upon these opinions might conceal fundamentally more important disagreements. For instance, one could ascribe Stern's term "classicist" to the ancient views of Aristotle, or to the medieval views of Thomas Aquinas, or to the modern views of Edmund Burke, all of whom recognized human limitation, respected tradition, distrusted radical change, and celebrated law. Yet, each of these men arrived at these opinions from very different starting points: the ultimate guide to right political opinions was ordered nature for Aristotle, divine revelation for Aquinas, and history or human tradition itself for Burke.[20] Indeed, it would be impossible to understand the thought of any of these men without understanding these profound differences, and the fact that they all held classicist or conservative political opinions is almost an obstacle to the comprehension of the "profundity of [their] ideas." In like manner, the claim that Melville is a classicist does not, in itself, tell us what I believe would be *the* critical thing about such a Melville, namely, *why* he held the conservative political opinions ascribed to him. Did Melville arrive at his presumed political classicism by way of ancient political philosophy, or medieval Christianity, or modern Burkean conservatism, or some other avenue? What was intended by Stern's speaking of conservative Melville's "sense of history"? The term "classicist" is faulty precisely because it does not address itself to, let alone allow one to answer, such questions.

The inadequacy of the term "classicist" is matched by the fundamental inadequacy of the term "romantic," and the general problem with the two terms is evidenced by Stern's presentation of Melville's conception of his role as an artist. When he denied that Melville was a romantic, Stern linked Melville to "a belief in the limited nature of human potential" and presumably denied that Melville held "a belief in inexhaustible human potential." When Stern describes Melville's view of the power of human art, however, it is in terms which suggest that men are capable, through art, of virtually unlimited creative accomplishment:

> The creation of measured forms became for Melville the highest expression of the human spirit in its struggle with the overwhelming, dark forces of an incomprehensible universe both inside and outside man. . . . There was something protoexistentialist about Melville. . . . He seemed to see the universe as enormously beyond a single unifying shape, meaning, or purpose, at least for the uses of human comprehension. Whatever ordered meaning, whatever formal shape, whatever moral purpose man saw in his existence, man put there. Man's fate, man's identity become what men make of themselves, and the making of man is in the terrible struggle of that weak, limited, mortal, animal creature to create out of raw existence the meaningful forms that are expressions of his own spirit.[21]

These remarks seem scarcely reconcilable with Stern's central argument that Melville was a classicist in his belief in human limitation. Stern presents Melville as politically conservative and yet portrays "Melville the artist" in protoexistentialist terms which suggest that at the same time that Melville believed that men were limited, he also believed they were capable, through art, of their own apotheosis. Now it may be that an artist can have quite opposing political and vocational stances, but certainly it would *seem* to be more consistent to view Melville as a political romantic and as an artistic protoexistentialist, thereby linking Melville both politically and aesthetically with the general belief in "inexhaustible human potential." And yet what could then be made of the antithetical implications of

Billy Budd, which Stern sees as Melville's "politically conservative tale"? Is there a form in which conservatism or classicism may be receptive to an existentialist world-view?[22] Clearly, the answer to this question would require the kind of philosophical precision about fundamentals which, again, the term "classicist" simply does not provide.

The basic difficulty with the terms "classic" and "romantic" is that they represent reinterpretations of the older terms "ancient," "medieval," and "modern,"[23] and certain underlying distinctions have been lost in the process of this reinterpretation. It is the loss of these distinctions that has caused the apparent inconsistency in Stern's portrayal of Melville's politics and artistic vision. The term "classic" blurs the distinctions between ancient, medieval, and modern political conservatism and therefore avoids the question of the different premises upon which that conservatism may be based. With this question ignored, no preparation could be made for Stern's claim that Melville was both a political conservative and an artistic proto-existentialist. Stern's presentation of Melville's view of the power of art locates Melville among those whom one might call the avant-garde of the modern project, while Stern's presentation of Melville's politics does not tell us where Melville stands on the differences between ancient, medieval, and modern political conservatism. Beginning with the terms "classicist" and "romantic," Stern could not show what a more apparently consistent position would have shown, namely, that Melville's political conservatism was of a decisively modern variety and therefore of precisely that variety which could be linked to decisively modern views on the nature of art. This more consistent and more precise position would then be that Melville was a *modern* political conservative and a *modern* artist who denied the older contentions that man ought to be guided by nature or God and who argued instead that man is and ought to be guided only by his own will, that is, by his creative capacity, operating in the light of his own history. This modern Melville would then believe, in short, that man, and not nature or God, "is the master of all things."[24]

The essential link here between modernity and the advocacy of human mastery accords well with the understanding of "the quarrel between the ancients and the moderns" in Jonathan Swift's *Battel of the Books*. According to Swift's tale, the argument between the ancients and the moderns is reflected in the argument between a bee and a spider. The "ancient" bee lives on the bounty of nature without causing the "least Injury" to natural beauty and without supposing that it is free of an obligation to "Heaven" for its "Flights" and for its "Musick." The "modern" spider, on the other hand, boasts of "being obliged to no other Creature, but of drawing, and spinning out all" from himself, and the spider supposes that his great skill in "Mathematicks" shows his superiority to or conquest of natural limitations.[25] For Swift, ancient philosophy is characterized by its bee-like devotion to nature and by its acceptance of nature as the ordered standard for its speculative flights and philosophic music, while modern philosophy is characterized by its spider-like celebration of its own self-sufficiency and its power to overcome or to ignore nature. Swift's symbolic representation of the moderns, among whom, incidentally, he numbers Aquinas,[26] is especially noteworthy because the characteristics of modernity he presents are in fact shared by the three most prominent representatives of modernity in *Billy Budd*. That is, the Enlightenment's faith in the unlimited power of reason and science, Romanticism's denial of fixed natural ends, and Burkean Conservatism's rejection of nature in favor of history and human tradition all result in the severing of the connection the ancients saw between man and the fixed standards of nature, all of which were thought to exist independently of human action or human will. Whatever differences may exist among these and the other forms of

modern thought, all the moderns are joined in common opposition to the ancient notion that ordered nature is *the* given
and unchanging standard for human activity *and* the unconquerable source of human limitation.[27]

We were led to this brief consideration of "the quarrel
between the ancients and the moderns" in the process of in-
vestigating Stern's views of Melville's political and artistic
persuasions. The antithesis between the ancients and the moderns, however, is not the final context in which I propose to
place *Billy Budd*, although this antithesis does lead us to make
the distinctions necessary for discovering the final context
which I have in mind. The battle between the ancients and the
moderns is, I believe, the context for understanding Swift, who
showed in *Gulliver's Travels* a deep understanding of the essential differences between ancient political theory and practice, on the one hand, and modern political theory and practice,
on the other, and who chose the side of the ancients.[28] Nevertheless, while Melville both understood and rejected modernity
in a way which is comparable to Swift, I do not believe that he
concluded, with Swift, that the proper alternative to the
modern theory of politics was the ancient theory of politics.
More positively, I believe that while Swift saw the point where
the moderns broke away from the ancients as the decisive break
in Western history, Melville believed that the moderns were
merely the final, horrible product of the rationalistic project
which they shared with the ancients. For Melville, that is, the
ancient philosophers may have been somewhat less corrupt
than the moderns, but the decisive event in Western history
was nevertheless the birth of philosophy itself, and both ancient
and modern philosophy must thus be understood finally in
opposition to what preceded philosophy. Further, I believe
that, for Melville, the birth of philosophy was an emphatically
tragic event, amounting to the Fall of Man, and that the history
of philosophy, culminating in modern philosophy, reveals the

full dimensions of that fall. Modern philosophy, according to Melville, merely made obvious to all the destructive effect upon natural human happiness of philosophy itself.

In the end, I would see *Billy Budd* in the context of the opposition of philosophy and poetry, rather than of antiquity and modernity, or of classicism and romanticism. By the opposition of philosophy and poetry I mean the quarrel which we can witness in the *Clouds* of Aristophanes, in Plato's *Republic*, or in Sir Philip Sidney's *An Apology for Poetry*. We would see in these works that philosophy attempts to comprehend universals and therefore questions particulars; the philosopher desires to know, to reason, and to live the life of the mind and contemplation. Poetry, on the other hand, gives living form to universals, enabling the poet to influence and direct human action. While the philosopher, in short, ultimately aims beyond morality and politics, the poet celebrates good acts and heroic men. The philosopher subverts the unenlightened city and the lives of its citizens, while the poet, to paraphrase now the narrator of *Billy Budd*, "embodies in verse" the very "exaltations of sentiment" upon which the unphilosophic political community depends and which the city's true rulers must "vitalize into acts."[29] Melville, I believe, stands decisively with the poets and the unenlightened city against philosophers and philosophy. He claims, in the end, not to be a protoexistentialist creator, but to be the possessor of a poetic vision of hostile nature, of natural greatness, and of natural human limitation. He claims too that this vision is undermined by the philosophic or rational attempt to comprehend the universe, and he believes that the result of philosophy's questioning of the poetic vision of man has been the tragedy of man.

This final context for *Billy Budd* is reached, however, only through a thorough analysis of the initial thrust of the novel, the critique of modernity. From the beginning, *Billy Budd* calls attention to major political events of the modern age; the novel is explicitly and implicitly populated by the giants of modern political and philosophical thought; and constant reference is made to modern technological and scientific advances. I suggest below that the ultimate purpose of the concentration upon such elements of modernity is to contrast modernity and, for example, modern character-types with the natural, prephilosophic world and its character-types. In direct opposition to the argument that Melville is a *modern* conservative, I will contend that this contrast indicates Melville's total rejection of the whole of modernity and that, in the end, it is modernity's variegated denial of nature which Melville sees as its underlying flaw. It is from this latter contention, added to Melville's argument that the human denial of nature was born with philosophy, that I have derived my views on Melville's attack on philosophy itself. Hence, in first calling attention to *Billy Budd*'s delineation of the limits of modernity, I do not imply that Melville's concern was for the problems of only one historical epoch. On the contrary, in his presentation of the limits of the modern age, Melville was led to the perennial questions of human life. *Billy Budd* begins with a critique of the condition of modern man and ends with a teaching on the human condition as such. While its initial concern is with the limits of modern politics, its ultimate concern is with the character and limits of political life in *any* age. *Billy Budd* is, I believe, the timeless work of a poet of nature who took a complex stand against the otherworldly faith of Christianity, the secular confidence of modern radicalism, the mere conventionalism of modern conservatism, and the human hubris implied by either rationalism or protoexistentialism.

Notes

¹ Herman Melville, *Billy Budd, Sailor (An Inside Narrative)*, Reading Text and Genetic Text, Edited from the Manuscript with Introduction and Notes by Harrison Hayford and Merton M. Sealts, Jr. (Chicago: University of Chicago Press, 1962), Preface, p. v. (Unless otherwise noted, all references to the text of *Billy Budd* will be to this edition and, unless accompanied by additional footnote material, will be indicated in brackets or parentheses in the body of my text; references to the editorial apparatus of this edition will be identified as *H&S* and, unless accompanied by additional footnote material, also will be indicated in brackets or parentheses in the body of my text.)

See the Appendix to the present study for a discussion of the reasons for my use of the text of Hayford and Sealts.

² See especially Kenneth Ledbetter, "The Ambiguity of *Billy Budd*," *Texas Studies in Literature and Language* 4 (Spring 1962): 130–34, and Paul Brodtkorb, Jr., "The Definitive *Billy Budd*: 'But aren't it all sham?'" *PMLA* 82 (December 1967): 602–12; however, compare these with Ray B. West, Jr., "The Unity of 'Billy Budd,'" *Hudson Review* 5 (Spring 1952): 120–27.

³ John Middleton Murry, "Herman Melville's Silence," *Times Literary Supplement*, no. 1173 (10 July 1924), p. 433.

⁴ John Freeman, *Herman Melville* (New York: Macmillan, 1926), p. 136; Raymond Weaver, ed., *Shorter Novels of Herman Melville* (New York: Liveright, 1928), Introduction, p. li; and Lewis Mumford, *Herman Melville* (New York: Harcourt, Brace, 1929), p. 357.

⁵ E. L. Grant Watson, "Melville's Testament of Acceptance," *New England Quarterly* 6 (June 1933): 322, 323.

⁶ See, for example, Watson's remarks, ibid., pp. 321, 323, 327, and the observations by Mumford, *Herman Melville*, pp. 356–57. For a somewhat later view of Billy as Christ, see Nathalia Wright,

Melville's Use of the Bible (Durham, N.C.: Duke University Press, 1949), pp. 128–35.

⁷ For an excellent, brief description of the elements of the "Whig model" in politics, see Alexander M. Bickel, "Notes on the Constitution," *Commentary* (August 1975), pp. 53–57.

The path of the "conservative" criticism shows both the persistence of the "Christian" reading and the effort to develop a more secular conservative reading of the novel; see, for instance, the following: F. O. Matthiessen, *American Renaissance: Art and Expression in the Age of Emerson and Whitman* (New York: Oxford University Press, 1941), pp. 500–514; Charles Weir, Jr., "Malice Reconciled: A Note on Melville's *Billy Budd*," *University of Toronto Quarterly* 13 (April 1944): 276–85; William Ellery Sedgwick, *Herman Melville: The Tragedy of Mind* (Cambridge, Mass.: Harvard University Press, 1944), pp. 231–49; Wendell Glick, "Expediency and Absolute Morality in *Billy Budd*," *PMLA* 68 (March 1953): 103–10; Richard Harter Fogle, "*Billy Budd*: The Order of the Fall," *Nineteenth-Century Fiction* 15 (December 1960): 189–205; Edward H. Rosenberry, "The Problem of *Billy Budd*," *PMLA* 80 (December 1965): 489–98; Jane Donahue, "Melville's Classicism: Law and Order in His Poetry," *Papers on Language and Literature* 5 (Winter 1969): 63–72; Janis Stout, "Melville's Use of the Book of Job," *Nineteenth-Century Fiction* 25 (June 1970): 69–83; and Christopher W. Sten, "Vere's Use of the 'Forms': Means and Ends in *Billy Budd*," *American Literature* 47 (March 1975): 37–51.

⁸ T. T. E., "Melville's *Billy Budd*," *Explicator* 2 (December 1943), Query 14.

⁹ Joseph Schiffman, "Melville's Final Stage, Irony: A Reexamination of *Billy Budd* Criticism," *American Literature* 22 (May 1950): 128–36.

¹⁰ Phil Withim, "*Billy Budd*: Testament of Resistance," *Modern Language Quarterly* 20 (June 1959): 115–27.

¹¹ Ibid., pp. 121, 127.

¹² According to Hayford and Sealts, "the opposing positions" of Burke and Paine "concerning the doctrine of abstract natural rights lie behind the dialectic of" the novel; see *H&S*, p. 138.

Notes

For additional elaboration and variations of the "resistance" reading, see the following: Arthur Sale, "Captain Vere's Reasons," *Cambridge Journal* 5 (October 1951): 3–18; Leonard Casper, "The Case against Captain Vere," *Perspective* 5 (Summer 1952): 146–52; Karl E. Zink, "Herman Melville and the Forms—Irony and Social Criticism in 'Billy Budd,'" *Accent* 12 (Summer 1952): 131–39; Lawrance Thompson, *Melville's Quarrel with God* (Princeton: Princeton University Press, 1952), pp. 355–414; Ray B. Browne, "*Billy Budd*: Gospel of Democracy," *Nineteenth-Century Fiction* 17 (March 1963): 321–37; and Kingsley Widmer, "The Perplexed Myths of Melville: *Billy Budd*," *Novel* 2 (Fall 1968): 25–35.

[13] Milton R. Stern, ed., *Billy Budd, Sailor (An Inside Narrative)* (Indianapolis: Bobbs-Merrill, 1975), Introduction, pp. xix–xx. (See the Appendix to the present study for a discussion of Stern's text.)

[14] Ibid., p. xlii.

[15] Ibid., pp. xxxix, xliv.

[16] Ibid., pp. xiv, xvii, xxxix, xxxiv. Stern's full argument that the Melville of *Billy Budd* was a "conservative" deserves very careful reading; see pp. xiv–xl.

[17] Ibid., pp. xviii, xx–xxi.

[18] For Stern's views on the "conservative tone" of *Billy Budd*, see ibid., pp. xxxi, xxxiv.
Compare Schiffman, "Melville's Final Stage, Irony" and Withim, "Testament of Resistance" with Thompson, *Melville's Quarrel with God* (especially pp. 360, 373) on the question of whether Melville himself speaks ironically in *Billy Budd*, or ironically uses a conservative narrator whose judgments he opposes.

[19] Stern, ed., *Billy Budd, Sailor*, Introduction, p. xxxiv.

[20] On the differences between Aristotle and St. Thomas, see Harry V. Jaffa, *Thomism and Aristotelianism* (Chicago: University of Chicago Press, 1952); on Burke's reliance upon tradition, see Leo Strauss, *Natural Right and History* (Chicago: University of Chicago Press, 1953), pp. 294–323.

[21] Stern, ed., *Billy Budd, Sailor*, Introduction, pp. xiv–xv.

²² Stern claims, and I believe that he is ultimately correct, that
it is not "inconsistent to identify a man as at once conservative and
protoexistentialist," although I do not believe that *Melville* was
such a man. It is also true, however, as Stern himself admits, that
"existentialism, with its view that man may achieve any possible
change and identity through the intense exercise of his will and
choice, is generally allied with radical and revolutionary postures."
Hence, it is necessary either to *show* in what form conservatism
may be allied with existentialism, or to demonstrate how an artist
can embody opposing political and vocational stances without
being inconsistent. A just complaint against "the tyranny of labels"
is an inadequate response to the "generally" held belief that "radical" and "existentialist" are the two more compatible labels. See
ibid., p. xviii.

²³ Leo Strauss, "The Three Waves of Modernity," in *Political
Philosophy: Six Essays by Leo Strauss*, ed. Hilail Gildin (Indianapolis: Bobbs-Merrill, 1975), p. 93.

²⁴ Ibid., p. 85.

²⁵ Jonathan Swift, *A Full and True Account of the Battel
Fought Last Friday Between the Antient and the Modern Books in
St. James's Library*, in *The Prose Works of Jonathan Swift*, ed.
Herbert Davis, 14 vols. (Oxford: Basil Blackwell, 1939–68),
1:149–50.

²⁶ Ibid., p. 152. In the chapters to follow, I argue that for Melville the Christian alternative also dropped from contention.

²⁷ See Leo Strauss, "On Classical Political Philosophy," in Gildin, ed., *Political Philosophy*, pp. 59–79, for a short statement on
the character of ancient political philosophy. See also "What is
Political Philosophy?" and "The Three Waves of Modernity,"
ibid., pp. 3–57, 81–98. The character of the quarrel between ancients and moderns is studied definitively in Professor Strauss's
Natural Right and History, and *Thoughts on Machiavelli* (Glencoe, Ill.: Free Press, 1958).

²⁸ Allan Bloom, "An Outline of *Gulliver's Travels*," in *Ancients
and Moderns*, ed. Joseph Cropsey (New York: Basic Books, 1964),
pp. 238–57.

²⁹ Compare Aristophanes *Clouds*; Plato *Republic* 595a–608c; Sir Philip Sidney, *An Apology for Poetry*, ed. Forrest G. Robinson (Indianapolis: Bobbs-Merrill, 1970), pp. 18–41; and *Billy Budd, Sailor*, p. 58. See also Leo Strauss, *Socrates and Aristophanes* (New York: Basic Books, 1966), pp. 3–8, 311–14.

For an indication of Melville's notions about "true poets" and the ability of poets to "master all mortals," see *Mardi: and a Voyage Thither*, in *The Writings of Herman Melville*, ed. Harrison Hayford, Hershel Parker, and G. Thomas Tanselle, 15 vols. (Evanston and Chicago: Northwestern University Press and The Newberry Library, 1968–   ), 3:397, 437–38. On the poet Melville's complex understanding of the differences between his own thoughtful "diving" and the ways of such "philosophers" as Emerson ("this Plato who talks thro' his nose"), see his letter to Evert A. Duyckinck, 3 March 1849, in *The Letters of Herman Melville*, ed. Merrell R. Davis and William H. Gilman (New Haven: Yale University Press, 1960), p. 79.

In the Time before Steamships

1

An Inside Narrative

I N CHAPTER 29 OF *Billy Budd*, the next to last chapter of
the novel, the narrator presents a journalistic account of
the story he has told and is about to complete. Having been
written within a "few weeks after the execution" of Billy Budd,
the news account "appeared in a naval chronicle of the time,
an authorized weekly publication." According to the narrator,
the journal's news story "was doubtless for the most part written in good faith, though the medium, partly rumor, through
which the facts must have reached the writer served to deflect
and in part falsify them." The chronicle's "account of the
affair" aboard H.M.S. *Bellipotent* is as follows:

"On the tenth of the last month a deplorable occurrence
took place on board H.M.S. *Bellipotent.* John Claggart, the
ship's master-at-arms, discovering that some sort of plot was
incipient among an inferior section of the ship's company,
and that the ringleader was one William Budd; he, Claggart,
in the act of arraigning the man before the captain, was
vindictively stabbed to the heart by the suddenly drawn
sheath knife of Budd.

"The deed and the implement employed sufficiently suggest that though mustered into the service under an English name the assassin was no Englishman, but one of those aliens adopting English cognomens whom the present extraordinary necessities of the service have caused to be admitted into it in considerable numbers.

"The enormity of the crime and the extreme depravity of the criminal appear the greater in view of the character of the victim, a middle-aged man respectable and discreet, belonging to that minor official grade, the petty officers, upon whom, as none know better than the commissioned gentlemen, the efficiency of His Majesty's navy so largely depends. His function was a responsible one, at once onerous and thankless; and his fidelity in it the greater because of his strong patriotic impulse. In this instance as in so many other instances in these days, the character of this unfortunate man signally refutes, if refutation were needed, that peevish saying attributed to the late Dr. Johnson, that patriotism is the last refuge of a scoundrel.

"The criminal paid the penalty of his crime. The promptitude of the punishment has proved salutary. Nothing amiss is now apprehended aboard H.M.S. *Bellipotent*."[1]

The news account sustains Claggart's charge against Billy Budd, incorrectly reports how Billy killed Claggart, praises the master-at-arms, and applauds Billy's swift execution. Also, the news story denies the English birth with which the narrator had definitely credited Billy and imputes a degree of patriotism to Claggart which implicitly cancels the narrator's earlier expressed doubts about the place of birth of the master-at-arms.[2] In any case, according to the narrator, this news item, "appearing in a publication now long ago superannuated and forgotten, is all that hitherto has stood in human record to attest what manner of men respectively were John Claggart and Billy Budd."[3]

The discrepancies between the "authorized" journal's

newspaper account of the events aboard H.M.S. *Bellipotent* and the narrator's own account of those events place his narrative in high relief and ultimately raise questions concerning Melville's intentions in writing the story. In the first place, the obvious contrasts between the newspaper record and the narrator's story have important implications for the narrator's statements concerning the veracity of his own account. He tells the reader that his story "is no romance," that "the symmetry of form attainable in pure fiction cannot so readily be achieved in a narration essentially having less to do with fable than with fact," and that his narration is "truth uncompromisingly told."[4] Thus, from the point of view of the narrator, his narrative and the chronicle's account are related as historical truth to historical falsehood. Both accounts are, however, parts of a work of fiction, *Billy Budd, Sailor (An Inside Narrative)*, and the reader must thus consider in turn the implications which Melville, as author, ultimately seeks to give to the narrator's words, "romance," "fiction," "fact," and "truth." The device of the contrasting journal's account thus both creates historical verisimilitude for the rendering of the main narrative and raises for the reader the question which Melville asked throughout his work, What is truth?

The distinction being made between the narrator and author, and hence the distinction beneath the problem of the levels of truth in *Billy Budd*, is particularly appropriate for Melville's works. Even in his most autobiographical novels, *Typee, Omoo, Redburn,* and *White-Jacket*, Melville carefully created a narrator sufficiently distinct from himself to allow considerable freedom for his artistic expression. In his first two works, Melville's "other self" was dictated partly by prudential considerations concerning his criticism of the South Seas missionaries and his erotic descriptions of life in Paradise, but he continued the practice even in the admittedly romantic *Mardi*, in which the narrator goes nameless until his apotheosis as the demigod Taji. In *Billy Budd,* the distinction between the narrator and the author is the background for the dialogs between the narrator and "an honest scholar, my senior" and "a writer whom few know," dialogs in which Melville is able to cite himself as authority.[5] In all, as used in *Billy Budd,* the device creates a tension between the author's fictional creation and the narrator's "authentic" tale, a tale which purports only to set the historical record straight on Billy Budd.

It is, in part, the failure to distinguish between narrator and author that has led some critics to see *Billy Budd* as Melville's thinly veiled contribution to the recurrent controversy surrounding the *Somers* mutiny affair in 1842. Charles R. Anderson, for instance, read the narrator's claims that his story was "no romance" and "fact" as equivalent to an assertion on Melville's part that *Billy Budd* was the "inside story" of the *Somers* affair, revealed to the author by his cousin, Lt. Gansevoort.[6] Such a reading of the story, however, would see *Billy Budd* as a historical work and, given the controversy over the historical truth about the *Somers* affair, would ultimately reduce Melville's novel to the standing of a mere partisan tract. Further, this reading ignores the implied lesson of the contrast between the naval chronicle and the narrator's tale, namely, that truth is not to be found in recorded history. In fact, the search for historical sources of *Billy Budd* as keys to its meaning actually reverses the lesson Melville would have his readers learn, for such a search assumes that recorded history can plumb the depths of art, while *Billy Budd* asserts in the end that only art can reveal the "inside" truth with which recorded history is unconcerned. Anderson himself, after the damage had been done, went on to say: "In *Billy Budd,* borrowing is reduced to a minimum, and imaginative invention counts for almost everything that makes it, as one critic declares, a masterpiece in miniature."[7]

The opposite reading, the assertion that the narrator and

the author of *Billy Budd* are simply and always opposed, was presented by Lawrance Thompson in *Melville's Quarrel with God*. Thompson's reading was an attempt to render an ironist interpretation of *Billy Budd* in the face of all the obstacles to such a reading by creating grounds for a wholesale reversal of the surface tone of the story. Thus, the narrator is seen as "stupid" and "bland," and his view of events and personalities aboard H.M.S. *Bellipotent* may be simply dismissed.[8] In effect, the dismissal of the surface reading of the story can allow the critic to replace the author as the creator of a work's meaning; the burden of proof for such an ironist reading thus must always rest upon the one who would read between the lines.[9] Thompson had good reasons to be dissatisfied with either the historical readings of *Billy Budd* or those readings which complacently set the narrator's story down as Melville's own conservative "testament of acceptance," thereby ignoring the levels of meaning that arise from the distinction between narrator and author. There are no grounds, however, for the assertion that Melville would have the reader simply disregard or reject the narrator's judgments entirely, and, as will be argued here, the effort to work a complete reversal of the story's surface tone in order to arrive at its "inner" truth is far too simplistic an approach to the novel.

In *Redburn*, Melville had one of his earlier narrators note how the historical record of human events, specifically as given by news accounts, drastically reduced the dimensions of human life. Having described the fatal workings of "a malignant fever" among the crowded and impoverished emigrants in the steerage of his ship, young Redburn observes:

> But the only account you obtain of such events is generally contained in a newspaper paragraph, under the shipping-head. *There* is the obituary of the destitute dead, who die on the sea. They die, like the billows that break on the shore, and no more are heard or seen. But in the events, thus merely

initialized in the catalogue of passing occurrences, and but glanced at by the readers of news, who are more taken up with paragraphs of fuller flavor; what a world of life and death, what a world of humanity and its woes, lies shrunk into a three-worded sentence! [10]

The naval chronicle's account of the affair aboard H.M.S. *Bellipotent* is witness to the fact that even a news story of more than "a three-worded sentence" can only shrink the "world of humanity." And the whole of which the naval chronicle is a part, the novel which Melville presents as "An Inside Narrative" should not be seen as merely another, albeit still longer "catalogue of passing occurrences," but rather as a different kind of writing altogether. What the narrator presents as a contrast between the historically accurate and the historically inaccurate is actually the author's means of approaching a truth which is beyond the purview of historical writing. The narrator's internal lesson, that a historical record of events does not reveal the truth, must be applied by the critic to Melville's creation, *Billy Budd, Sailor*, as a whole. The narrator's "truth uncompromisingly told" thus speaks, for the author, of a truth beyond history, and when the narrator says his story is "restricted . . . to the inner life of one particular ship and the career of an individual sailor," the reader hears of an "inner life" which is something beyond a historical record, accurate or inaccurate, of passing events.[11]

Furthermore, the negative view of recorded history which rises out of the "Inside Narrative's" contrasting accounts of the story of Billy Budd is consistent with Melville's fuller portrayal of history and the historian in *Mardi*. There the narrator, going among the Mardians as the demigod Taji, is joined by a king, a philosopher, a poet, and a historian in the search for the lost maiden, Yillah. The search through the Mardian universe allows the author to create a continuous seminar on politics, philosophy, poetry, and history, the latter embodied in the legend-teller Mohi, the "Herodotus" and "Diodorus" of the group.[12] At one point, an argument arises between Mohi and the group's poet, Yoomy, over who shall claim the honor of relating the legend of a mysterious islet. In answer to Mohi's charge that poets are too silly to relate a plain tale, Yoomy asserts:

> Much truth is not in thee, historian. Besides, Mohi: my songs perpetuate many things which you sage scribes entirely overlook. Have you not oftentimes come to me, and my ever dewy ballads for information, in which you and your musty old chronicles were deficient? In much that is precious, Mohi, we poets are the true historians; we embalm; you corrode.

While it is, of course, hazardous simply to identify Yoomy's expressed opinion with Melville's, the implication throughout *Mardi* is that Melville was using his characters' negative judgments of each other to reveal his own opinions of the limitations of each character type, without necessarily endorsing the characters' positive views of themselves. Thus, it is significant that after the above observation of Yoomy, the philosopher Babbalanja interrupts, saying, "Peace, rivals . . . you are each nearest the right, when you speak of the other; and furthest therefrom, when you speak of yourselves."[13] The authorized naval journal indicates that the author of *Billy Budd* still agreed with Yoomy's opinion of history and historians and thus that the truth of the novel which he subtitled "An Inside Narrative" is again a truth which transcends history and corrosive historical writing.

Further insight into the importance and the implications of the subtitle to the story may be had through a consideration of Melville's mood as he wrote *Billy Budd*. Writing in literary obscurity and leisurely retirement as he approached and then passed his seventieth year, Melville apparently created the novel in an atmosphere of intense retrospection about his seafaring past.[14] These youthful memories, and the care he could and naturally would give his work in the final years of his life combine both to indicate the importance of the details of *Billy Budd*, including the subtitle, and to suggest Melville's literary youth as a further source of insight into that subtitle's significance.

Melville had confronted the problem of the truth of a "narrative" in his very first novel, *Typee*. The work was published in England by John Murray, whose "Colonial and Home Library" specialized in "true adventure" narratives, and from the first, Murray had doubts about the veracity of Melville's story. The debate over the truth of *Typee* was joined by critics on both sides of the Atlantic, in large measure because Melville's artistic ability was considered to be too great to be the product of a mutinous "ordinary seaman."[15] In the Preface to *Typee*, Melville addressed himself to the question of his narrative's veracity and at the same time defended himself for his harsh words about the South Seas missionaries. To sailors, he wrote, "many things which to fire-side people appear strange and romantic . . . seem as common-place as a jacket out at elbows." And if the things narrated seem "entirely incomprehensible" to the reader, the author can only assure him that "he has stated such matters just as they occurred, and leaves every one to form his own opinion concerning them; trusting that his anxious desire to speak the unvarnished truth will gain for him the confidence of his readers."[16]

Melville was obviously on the defensive after Murray expressed his doubts about *Typee*; and while he claimed he had desired to speak only the "unvarnished truth," he refrained, as Leon Howard noted, from claiming in his Preface that he had *done* so. He appears to have been exasperated by his editor's concentration on the question of the "truth" of his story, and as Howard also noted, faced with this "demand that his 'yarn' be certified as the 'truth,' he could only ask, with jesting

Pilate, 'What is truth?' and evade, as best he could, the answer."[17] Melville realized, that is, that his story was not "true" in the sense the publisher and critics demanded because he had taken many artistic liberties in writing his experiences into a "yarn." He was determined, however, to defend his published work, and he therefore capitalized on his ability to assert with honesty that his story was basically "authentic." Since he also knew that the "unvarnished truth" was not identical to the historical "truth" demanded by his critics, he could respond to their charges on their own ground and simultaneously assert, quietly, that his interests were other than those of the mere historian.

Melville entitled his second work, *Omoo: A Narrative of Adventures in the South Seas*, published a year after *Typee*, in 1847. In the Preface to *Omoo*, Melville said he was presenting "a circumstantial history of adventures befalling the author" and offering "a *familiar* account of the present condition of the converted Polynesians." But he went on to apologize for his lack of "precision with respect to dates," thereby attempting to defend himself in advance for the liberties he had taken with the time span of his "circumstantial history." And in ending his Preface, he subtly admitted to the reader that his work was something more than history:

> In no respect does the author make pretensions to philosophic research. In a familiar way, he has merely described what he has seen; and if reflections are occasionally indulged in, they are spontaneous, and such as would, very probably, suggest themselves to the most casual observer.[18]

His "spontaneous reflections," of course, were far deeper than casual observations, and *Omoo* makes clear that its author was interested in making some very thoughtful observations in a work otherwise, as Melville wrote to his publisher, "calculated for popular reading."[19] *Omoo* was, in fact, a combination of

Melville's desire to speak the truth about enlightened civilization and its effect on Polynesia and his calculated effort to compete in the market for "true adventure" stories. He wrote, therefore, for two audiences.

Melville's continued annoyance with his critics' incredulity climaxed in his Preface to *Mardi*, which he began as a sequel to *Typee* and *Omoo* but developed into "a real romance." Addressing himself again to the problem of narratives and truth, he wrote:

> Not long ago, having published two narratives of voyages in the Pacific, which, in many quarters, were received with incredulity, the thought occurred to me, of indeed writing a romance of Polynesian adventure, and publishing it as such; to see whether, the fiction might not, possibly, be received for a verity: in some degree the reverse of my previous experience.[20]

In speaking of "a verity" in a book like *Mardi*, in which the verities sought are eternal, Melville was obviously using his Preface to shift the grounds of the debate over his works' veracity. His "true adventures" had been received as fictions, thereby obscuring the real truth of what their author had to say, and he now hoped his fiction might be accepted as *truth*. The dry humor of Melville's remark in the Preface served both to reveal and conceal the author's intentions, the effect depending upon the interests and attention of his readers. In the text of *Mardi* itself, and in the context of *its* true universe, the philosopher Babbalanja spoke what must have been Melville's own thoughts: "I . . . assert that what are vulgarly called fictions are as much realities as the gross mattock of Dididi, the digger of trenches."[21]

Mardi was a critical failure, most reviewers decrying the metaphysical gymnastics of the storyteller who had given them *Typee* and *Omoo*. Melville's failure to please the critics had immediate financial consequences, and he undertook *Redburn* and *White-Jacket* in an effort to meet his monetary obligations and regain his lost popularity. Yet he attempted to do so only by taming his wildest flourishes and not by surrendering his true goals. A letter to his father-in-law, Chief Justice Lemuel Shaw, reveals Melville's mind:

> For Redburn I anticipate no particular reception of any kind. It may be deemed a book of tolerable entertainment; —& may be accounted dull.—As for the other book, it will be sure to be attacked in some quarters. But no reputation that is gratifying to me, can possibly be achieved by either of these books. They are two *jobs*, which I have done for the money—being forced to it, as other men are to sawing wood. And while I have felt obliged to refrain from writing the kind of book I would wish to; yet, in writing these two books, I have not repressed myself much—so far as *they* are concerned; but have spoken pretty much as I feel.—Being books, then, written in this way, my only desire for their "success" (as it is called) springs from my pocket, & not from my heart. So far as I am individually concerned, & independent of my pocket, it is my earnest desire to write those sort of books which are said to "fail."—Pardon this egotism.[22]

Melville was thus clearly attempting to satisfy the demands of the public and the strivings of his mind at the same time. His works were thus both tales meant to be "tolerable entertainment" and quieter means of speaking "pretty much" as he felt. He summed up his situation in a letter to Nathaniel Hawthorne, written just before the publication of *Moby-Dick* in 1851:

> What I feel most moved to write, that is banned,—it will not pay. Yet, altogether, write the *other* way I cannot. So the product is a final hash, and all my books are botches.[23]

Celebrated as a writer of "true adventures," Melville was frustratingly unpopular as the kind of writer he wished to be.

Indeed, whenever he strayed from his "botches" after *Moby-Dick* and attempted to experiment in less rousing literary worlds, he met with critical and popular disapproval, and he was eventually forced to abandon the life of the professional author for the security of the life of an inspector of customs.

Some four decades after *Moby-Dick*, Melville worked intently on *Billy Budd, Sailor*, an "Inside Narrative" once again aimed at the "uncompromising truth." Returning in his retirement to a tale of the sea, Melville contrasted some fictional events with a fictional news account of those events to see again whether fiction could yield "a verity." A novel which, on its own terms and within its own universe, merely told the true story of Billy Budd, was again a narrative about a far more profound truth. In all, thus, Melville's final novel must be read with the same care and subtlety with which the younger Melville read another great poet:

For in this world of lies, Truth is forced to fly like a scared white doe in the woodlands; and only by cunning glimpses will she reveal herself, as in Shakespeare and other masters of the great Art of Telling the Truth,—even though it be covertly and by snatches.[24]

Notes

[1] Pp. 130–31. Hayford and Sealts point out that the chronicle's account does not mention Vere by name nor refer to the captain's subsequent death. They attribute these omissions to the fact that "the substance of the present chapter" antedates Melville's later elaboration of Vere's character, and hence the editors imply that Melville would have corrected these omissions had he lived to "finish" the substance of *Billy Budd*. In light of the other, deliberate inaccuracies in the chronicle's account, however, there is no reason to conclude that these so-called "inconsistencies," in themselves, "are evidence that *Billy Budd* was literally 'unfinished'—Mrs. Melville's term . . . —at the time of [Melville's] death." See *H&S*, p. 200.

[2] For Billy's lineage, see p. 51, and for Claggart's, p. 65.

[3] P. 131. Hayford and Sealts regard this statement as inconsistent with the next chapter's presentation of the ballad, "Billy in the Darbies," as having been "printed at Portsmouth." Nevertheless, "human record" suggests some kind of historiographical writing, and thus the accuracy of the narrator's statement here may not be affected by the existence of a sailor's ballad. See again *H&S*, p. 200.

[4] Pp. 53, 128. As background for the following observations about the implications of Melville's use of his titles, see the letters to John Murray of 15 July 1846 and 29 January 1847 in *The Letters of Herman Melville*, ed. Merrell R. Davis and William H. Gilman (New Haven: Yale University Press, 1960), pp. 40, 53; see also *H&S*, plates V and VI (following p. 4) and pp. 19–20.

[5] Pp. 74, 114; see *H&S*, pp. 38, 161, 183. On the general problem of narrator and author, see Wayne C. Booth, *The Rhetoric of Fiction* (Chicago: University of Chicago Press, 1961), pp. 149–65. Concerning Melville's narrators, see Warner Berthoff, *The Example of Melville* (Princeton: Princeton University Press, 1962), pp. 115–32. Also, compare the internal dialogue of *Billy Budd* with Taji's talk with his "Mentor" in *Mardi: and a Voyage Thither*, in

[*15*]

The Writings of Herman Melville, ed. Harrison Hayford, Hershel Parker, and G. Thomas Tanselle, 15 vols. (Evanston and Chicago: Northwestern University Press and The Newberry Library, 1968–), 3:174–77.

⁶ Charles R. Anderson, "The Genesis of *Billy Budd*," *American Literature* 12 (November 1940): 335, 338, 340. See also Newton Arvin, "A Note on the Background of *Billy Budd*," *American Literature* 20 (March 1948): 51–55.

⁷ Anderson, "The Genesis of *Billy Budd*," p. 346. For the narrator's mention of the *Somers* affair and his reminder that "the circumstances on board the *Somers* were different from those on board the *Bellipotent*," see *Billy Budd*, pp. 113–14. Finally, on the *Somers* affair, see *H&S*, pp. 28–30.

⁸ Lawrance Thompson, *Melville's Quarrel with God* (Princeton: Princeton University Press, 1952), pp. 360, 373.

⁹ Leo Strauss, *Persecution and the Art of Writing* (Glencoe, Ill.: Free Press, 1952), pp. 29–30ff.; Booth, *The Rhetoric of Fiction*, pp. 364–74. Criticism of Thompson on this point may be found in Richard Harter Fogle, "*Billy Budd*: The Order of the Fall," *Nineteenth-Century Fiction* 15 (December 1960): 189–205; and in Edward H. Rosenberry, "The Problem of *Billy Budd*," *PMLA* 80 (December 1965): 489–98. The best short criticism of the ironist readings of Billy Budd is Richard Harter Fogle, "*Billy Budd* —Acceptance or Irony," *Tulane Studies in English* 8 (1958): 107–13.

¹⁰ *Redburn: His First Voyage*, in *The Writings of Herman Melville*, ed. Harrison Hayford, Hershel Parker, and G. Thomas Tanselle, 15 vols. (Evanston and Chicago: Northwestern University Press and The Newberry Library, 1968–), 4:292.

¹¹ P. 54. Hayford and Sealts discount any meaning for "An Inside Narrative" which goes beyond the claim of being merely the "*inside* story" of "what *really* happened." In this they follow Sidney Kaplan, "Explication," *Melville Society Newsletter* 13, no. 2 (Summer 1957): [3]. The editors' citation of the statement quoted here concerning the "inner life of one particular ship" to justify this reading only begs the question since it is precisely the

meaning of "inner life" that is at issue. To read the story as merely "what *really* happened" requires that the reader remain within the story's own universe and ignores Melville's universe, of which the story is a created part. (See *H&S*, 134–35).

[12] *Mardi*, pp. 269, 461. Mohi's legends are called "incredible" at p. 213. See also the remark on "the occasional credulity" of historians at p. 332.

[13] Ibid., pp. 280–81.

[14] See Leon Howard, *Herman Melville: A Biography* (Berkeley: University of California Press, 1951), p. 320; *H&S*, p. 33; and Milton R. Stern, ed., *Billy Budd, Sailor (An Inside Narrative)* (Indianapolis: Bobbs-Merrill, 1975), Introduction, p. viii.

For a study which argues that the subtitle indicates an internal conflict in Melville's own soul, see William Braswell, "Melville's *Billy Budd* as 'An Inside Narrative'," *American Literature* 29 (May 1957): 133–46. See also Eugenio Montale, "An Introduction to *Billy Budd* (1942)," *Sewanee Review* 68 (Summer 1960): 421.

[15] For an account of Melville's troubles with *Typee*, see Leon Howard's Historical Note in *Typee: A Peep at Polynesian Life*, in *The Writings of Herman Melville*, ed. Harrison Hayford, Hershel Parker, and G. Thomas Tanselle, 15 vols. (Evanston and Chicago: Northwestern University Press and The Newberry Library, 1968–), 1:277–301.

[16] Ibid., Preface, pp. xiii–xiv. See also *Mardi*, p. 7, for a remark on the "romantic" real events in the Pacific.

[17] *Typee*, Historical Note, p. 293. For Melville's reactions to the demands of his publishers and critics, see *The Letters of Herman Melville*, pp. 24–29, 35–47.

[18] *Omoo: A Narrative of Adventures in the South Seas*, in *The Writings of Herman Melville*, ed. Harrison Hayford, Hershel Parker, and G. Thomas Tanselle, 15 vols. (Evanston and Chicago: Northwestern University Press and The Newberry Library, 1968–), Preface, 2:xiii–xv. For the background history of *Omoo*, see Gordon Roper's Historical Note in this edition, pp. 319–44, and for an apology for the fictional character of an event in *Omoo*, see p. 95.

[19] Letter to John Murray, 29 January 1847, in *The Letters of Herman Melville*, p. 53.

[20] *Mardi*, Preface, p. xvii. For the historical background of *Mardi*, see Elizabeth S. Foster's Historical Note in the edition cited, pp. 657–81.

[21] Ibid., p. 283. The context of the remark is the discussion of the truth of the airy conceits of Yoomy's tale of the mysterious islet. See also the comment on "shallow-minded readers" in *Redburn*, p. 150.

[22] Letter to Lemuel Shaw, 6 October 1849, in *The Letters of Herman Melville*, pp. 91–92. For a discussion of the background to *Redburn*, see the Historical Note by Hershel Parker in the edition cited, pp. 315–52.

[23] Letter to Nathaniel Hawthorne, 1? June 1851, in *The Letters of Herman Melville*, p. 128. See also *Redburn*, p. 115, on the way "most books are manufactured."

[24] "Hawthorne and His Mosses," in Raymond W. Weaver, ed., *Billy Budd and Other Prose Pieces*, in *The Works of Herman Melville*, 16 vols. (London: Constable, 1922–24), 13:131.

On the relation of fiction to truth, see also Herman Melville, *The Confidence-Man: His Masquerade*, ed. Elizabeth S. Foster (New York: Hendricks House, 1954), pp. 76–79, 206–7, 270–71.

For a different view of Melville's understanding of the implications of the words "narrative" and "romance," see Helen P. Trimpi, "Conventions of Romance in *Moby-Dick*," *Southern Review* 7, New Series (January 1971): 115–29.

2

Upright Barbarians

WHILE WRITING *Billy Budd, Sailor* during his last years, Melville may well have been suspended between a retrospective mood in which he conjured up memories of his seafaring past and a prospective mood in which he once again attempted to secure remembrance in the future. In any case, *Billy Budd* itself points emphatically to the past, and the critique of the modern age which is part of the core of the story is based upon a certain understanding or teaching concerning the past. This concern with the past is signalled by the very first words of the "Inside Narrative," and the whole first paragraph, in fact, serves as an introduction to the intended teaching about the past:

> In the time before steamships, or then more frequently than now, a stroller along the docks of any considerable seaport would occasionally have his attention arrested by a group of bronzed mariners, man-of-war's men or merchant sailors in holiday attire, ashore on liberty. In certain instances they would flank, or like a bodyguard quite surround, some superior figure of their own class, moving along with them like

Aldebaran among the lesser lights of his constellation. That signal object was the "Handsome Sailor" of the less prosaic time alike of the military and merchant navies. With no perceptible trace of the vainglorious about him, rather with the offhand unaffectedness of natural regality, he seemed to accept the spontaneous homage of his shipmates. [P. 43]

The "Handsome Sailor" is a character type out of the past, the time before the advance of the technology and the prosaic science that have produced the steamship. In the present time of advanced technology, "Handsome Sailors" are nonexistent or, at least, rare. In some manner, the time of steamships has proven to be inimical to the unaffected "natural regality" embodied in the "Handsome Sailor." The contrast between the less scientific past and the technologically advanced present which underlies these facts is thus the initial theme of the narrative and, as will be shown, is a primary element in the background for the character sketches and events of the story.

A full understanding of the character of the "Handsome Sailor" depends upon the realization that he is not merely a particular phenomenon of the recent historical past. This fact is somewhat concealed because the narrator suggests it by describing one very particular instance of a "Handsome Sailor" in his own lifetime:

A somewhat remarkable instance recurs to me. In Liverpool, now half a century ago, I saw under the shadow of the great dingy street-wall of Prince's Dock (an obstruction long since removed) a common sailor so intensely black that he must needs have been a native African of the unadulterate blood of Ham—a symmetric figure much above the average height. The two ends of a gay silk handkerchief thrown loose about the neck danced upon the displayed ebony of his chest, in his ears were big hoops of gold, and a Highland bonnet with a tartan band set off his shapely head. It was a hot noon in July; and his face, lustrous with perspiration, beamed with barbaric good humor. In jovial sallies right and left, his white teeth flashing into view, he rollicked along, the center of a company of his shipmates. These were made up of such an assortment of tribes and complexions as would have well fitted them to be marched up by Anacharsis Cloots before the bar of the first French Assembly as Representatives of the Human Race. At each spontaneous tribute rendered by the wayfarers to this black pagod of a fellow—the tribute of a pause and stare, and less frequently an exclamation—the motley retinue showed that they took that sort of pride in the evoker of it which the Assyrian priests doubtless showed for their grand sculptured Bull when the faithful prostrated themselves.[1]

The narrator's recollection of the black Handsome Sailor, who was admired by members of so many "tribes and complexions," universalizes the character type to which he has referred. Moreover, the narrator's comparison of the adoration given the black Handsome Sailor, a "pagod of a fellow," and the adoration given the Assyrian idol suggests that the "Handsome Sailor" character is a representation of an archetype which harkens back at least to the earliest historic past. That is, the "Handsome Sailor" type, initially and significantly compared to "Aldebaran," the star which is the eye of the constellation Taurus, the Bull, recalls the distant time of the Assyrian Bull. Indeed, that time suggests a nearly immemorial age, the turning point between myth and history. The particular instance of the black Handsome Sailor thus serves to reveal both the persistent universality and the mythic antiquity of the archetype of which he is so "remarkable" an instance.[2]

The primary characteristic of this universal and ancient archetype is an attunement to nature. Thus, the "Handsome Sailor" embodies unaffected "natural regality" without artificial vainglory. Moreover, the case of the "unadulterate" and "barbaric" black Handsome Sailor suggests that the superior

[*21*]

stature of the archetype represented in the "Handsome Sailor" can transcend the merely conventional national and ethnic distinctions which may otherwise divide his admirers. Since his superiority is according to nature, the black Handsome Sailor evokes "spontaneous tribute" rather than conventionally enforced suspicion or prejudice. Finally, since this superiority is a natural endowment, the "Handsome Sailor" type represents a form of natural leadership which belies any artificial and merely conventional hierarchy which would assign a representative of the type to the rank of a mere common sailor.

The natural superiority of the "Handsome Sailor" authorizes his right to rule over his shipmates, who, as the instance of the black Handsome Sailor shows, represent the whole human race. The archetypical "Handsome Sailor," the "Aldebaran" who embodies "natural regality," rules as idol and king by natural and divine right. This claim to rule is in startling contrast to the egalitarianism of the first French Assembly to which Cloots brought his Representatives of the Human Race and by which both divinity and regality were abjured. While the Assembly denies any natural right to rule, the "Handsome Sailor" represents the ancient claim to temporal and spiritual rule as both king and idol. This phenomenon of "the less prosaic time" thus embodied a natural hierarchy which distinguished a divinely authorized ruler from the ruled, a hierarchy rejected by modern egalitarianism and atheism.[3]

Returning to his description of the "Handsome Sailor" type, the narrator first indicates that the character's natural distinction was based upon certain physical characteristics. The reader has already been shown the lustrous ebony beauty of the black Liverpool idol, but he now learns that the "Handsome Sailor's" physical distinction embraces more than his imposing appearance. "Invariably a proficient in his perilous calling, he was also more or less of a mighty boxer or wrestler. It was strength and beauty." The "Handsome Sailor" is both beautiful in appearance and proficient in action. "Ashore he was the champion; afloat the spokesman; on every suitable occasion always foremost." In a gale, he could be seen "astride the weather yardarm-end, . . . in very much the attitude of young Alexander curbing the fiery Bucephalus" (p. 44).

The natural ruling ability of this young Alexander, although grounded thus in his remarkable beauty and proficient strength, depended also upon his capacity to bring order to his phenomenal physical attributes. The natural ruler also possessed a certain moral character:

> The moral nature was seldom out of keeping with the physical make. Indeed, except as toned by the former, the comeliness and power, always attractive in masculine conjunction, hardly could have drawn the sort of honest homage the Handsome Sailor in some examples received from his less gifted associates.[4]

In all, the archetype represented by the "Handsome Sailor" reveals a natural physical and moral superiority which authorizes the rule of an idol-king among men. This archetypical form of rule is prescientific, natural, physical, moral, and religious. It depends upon natural endowment rather than upon conventional distinction, and it was effectively or fully incarnate in the universalized and mythologized past rather than in the immediate historical past or present. This natural form of rule is described not only without reference to modern intellectuality, but it in fact stems from a time prior to the existence of rational intellectuality as such; that is, it stems from the time of Assyrian myths. That is to say, the naturally right form of rule is independent of rationality and existed before philosophy.

The narrator suggests that the contemporary world is no longer hospitable to the "natural regality" of the "Handsome Sailor," and he implicitly criticizes the atheistic egalitarianism which his world has offered as a substitute for that regality. Men, according to nature, are divided into rulers and ruled: kings, priests, and faithful. The fact that the prosaic, scientific world operates with other kinds of hierarchies cannot conceal the natural truth, nor can enlightened philosophy refute it. The "Handsome Sailor" types may be relegated to the lower ranks or destroyed, but the naturally right rule represented in the type cannot be controverted. Modern technological science and enlightened philosophy, and perhaps science and philosophy themselves, have almost emptied the world of "Handsome Sailors," but they thereby have eliminated the possibility of naturally just rule.

The narrator's matter-of-fact descriptions of the "Handsome Sailor" type and the black Handsome Sailor in particular thus serve as devices by which Melville raises the first crucial issues of his novel: the contrasts between prescientific past and technologically advanced present, the natural and the conventional, the claims of natural authority and the claims of the French Enlightenment. In the past time within the narrator's memory, the "Handsome Sailor" existed as an anachronism, harkening back to the time of Assyrian priests and cities ruled by god-kings. The "Handsome Sailor" existed, that is, as an anomalous natural king in the garb of a common sailor. The reader may speculate that the political decline of other representatives of the archetype embodied by the "Handsome Sailor" may have been caused by the same force which, within the narrator's lifetime, has made the "Handsome Sailor" himself more rare, that is, the force of modern science and its technology. The reader may speculate further that Melville suggests through his narrator that there is an inherent conflict between the paradigm of naturally right rule and science or philosophy itself. In any case, it is sufficient so far to note the admirable portrait of the "Handsome Sailor" archetype, a portrait of past, natural authority to which the characters of *Billy Budd, Sailor* will be compared or related.

The narrator explicitly invites comparison between the "Handsome Sailor" and Billy Budd. Immediately following his description of the former, the narrator says:

Such a cynosure, at least in aspect, and something such too in nature, though with important variations made apparent as the story proceeds, was welkin-eyed Billy Budd—or Baby Budd, as more familiarly, under circumstances hereafter to be given, he at last came to be called—aged twenty-one, a foretopman of the British fleet toward the close of the last decade of the eighteenth century. [P. 44]

Billy has the aspect of the "Handsome Sailor" and something of his nature, but "with important *variations*." The nature of Billy Budd is thus to be understood as it compares to and contrasts with that of the "Handsome Sailor." Billy Budd will be both similar to and different from the "Handsome Sailor" type.

Billy is "welkin-eyed," and in this, his celestial aspect, he clearly resembles the "Handsome Sailor." But the reader quickly learns that Billy lacks something of the "Handsome Sailor's" apparent ability to master his own immediate fate. Billy is "foremost" not as "champion," but as plunder. When he alone was chosen to be "impressed on the Narrow Seas from a homeward-bound English merchantman into a seventy-four outward bound, H.M.S. *Bellipotent*, . . . Billy made no demur. But, indeed, any demur would have been as idle as the protest of a goldfinch popped into a cage" (pp. 44–45). Also, this is the first of a series of images which compare Billy to animals, but unlike the comparison of the black Handsome Sailor to the Assyrian Bull, the comparisons in Billy's case point to his real affinity to the lower animals rather than to his ostensible incarnation of the divine. "Like the animals," the narrator says,

"though no philosopher, he was, without knowing it, practically a fatalist," and the narrator later adds, "Of self-consciousness
he seemed to have little or none, or about as much as we may
reasonably impute to a dog of Saint Bernard's breed." In Billy,
therefore, the "Handsome Sailor's" embodiment of human excellence and divine influence becomes instead an embodiment
of animal instinct and innocence.

It is in his physical attributes that Billy is unquestionably a
"Handsome Sailor." He is "rated as an able seaman," and is
therefore "a proficient in his perilous calling." He is a "mighty
boxer" who easily drubbed the annoying Red Whiskers. But
mostly, Billy has the *appearance* of a "Handsome Sailor." "Cast
in a mold peculiar to the finest physical examples of those
Englishmen in whom the Saxon strain would seem not at all to
partake of any Norman or other admixture, he showed in face
that humane look of reposeful good nature which the Greek
sculptor in some instances gave to his heroic strong man, Hercules." Billy is a fine physical specimen of unknown paternal
origin, "a foundling, a presumable by-blow, and, evidently,
no ignoble one. Noble descent was as evident in him as in a
blood horse." The narrator thus returns to Billy's similarity to
the lower animals in the very place in which he describes Billy's
most striking similarity to the "Handsome Sailor."[6] The "important variations" between Billy and the "Handsome Sailor,"
again, are to be found in the differences in "moral nature"
which lie beneath their striking physical similarities.

The narrator emphasizes Billy's lack of the refinements of
civilized human existence. His similarity to the animals is thus
that similarity which presumably marked nascent man. Billy
is, as his nickname reminds the reader, a baby bud of humanity:

> . . . with little or no sharpness of faculty or any trace of the
> wisdom of the serpent, nor yet quite a dove, he possessed that
> kind and degree of intelligence going along with the uncon-
> ventional rectitude of a sound human creature, one to whom

not yet has been proferred the questionable apple of knowledge. He was illiterate; he could not read, but he could sing,
and like the illiterate nightingale was sometimes the com-
poser of his own song.

Like that of the "Handsome Sailor," Billy's nature is seemingly
dependent on an absence of progress in science or rationality
for its ability to exist in human form. The "apple of knowledge" is "questionable" precisely because it kills off the "Handsome Sailors" and Billy Budds. But Billy markedly differs from
the "Handsome Sailor" in that he does not possess any of the
"Handsome Sailor's" residual or actual political nature. Billy's
natural habitat is not in the center of a ship's society. "By his
original constitution aided by the co-operating influences of his
lot, Billy in many respects was little more than a sort of upright barbarian, much such perhaps as Adam presumably might
have been ere the urbane Serpent wriggled himself into his
company." Untouched by the *urbane* Serpent, Billy is a throwback:

> And here be it submitted that apparently going to corrobo-
> rate the doctrine of man's Fall, a doctrine now popularly
> ignored, it is observable that where certain virtues pristine
> and unadulterate peculiarly characterize anybody in the
> external uniform of civilization, they will upon scrutiny
> seem not to be derived from custom or convention, but
> rather to be out of keeping with these, as if indeed excep-
> tionally transmitted from a period prior to Cain's city and
> citified man. [Pp. 52–53]

It is important to note that the narrator's references to the
Bible suggest an *interpretation* of the biblical images. The comparison of Billy to prelapsarian Adam is made in the context of
a series of images which relate a secular version of "the doctrine
of man's Fall," namely the doctrine which contrasts a barbarian
state of nature to the state of civilization. As one critic stated,
"The analogies Melville brings forward in support of his story

... prove nothing in themselves about either his intention or his achievement."[7] The narrator's analogy to Adam thus must not obscure the fact that Billy is subtly contrasted with both *Christian* civilization and civilization in general. Billy is not ultimately the Christian Adam, old or new; he is a stranger to Christianity *and* to civilization:

> The character marked by such qualities has to an unvitiated taste an untampered-with flavor like that of berries, while the man thoroughly civilized, even in a fair specimen of the breed, has to the same moral palate a questionable smack as of a compounded wine. To any stray inheritor of these primitive qualities found, like Casper Hauser, wandering dazed in any *Christian* capital of our time, the good-natured poet's famous invocation, near two thousand years ago, of the good rustic out of his latitude in the Rome of the Caesars, still appropriately holds:
>
>> Honest and poor, faithful in word and thought,
>> What hath thee, Fabian, to the city brought?[8]

In his physical robustness, his similarity to the animals, his lack of knowledge and wisdom, his apolitical character, and his natural barbarity, Billy Budd clearly reminds one of Rousseau's noble savage. According to Rousseau, "The savage man's body being the only implement he knows, he employs it for various uses of which, through lack of training, our bodies are incapable; our industry deprives us of the strength and agility that necessity obliges him to acquire." Savage man, "strong and robust," is "the most advantageously organized" animal of all. Also, "by nature committed to instinct alone," savage man "will therefore begin with purely animal functions." This natural man thus lacks any intellectual consciousness; his mind is "found to have dullness and stupidity," and indeed, as Rousseau would have it, "I almost dare affirm that the state of reflection is a state contrary to nature and that the man who meditates is a depraved animal."[9]

[2 8]

Billy is Rousseau's noble savage par excellence in that he was "apt to develop an organic hesitancy" in speech, "more or less of a stutter or even worse." [10] This speaking inability is a throwback to that state of Rousseauean natural man which he so thoroughly approximates, and when it is remembered that speech or *logos* is the classical foundation for man's existence as a political animal, Billy's speaking difficulty becomes the symbol of his existence outside of the city of men. As Rousseau described primitive man, he was an apolitical animal: "In the primitive state, having neither houses, nor huts, nor property of any kind, everyone took up his lodging by chance and often for only one night." The state of nature is without family or communal bonds. "Males and females united fortuitously, depending on encounter, occasion, and desire, without speech being a very necessary interpreter of the things they had to say to each other; they left each other with the same ease." [11] And so, Billy Budd, a foundling with unknown parents, is neither a product of a family bond nor a member of a civilized society. He is an "upright barbarian" fresh from the state of nature.

This sketch of a Rousseauean noble savage in *Billy Budd* markedly differs from the noble savage of Melville's earlier excursion into the "state of Nature" in *Typee*, and this difference both highlights the character of Billy Budd and sheds light upon the dialectic of Melville's final work. Describing the inhabitants of the island of Nukuheva, Tommo explicitly stated that "they retain their original primitive character, remaining very nearly in the same state of nature in which they were first beheld by white men." But Tommo found that the state of nature displayed a highly organized political community in which all were under the law of the all-pervasive Taboo. And Tommo found a "noble savage," but he was Mehevi, the chief "highest in rank," "one of Nature's noblemen." That is, Tommo found that in man's natural condition, nature distinguished the truly noble man from the many by both "the excellence of his physical proportions" and his capacity for leadership. The noble savage was a political leader and a "distinguished personage, the natives regarding him with the utmost deference, and making room for him as he approached."[12]

The noble savage of Melville's early artistic experience in *Typee*'s state of nature is thus the political "champion" and "spokesman" whose shadow was still cast, albeit dimly, by *Billy Budd*'s "Handsome Sailor" type. He is, in nature, opposed to the Rousseauean noble savage, Billy Budd. The differences are the more remarkable because in most other respects the Melville of *Typee* pictured the state of nature as conforming to the principles of Rousseau; for example, "sickness was almost unknown" among the Typees, who lived in "thoughtless happiness" amid natural plenty.[13] Melville's disagreements with Rousseau apparently center upon the most politically critical aspects or dimensions of Rousseau's teachings, Melville apparently claiming that man is by nature political and that nature authorizes a human political hierarchy.

Melville's agreement with Rousseau on other aspects of the state of nature is related to a similarity in a central theme in *Typee*, *Billy Budd*, and Rousseau's *Discourse on the Sciences and Arts*. In Melville's first work, Tommo engaged in a continuing attack on Christian civilization's "enlightened" intervention in Polynesia. He saw Christian civilization as the purveyor of European Enlightenment, and he continually dared to doubt the value of this civilizational progress:

Let the once smiling and populous Hawaiian islands, with their now diseased, starving, and dying natives, answer the question. The missionaries may seek to disguise the matter as they will, but the facts are incontrovertible; and the devoutest Christian who visits the group with an unbiased mind, must go away mournfully asking—"Are these, alas! the fruits of twenty-five years of enlightening?"[14]

As has been shown above, in *Billy Budd* this theme reappears in the contrast between the "less prosaic" time of the "Handsome Sailor" (and by extension, of the idol-king he represents) and the time of prosaic, enlightened science in which the narrator now lives. In either case, the theme is closely related to the attack on the Enlightenment in the *First Discourse*, in which Rousseau detailed how "our souls have been corrupted in proportion to the advancement of our sciences and arts toward perfection."[15] In other words, the Melville of both *Typee* and *Billy Budd* portrays Rousseau's contention that enlightenment destroys the natural endowments of man. Again, their disagreement apparently concerns *what* has been destroyed: a natural political leader, or a natural apolitical state of merely animal happiness.

The merchantman from which Billy is impressed is the *Rights-of-Man*, and this fact may lead the reader to speculate further about the relationship between Melville, Rousseau, and the Enlightenment. Billy's initial position aboard the *Rights* may suggest that it is Melville's contention that the Enlightenment's gospel of the Rights of Man has as its real secular hero a noble savage of Rousseau's description and not the new Adam of Reason which enlightened philosophy expected and celebrated. Billy Budd may serve in this way as Melville's correction of the Enlightenment's portrait of natural man. Thus, Melville's disagreement with Rousseau concerning the nature of natural man may not have prevented him from seeing that, given the Enlightened premise that man is not political by nature, Rousseau is more consistent in stripping his own natural man of *all* the traits of corrupt civilization, especially Reason.[16]

In any case, the character sketches of the "Handsome Sailor" and Billy Budd certainly combine to suggest Melville's total rejection of the dominant thought of the Enlightenment: the "Handsome Sailor" is contrasted with enlightened atheistic egalitarianism, and Billy Budd is contrasted with enlightened

faith in Reason. The sketch of the "Handsome Sailor," contrasted in turn with the sketch of Billy Budd, sets the stage
then for Melville's demonstration of the limitations and errors
of Rousseau's alternative to the Enlightenment, and with the
action of the story which will reveal these limitations and
errors, Melville will indicate his rejection of the modernity of
Rousseau along with that of the Enlightenment.

Aboard the *Rights*, Billy was the center of attraction in a
world that presumably existed in accordance with the principles announced by that ship's name. Dealing with commercial
intercourse among men, and therefore in accordance with
Thomas Paine's natural laws of human interest, the *Rights-of-
Man* is marked by tranquility, embodied in Captain Graveling,
of whom the narrator says, "there was nothing this honest soul
at heart loved better than simple peace and quiet."[17] Aboard
the *Rights-of-Man*, that is, within Paine's tolerant regime,
Billy could live the peaceful life of Rousseau's noble savage,
"his soul, agitated by nothing, . . . given over to the sole sentiment of its present existence without any idea of the future."[18]
But the future comes, in the form of Billy's "arbitrary enlistment" onto the *Bellipotent*, a man-of-war. There he meets
untempered urbanity in the form of a society highly structured
and disciplined due to the exigencies of war, the unreasonable
evil which presumably would be eliminated by universal acceptance of the Rights of Man; thus, Billy will be tested for his
ability to exist on a military vessel, as did the "Handsome
Sailor," "alike of the military and merchant navies."[19]

Billy's enlistment is his civilization. The *Rights-of-Man* had
been named by its "hardheaded Dundee owner" in admiration
of Thomas Paine. The narrator notes that this style of chris-
tening was employed by Stephen Girard of Philadelphia, who
had named his ships after "the liberal philosophers . . . Vol-
taire, Diderot, and so forth." The exclusion of Rousseau here
from those mentioned as "liberal philosophers" is itself note-

worthy—one of Girard's three finest ships was the *Rousseau*.[20] As witnessed by the arational character of the noble savage, Billy Budd, Rousseau's inclusion on a list of enlightened philosophers would be problematic. In any case, Billy had inhabited the world of these liberal philosophers, embodying not Reason, but what Rousseauean philosophy revealed man to be. He is Rousseau's answer *ante* to Paine's "Adam of the new world."[21] But in *Billy Budd*, this Adam falls into the hands of a seventy-four-gun ship of war. In line with the narrator's quotation from the poem by Martial, he tells us, "Billy Budd's position aboard the seventy-four was something analogous to that of a rustic beauty transplanted from the provinces and brought into competition with the highborn dames of the court." The competition comes from "several individuals who however inferior in grade were of no common natural stamp, sailors more signally susceptive of that air which continuous martial discipline and repeated presence in battle can in some degree impart even to the average man" (pp. 50–51). Billy's position as "Handsome Sailor" is thus made questionable by his differences in nature and his lack of military character, the latter made apparent by his presence among the seasoned warriors of civilization. And Billy's salute to his old ship, though "to deal in double meanings and insinuations of any sort was quite foreign to his nature," is nevertheless an insightful comment upon his new predicament: "And good-bye to you too, old *Rights-of-Man*" (p. 49).

Civilized onto the *Bellipotent*, Billy Budd is put in a precarious position, but he is protected from concern by his naiveté. "He was soon at home in the service, not at all disliked for his unpretentious good looks and a sort of genial happy-go-lucky air. No merrier man in his mess." He "scarce noted" his change of circumstance, "an ambiguous smile in one or two" of the sailors, or "the peculiar favorable effect his person and demeanor had upon the more intelligent gentlemen of the quarter-deck."²² His fate in martial civilization will not be the fate of attained goodness, but of pristine innocence. His "simple nature remained unsophisticated by those moral obliquities which are not in every case incompatible with that manufacturable thing known as respectability." Like the vices of all sailors, Billy's are but "frank manifestations in accordance with natural law" (p. 52). What will befall this Rousseauean phenomenon in real civilization is, of course, the story of *Billy Budd*.

Billy's similarity to Rousseau's noble savage and his differences from the "Handsome Sailor" type are thus the first keys to the dialectic of the novel. The "Handsome Sailor" appears as the embodiment of natural authority. His incongruous existence in the time of the narrator's memory leaves open the question of whether or not natural authority existed then in some other form, in a position of political authority. However that may be, the "Handsome Sailor" serves both as a counterpoint to enlightened egalitarianism and as Melville's answer to Rousseau: the author's artistic vision reveals that the philosopher erred in describing men as naturally apolitical and equal. With Rousseau, however, Melville takes up the fight against the Enlightenment: he presents Billy Budd as the hero of natural rights philosophy, even though the liberal philosophers themselves may not claim him as their own. Billy's essential difference from the "Handsome Sailor," his inability to be "champion" and "spokesman" because of his defect of speech, thus acts as a correction of the liberal philosophers and sets the stage for the realization of what they unwittingly and Rousseau consciously have wrought. Billy's speech impediment leads the narrator to say, "The avowal of such an imperfection in the Handsome Sailor should be evidence not alone that he is not presented as a conventional hero, but also that the story in which he is the main figure is no romance" (p. 53). And the narration in the end will not in fact romanticize an *imperfect* "Handsome Sailor" but will show the tragedy of a Rousseauean noble savage.

The intricacies of the above discussion should not obscure the power of Melville's art. Indeed, the description of Billy Budd is artistically so effective in arousing the readers' emotions that, as one critic noted in the course of his argument, "there is danger that the readers' admiration for Billy's integrity may be submerged beneath their contempt for his simplicity."[23] Melville's ability to induce admiration *or* contempt in his readers, and the resultant struggle within the readers' hearts, are the marks of his great artistry. But Melville speaks both to the heart and of the truth, and the careful reader must thus dive into the narrator's straightforward remarks in quest of the truth. The appeal to the reader's passions must not obscure the fact that Melville proves thereby his knowledge of the soul and its strivings; Melville claims to tell the truth in the very act of appealing to the reader's heart. What the narrator later says of the main character of the story thus serves as a warning for understanding the story itself: "But something more, or rather something else than mere shrewdness is perhaps needful for the due understanding of such a character as Billy Budd's" (p. 90).

Notes

¹ Pp. 43–44. Melville himself had been to Liverpool about fifty years before writing *Billy Budd*, from 2 July to 13 August 1839. In *Redburn*, which was based in part on this visit, Redburn noted "the absence of negroes" in Liverpool, where usually "not a negro was to be seen"; a negro who did come on an American ship could, however, walk "with a prouder pace" than in the United States and raise "his head like a man." See *Redburn: His First Voyage*, in *The Writings of Herman Melville*, ed. Harrison Hayford, Hershel Parker, and G. Thomas Tanselle, 15 vols. (Evanston and Chicago: Northwestern University Press and The Newberry Library, 1968–), 4:201–2. Hayford and Sealts note that the similarity here between the experiences of Melville (that is, as Redburn) and his narrator tends "to discredit the view advanced by [Lawrance] Thompson . . . that . . . [Melville] was deliberately creating a 'narrator' other than his own person." (See *H&S*, pp. 135–36). The *differences* in the fictional accounts of those experiences, however, show that Melville altered his own experiences to suit his narrators when it served his artistic purposes. The narrator of *Billy Budd* is thus not Melville's virtual opposite (as Thompson would have it), but neither is he simply identical to the author. In general, Melville is using his narrator to serve his larger purposes.

F. O. Matthiessen points out that the motif of the multinational and multiracial crew representing the human race "is an integral part of Melville's conception of the world as 'a ship on its passage out'." See *American Renaissance: Art and Expression in the Age of Emerson and Whitman* (New York: Oxford University Press, 1941), p. 410.

² On the universalized Black Handsome Sailor, see Milton R. Stern, *The Fine Hammered Steel of Herman Melville* (Urbana, Ill.: University of Illinois Press, 1957), p. 214; also, on the "mythical proportions" of the "Handsome Sailor," see Richard Harter Fogle, "*Billy Budd*—Acceptance or Irony," *Tulane Studies in English* 8 (1958): 110.

³ Melville apparently read of the Cloots episode in Carlyle's *French Revolution*. (See *H&S*, p. 136.) The intimate connection between regicide and deicide in the minds of Cloots and the more prominent French revolutionaries is explored by Albert Camus in *The Rebel: An Essay on Man in Revolt*, trans. Anthony Bower (New York: Random House, Vintage Books, 1956), pp. 105–32.

⁴ P. 44. Compare the description of the "Handsome Sailor" with Aristotle *Politics* 1254b 27–39.

⁵ Pp. 49, 52. In the course of the novel, Billy is compared to a goldfinch, a dog, a horse, and a nightingale.

⁶ Pp. 51, 52. Captain Graveling relates the Red Whiskers episode at p. 47. Also, on the obscurity of heroes' "early history," see *Omoo: A Narrative of Adventures in the South Seas*, in *The Writings of Herman Melville*, ed. Harrison Hayford, Hershel Parker, and G. Thomas Tanselle, 15 vols. (Evanston and Chicago: Northwestern University Press and The Newberry Library, 1968–   ), 2:12.

⁷ Warner Berthoff, " 'Certain Phenomenal Men': The Example of *Billy Budd*," *ELH* 27 (December 1960): 337.

⁸ P. 53, italics added. Note also, thus, Billy's comparison to such pre-Christian heroes as Hercules and Achilles (pp. 51, 71).

⁹ Jean-Jacques Rousseau, *Discourse on the Origin and Foundations of Inequality Among Men*, in *The First and Second Discourses*, ed. Roger D. Masters and trans. Roger D. and Judith R. Masters (New York: St. Martin's, 1964), pp. 105, 106, 110, 115, 119.

¹⁰ P. 53. Billy's speech defect is compared here to the crimson blemish on Georgiana's cheek in Hawthorne's "The Birthmark." Note that Georgiana was killed by her scientific husband, Aylmer. (See *H&S*, p. 143.)

¹¹ Rousseau, *Discourse on Inequality*, pp. 120–21.

¹² *Typee: A Peep at Polynesian Life*, in *The Writings of Herman Melville*, ed. Harrison Hayford, Hershel Parker, and G. Thomas Tanselle, 15 vols. (Evanston and Chicago: Northwestern University Press and The Newberry Library, 1968–   ), 1:11, 71, 77, 78, 90. The apparent lawlessness of the Typees (pp. 177, 200)

is shown to be illusory by Tommo's subsequent remarks on the Taboo at p. 224.

¹³ Ibid., pp. 127, 204. See p. 185 on the general "equality of condition" among the Typees.

¹⁴ Ibid., p. 124. See chap. 17 in general on this point, as well as pp. 15, 29, 112. I treat this and other aspects of *Typee* in my article, "Tragedy in the State of Nature: Melville's *Typee*," forthcoming in *Interpretation* 8 (January 1979).

¹⁵ Rousseau, *Discourse on the Sciences and Arts*, in *The First and Second Discourses*, p. 39.

Despite the strong internal evidence of Melville's familiarity with the ideas of the *Discourses*, there is no external evidence that he read or owned texts containing them. Melville did, however, buy and read a "much desired" copy of Rousseau's *Confessions*. See *Journal of a Visit to London and the Continent by Herman Melville, 1849–1850*, ed. Eleanor Melville Metcalf (Cambridge, Mass.: Harvard University Press, 1948), pp. 70, 84, 85. Rousseau was also apparently on Melville's mind as a subject for study at the end of his 1856–57 voyage, as witnessed by his notation in *Journal of a Visit to Europe and the Levant, October 11, 1856–May 6, 1857, by Herman Melville*, ed. Howard C. Horsford (Princeton: Princeton University Press, 1955), p. 262. As an indication that internal evidence must be given priority over external evidence, however, note that Melville directly refers to Rousseau in his first book, *prior* to his purchase of the *Confessions*: see *Typee*, p. 127.

Also, on Melville's familiarity with Rousseau's works, see Charles Roberts Anderson, *Melville in the South Seas*, Columbia University Studies in English and Comparative Literature, no. 138 (New York: Columbia University Press, 1949), p. 178; and on Billy's similarity to Rousseau's savage, in connection with a discussion of the political standing of pity or compassion in modernity, see Hannah Arendt, *On Revolution* (New York: Viking, 1965), pp. 74–83.

¹⁶ Rousseau, *Discourse on Inequality*, pp. 102, 129. In the latter reference, Rousseau directs himself specifically against Hobbes and his inclusion "in the savage man's care of self-preservation the need to satisfy a multitude of passions which are the product of society."

[17] P. 45. Cf. Thomas Paine, *The Rights of Man*, in *Complete Writings of Thomas Paine*, ed. Philip S. Foner, 2 vols. (New York: Citadel, 1945), 1:359.

[18] Rousseau, *Discourse on Inequality*, p. 117.

[19] Cf. p. 43 and Paine, *The Rights of Man*, p. 449.

[20] See p. 48 and *H&S*, p. 138.

[21] Paine, *The Rights of Man*, p. 449.

[22] Pp. 49 and 51. See also p. 88, where the narrator says of Billy, "innocence was his blinder."

[23] Wayne C. Booth, *The Rhetoric of Fiction* (Chicago: University of Chicago Press, 1961), p. 178.

3

Aristocratic Virtue

THE DESCRIPTION OF THE "HANDSOME SAILOR" contained time and character references which served as background for the introduction of Billy Budd; in like manner, the novel's second major figure, Captain Vere, is introduced by references to a certain time and a certain phenomenal character. In the case of Billy Budd, the background references were to the mythically distant, prescientific, and technologically backward past and to a character embodying "natural regality"; the nature of Billy Budd was revealed as it compared to and contrasted with the nature of the unsophisticated and naturally regal "Handsome Sailor." In the case of Captain Vere, the background time reference is to the major political event of the modern age, the French Revolution, and the background character reference is to the Great Sailor, Lord Nelson; it is to be expected, thus, that the nature of Captain Vere will be revealed as it compares to and contrasts with the nature of the politically heroic figure of Lord Nelson.

The narrator first observes that at the time of Billy's "arbitrary enlistment," the *Bellipotent* was on the way to her position in the Mediterranean fleet and that "her superior sailing qualities" often distinguished her for "separate duty as a scout" or for "less temporary [special] service." The narrator then observes, "But with all this the story has little concernment, restricted as it is to the inner life of one particular ship and the career of an individual sailor" (p. 54). This disclaimer is belied, however, not only by the fact that the *Bellipotent*'s service away from the fleet is a crucial element in the plot of *Billy Budd*, but also by the fact that the disclaimer occurs at the beginning of three chapters which deal only with "all this" supposedly extraneous material. The material on the Great Mutiny, the French Revolution, and Lord Nelson given in these chapters is, of course, the absolutely necessary prologue to the two-chapter introduction of Captain Vere.

The narrator gives the historical background in a long paragraph in which a relationship is established between the mutiny within the British fleet and the war raging outside with revolutionary France:

It was the summer of 1797. In the April of that year had occurred the commotion at Spithead followed in May by a second and yet more serious outbreak in the fleet at the Nore. The latter is known, and without exaggeration in the epithet, as "the Great Mutiny." It was indeed a demonstration more menacing to England than the contemporary manifestoes and conquering and proselyting armies of the French Directory. To the British Empire the Nore Mutiny was what a strike in the fire brigade would be to London threatened by general arson. In a crisis when the kingdom might well have anticipated the famous signal that some years later published along the naval line of battle what it was that upon occasion England expected to Englishmen; *that* was the time when at the mastheads of the three-deckers and seventy-fours moored in her own roadstead—a fleet the right arm of a Power then all but the sole free conservative one of the Old World

—the bluejackets, to be numbered by thousands, ran up with huzzas the British colors with the union and cross wiped out; by that cancellation transmuting the flag of founded law and freedom defined, into the enemy's red meteor of unbridled and unbounded revolt. Reasonable discontent growing out of practical grievances in the fleet had been ignited into irrational combustion as by live cinders blown across the Channel from France in flames. [P. 54]

The spring mutinies occurred at a time when Britain was threatened by the likes of "general arson" and "France in flames." While the French Directory and its "conquering and proselyting armies" constituted the direct threat to England, the mutinies endangered England's ability to meet that threat. The narrator does not present England as a merely reactionary force against revolutionary France, but rather as a "*free* conservative" power, displaying a flag of "founded law and *freedom* defined." That is, Britain is seen as a defender of a certain kind of freedom against "unbridled and unbounded revolt." The narrator's defense does not lead him to deny the fact that the mutinies grew out of very real "practical grievances." Later he notes that these grievances were such things as "shoddy cloth, rations not sound, or false in the measure," and especially, "impressment" (p. 58). But what might have been an agitation for practical reform was "ignited into irrational combustion," and what the government saw as the resulting "inadmissible" and "aggressively insolent" demands of the bluejackets "indicated—if the Red Flag did not sufficiently do so— what was the spirit animating the men" (p. 55). That is to say, the course which the sailors' discontent took revealed that their real grievances served also as vehicles for revolutionary agitation. Thus, although the conquering armies of revolutionary France could not cross the Channel while the British fleet survived, the *spirit* of the revolution could leap the Channel and infect the British Empire's fleet and well-being. "To some extent," the narrator remarks, "the Nore Mutiny may be regarded as analogous to the distempering irruption of contagious fever in a frame constitutionally sound, and which anon throws it off" (p. 55).

The narrator observes that details about the Great Mutiny are difficult to find because the event was such that "national pride along with views of policy would fain shade it off into the historical background." Nevertheless, the narrator says, "Such events cannot be ignored, but there is a considerate way of historically treating them."[1] And Melville uses the narrator's biased, but considerate and thoughtful presentation of the difficulties facing Great Britain to present a historical account of the times which does not succumb to the fastidiousness of national pride. Moreover, the narrator's various asides combine to present the situation in 1797 as one of complex difficulties, irrespective of one's ideological preference for Britain or France. There were *real* grievances in the British fleet, and the injustice of impressment *did* particularly undermine the fleet's morale. But impressment was "sanctioned for centuries" by custom and "judicially maintained by a Lord Chancellor as late as Mansfield," thus giving the most powerful endorsements of a regime of "founded law" to the nevertheless unjust practice. Moreover, the war with France was a *fact* that added to the complicated status of impressment: "its abrogation would have crippled the indispensable fleet, . . . worked by muscle alone; a fleet the more insatiate in demand for men, because then multiplying its ships of all grades against contingencies present and to come of the convulsed Continent" (pp. 58–59). In all, thus, the narrator's account serves as Melville's way of presenting the nonpartisan given facts of the situation in 1797: war and injustice, mutiny and revolution, national pride and national danger. As that time was lived, the situation was fluid, complex, and enigmatic: "That era appears measurably clear to us who look back at it, and but read of it. But to the grandfathers of us graybeards, the more thoughtful of them, the genius of it presented an aspect like that of Camöens' Spirit of the Cape, an eclipsing menace mysterious and prodigious" (p. 66).

Melville suggests in this way that human events are complexes of various forces and counterforces, and he implies that the true story of any era will not support the certainty beneath *mere* partisanship; indeed, even the narrator's partisanship—presumably he is an Englishman, and he is clearly English in his sympathies—is tempered by his impartial admission of real injustices in the fleet, placing him in contrast to the authorized naval chronicle's smug complacency. The degree of bias in the narrator is such as befits his role as the ostensible chronicler of particular events and personages. The author, however, retains the point of view of one who seeks ultimately the perennial and universal truth. The given fact about human events is that they are "mysterious and prodigious." This is the reality in which men act, and this is the reality in which Melville's characters in *Billy Budd* reveal their natures.[2]

The spring mutinies were finally suppressed, and the mutineers went on "to win a coronet for Nelson at the Nile, and the naval crown of crowns for him at Trafalgar." The subject of Nelson is thus raised in reference to this "plenary absolution" (p. 56) of the British mutineers, and a quasi-soteriological relationship between the Great Sailor and the dangerous straits of the Empire is clearly suggested. The importance of Nelson in the story is further revealed, again obliquely, by the device of having the narrator's explicit words suggest an alternate reading:

In this matter of writing, resolve as one may to keep to the main road, some bypaths have an enticement not readily to be withstood. I am going to err into such a bypath. If the reader will keep me company I shall be glad. At the least, we

can promise ourselves that pleasure which is wickedly said
to be in sinning, for a literary sin the divergence will be.
[P. 56]

Actually, the "divergence," as Milton R. Stern noted, is instead
a "direct road into the center of this 'inside narrative'."[3]

The discussion of Nelson is preceded by a return to the
theme of the first sentence of the novel: the contrast between
the advance of science or technology and the decline of certain
virtuous human characteristics. "Very likely," begins the narrator, "it is no new remark that the inventions of our time have
at last brought about a change in sea warfare in degree corresponding to the revolution in all warfare effected by the original introduction from China into Europe of gunpowder." The
narrator then notes that the first firearm was "scouted by no
few of the knights as a base implement, good enough peradventure for weavers too craven to stand up crossing steel with
steel in frank fight." This statement and a further one, that
"nowadays in encounters [on the sea] a certain kind of displayed gallantry [has] fallen out of date as hardly applicable
under changed circumstances," are actually extraneous to and
inconsistent with the apparent point of the paragraph. The
heart of the paragraph is the narrator's assertion that although
sea warfare *has* changed along with advanced technology in the
way land warfare has changed, nonetheless, just "as ashore
knightly valor . . . did not cease with the knights, neither on
the seas . . . did the nobler qualities of . . . naval magnates . . .
become obsolete with their wooden walls" (p. 56). The ap-
pended statements about the knights' scorn for firearms and the
decline of "displayed gallantry" run counter to the paragraph's
core in that they suggest a view of courage and its present
enervation which contradicts the narrator's ostensible certainty
that the "nobler qualities" of naval heroes have *not* "become
obsolete." That is, the narrator *implicitly* suggests that the

technological advances *have* in fact made certain qualities of valor and gallantry obsolete.

The narrator's real concern is continued, while the purported defense of the continued existence of naval valor is dropped. "To anybody who can hold the Present at its worth without being inappreciative of the Past, . . . the solitary old hulk at Portsmouth, Nelson's *Victory*, seems to float there, not alone as the decaying monument of a fame incorruptible, but also as a poetic reproach . . . to the *Monitors* and yet mightier hulls of the European ironclads." Some others may choose to parry this symbol "on behalf of the new order":

> For example, prompted by the sight of the star inserted in the *Victory*'s quarter-deck designating the spot where the Great Sailor fell, these martial utilitarians may suggest considerations implying that Nelson's ornate publication of his person in battle was not only unnecessary, but not military, nay, savored of foolhardiness and vanity . . . and that but for his bravado the victorious admiral might possibly have survived the battle, and so, instead of having his sagacious dying injunctions overruled by his immediate successor in command, he himself when the contest was decided might have brought his shattered fleet to anchor, a proceeding which might have averted the deplorable loss of life by shipwreck in the elemental tempest that followed the martial one. [P. 57]

According to the narrator, those who would make this argument—these "Benthamites of war"—simply ignore the fact that the actual occurrence of events limited the real possibilities of action at Trafalgar. Even granting the "more than disputable" possibility of anchoring the fleet, their argument rests upon mere conjectures, and "the *might-have-been* is but boggy ground to build on." But the narrator goes on to make an observation in defense of Nelson which is of an entirely different character. He shows that Nelson was capable of placing safety first, but only when other events and other duty called for it: "In foresight as to the larger issue of an encounter, and anxious preparations for it—buoying the deadly way and mapping it out, as at Copenhagen—few commanders have been so pains-takingly circumspect as this same reckless declarer of his per-son in fight" (pp. 57–58). The "martial utilitarians" thus do not see that the Great Sailor acts in terms of an end (ultimate victory) and subordinates all means and methods to that end; they do not see, indeed, that the greatest victory may call for the greatest sacrifice or that different situations may call for opposite tactics. The "Benthamites of war," while purporting to make only utilitarian criticisms, actually presuppose another highest good, the end of self-preservation, which Nelson's highest good places at a lesser value.

The narrator suggests that Tennyson's invocation of Nel-son as "the greatest sailor since our world began" may be understood "from the above." Nelson embodied this dictate: "Personal prudence, even when dictated by quite other than selfish considerations, surely is no special virtue in a military man; while an excessive love of glory, impassioning a less burning impulse, the honest sense of duty, is the first." The glory and duty that moved Nelson at Trafalgar, the battle which absolved the sins of the mutineers, demanded a quasi-religious act, the implicitly deliberate act of consecrating the greatest victory with a sacrifice and thereby winning spiritual approval, forgiveness, and immortality for the victorious:

At Trafalgar Nelson on the brink of opening the fight sat down and wrote his last brief will and testament. If under the presentiment of the most magnificent of all victories to be crowned by his own glorious death, a sort of priestly motive led him to dress his person in the jewelled vouchers of his own shining deeds; if thus to have adorned himself for the altar and the sacrifice were indeed vainglory, then affecta-tion and fustian is each more heroic line in the great epics and dramas, since in such lines the poet but embodies in verse those exaltations of sentiment that a nature like Nelson, the opportunity being given, vitalizes into acts. [P. 58]

It is the *poet*, like the creator of *Billy Budd*, who embodies the glory of the Great Sailor in his verse. For this poet, the Great Sailor exists as a paradigm of courage and honor, a paradigm by which allegiance is secured in the present and, perchance, in "the most magnificent of all victories," for all time. The end for which the Great Sailor acts is the preservation of the political community, and the actions he follows toward that end are scaled from those that concern individual units of the commonwealth to those that concern the whole's ultimate historical existence. At Trafalgar, Nelson dealt with the latter, but in "the same year with this story," he also showed his capacity for meeting a more particular crisis. Nelson was ordered from the *Captain* to the *Theseus*, "and for this reason: that the latter ship having newly arrived on the station from home, where it had taken part in the Great Mutiny, danger was apprehended from the temper of the men; and it was thought that an officer like Nelson was the one, not indeed to terrorize the crew into base subjection, but to win them, by force of his mere presence and heroic personality, back to an allegiance if not as enthusiastic as his own yet as true."[4]

What Melville holds up as an example is the Great Sailor who acts for the common good. In nature, the Great Sailor type is above national distinctions: the "naval magnates" mentioned before are represented by "Don John of Austria, Doria, Van Tromp, Jean Bart, the long line of British admirals, and the American Decaturs of 1812."[5] Nelson is singled out as the greatest of the Great Sailors, and he was a long-time hero of Melville's. One sees in Nelson at Trafalgar the most obvious and spectacular instance of the nature of a Great Sailor, and the sketch of Nelson thus serves as another archetype with

[*49*]

which the characters of *Billy Budd* are to be compared. The fact that the archetype of the Great Sailor transcends national distinctions serves the author's purpose of remaining above the narrator's concern with particular events and political conflicts and also suggests the need to distinguish the Great Sailor from the also-universalized "Handsome Sailor." The contrast between Nelson's disciplinary effect on the *Theseus* and Billy Budd's tranquilizing effect on the *Rights-of-Man* further highlights the nature of the Great Sailor and finally completes the scene for the introduction of Captain Vere and his own comparison to the Great Sailor.

The "Handsome Sailor" won allegiance to his own person by his beauty, prowess, and moral nature: he founded a political community. He existed as an anomaly in modern times, an anomaly because he embodied a prescientific natural regality and divinity of the kind found in Assyrian city-states but was now relegated to the status of a mere common sailor. His ability to exist as the actual god-king depended upon a prescientific cosmology, and his status in the scientific world had correspondingly deteriorated; the more science progressed, the rarer became the "Handsome Sailor." Thus, the archetype to which the "Handsome Sailor" harkened back was the victim of the apparently irresistible progress of science and technology, and the ability of a political leader to hold the seal of divine approbation in his very person was, perhaps forever, lost.

The Great Sailor, on the other hand, wins allegiance to the political community as an entity, even in modern times. He preserves the work of the founder, the *Theseus*. He does so by "his mere presence and heroic personality," and unlike the "Handsome Sailor's" "barbaric" regality, the Great Sailor's status is embellished by the conventional "jewelled vouchers of his own shining deeds." Thus, although he is a universal phenomenon, the Great Sailor is always able to be identified with a particular nation, that is, with a particular set of conventions. If his courageous endowments are a natural gift, his energies are expended for the sake of both personal and national honor. His actions, like those of Aristotle's great-souled man, whom he recalls, are motivated by his own pride in his moral potential and honored through his willingness to accept the citations of his community.[6] Also, unlike the "Handsome Sailor," the Great Sailor, whenever he exists, is always capable of attaining that actual station in life which is commensurate with his nature. He appears, however, from the discussion of advanced naval warfare and the listing of only past naval magnates, to be subject to the same adverse effects of progressing science as is the "Handsome Sailor." Finally, but not less importantly, his ability to carry the stamp of divine approval in his actions stems from sacrificial calculation and not from his own incarnation of that divine approval. In all, he is not god and king, but priest and nobleman.

Billy Budd, the noble savage, could win neither personal nor communal allegiance. He could not be the "spokesman" nor could he establish a position of leadership in a society. His was the virtue of bringing about not an active loyalty, but a quiescent harmony, or a thoughtless harmony accidentally in phase with the enlightened philosophers' rationalistic expectations. Captain Graveling says of him:

"Before I shipped that young fellow, my forecastle was a rat-pit of quarrels. It was black times, I tell you, aboard the *Rights* here. I was worried to that degree my pipe had no comfort for me. But Billy came; and it was like a Catholic priest striking peace in an Irish shindy. Not that he preached to them or said or did anything in particular; but a virtue went out of him, sugaring the sour ones. . . . But now, Lieutenant, if that young fellow goes—I know how it will be aboard the *Rights*. Not again very soon shall I, coming up from dinner, lean over the capstan smoking a quiet pipe—

no, not very soon again, I think. Ay, Lieutenant, you are going to take away the jewel of 'em; you are going to take away my peacemaker!" [Pp. 46–47]

This peaceful virtue, existing independently of Billy's words and deeds, is Billy Budd's offering, and it is this which distinguishes him from the active "Handsome Sailor" and Great Sailor, the former of whom could be found in *both* merchant and military navies and the latter of whom indeed thrives on warfare. The fate of Billy, according to Melville the real hero of natural rights philosophy, will reveal that he needed the peace of the orderly merchant service as much as he helped create it, and *Billy Budd* thus will tell the story of the fate of the noble savage in a world which is marked, as Melville shows, not by peace, but by "the complexities of factitious life" (p. 50).

It is among these phenomenal human types and into this situation that Captain Vere is introduced. Vere is to be compared with and contrasted to the Great Sailor as he acts in a situation in which "it was not unreasonable to apprehend some return of trouble sporadic or general" (p. 59). Vere's fate in this situation will reveal the limitations of another modern human type in the man-of-war world.

Because of the recent trouble, "precautionary vigilance was strained against relapse" aboard many British vessels. Indeed, in some instances, "the lieutenants assigned to batteries felt it incumbent on them . . . to stand with drawn swords behind the men working the guns" (p. 59). However, aboard H.M.S. *Bellipotent* "very little in the manner of the men and nothing obvious in the demeanor of the officers would have suggested to an ordinary observer that the Great Mutiny was a recent event." This lack of anxiety on the part of the officers and the concomitant calm of the men stem from one fact: "In their general bearing and conduct the commissioned officers of a warship naturally take their tone from the commander, that is if he have that ascendancy of character that ought to be his."[7] Captain Vere's relationship to the officers and men is thus from the first pictured as exemplary: his "ascendancy of character" allows the *Bellipotent* to escape both abrasive "precautionary" tactics by the officers and overt hostility on the part of the crew. Where there was discontent and war, Captain Vere has brought calm and attention to duty.

Melville had described the position of a captain aboard a man-of-war in *White-Jacket*. There the narrator notes that "a ship is a bit of terra firma cut off from the main; it is a state in itself; and the captain is its king." Not a "limited monarchy," the captain's rule is "almost a despotism," his "word is law," and in all, "no mortal man has more reason to feel such an intense sense of his own personal consequence, as the captain of a man-of-war at sea."[8] It is for these reasons that the situation aboard H.M.S. *Bellipotent* is attributable directly to Captain Vere and his character. Also, Vere's position as "king" of a state in the man-of-war world makes him the embodiment of conventional authority in what Melville claims to be the real world.

Vere's rank distinguishes him from the "Handsome Sailor," and the narrator's description of Vere shows that his are the qualifications of a Great Sailor:

Captain the Honorable Edward Fairfax Vere, to give his full title, was a bachelor of forty or thereabouts, a sailor of distinction even in a time prolific of renowned seamen. Though allied to the higher nobility, his advancement had not been altogether owing to influences connected with that circumstance. He had seen much service, been in various engagements, always acquitting himself as an officer mindful of the welfare of his men, but never tolerating an infraction of discipline; thoroughly versed in the science of his profession, and intrepid to the verge of temerity, though never injudiciously so. For his gallantry in the West Indian waters as flag lieutenant under Rodney in that admiral's crowning victory over De Grasse, he was made a post captain. [P. 60]

Vere is thus a sailor of unquestioned ability, a nobleman implicitly willing to use *some* influence to assure that his natural endowments won conventional stature, and a courageous disciplinarian. His intolerance of disciplinary infractions must be judged in the light of the description of the situation aboard H.M.S. *Bellipotent*: like Nelson, Vere apparently is able to win allegiance and discipline without resorting to practices which "terrorize the crew into base subjection." Moreover, in a man-of-war world, discipline is an absolute necessity; without discipline and regulations, White-Jacket tells his readers, "a man-of-war's crew would be nothing but a mob."[9] Thus, while Captain Vere's authority is plenary, his reign does not descend to the level of despotism.

While Vere wears his rank well, both in the fleet and in society, he is capable of shedding the signs of his professional stature and yet retaining his personal status. "Ashore, in the garb of a civilian, scarce anyone would have taken him for a sailor," and at quiet times at sea, "he was the most undemonstrative of men." In fact, his character is such that it carries its own signs of social stature:

Any landsman observing this gentleman not conspicuous by his stature and wearing no pronounced insignia, emerging from his cabin to the open deck, and noting the silent deference of the officers retiring to leeward, might have taken him for the King's guest, a civilian aboard the King's ship, some highly honorable discreet envoy on his way to an important post. But in fact this unobtrusiveness of demeanor may have proceeded from a certain unaffected modesty of manhood sometimes accompanying a resolute nature, a modesty evinced at all times not calling for pronounced action, which shown in any rank of life suggests a virtue aristocratic in kind.[10]

Vere is thus a nobleman, but one in a conventionally hierarchical society. Unlike the noble savage Mehevi in *Typee*, he is not simply one of "Nature's noblemen," but his abilities are nonetheless natural endowments. In Vere, nature and convention meet to distinguish one man from the mass of men. Whereas Billy's nobility is that of a "blood horse," Vere's is that of a born aristocrat. But Vere's standing as an aristocrat is more than just social and political. His popular nickname is "Starry Vere," and the narrator notes that this appellation is somewhat incongruous for "one who whatever his sterling qualities was without any brilliant ones." "Brilliant" and "Starry" in this sense are the opposites of "undemonstrative," "unobtrusive," and "unaffected"; the incongruity of the nickname lies in Vere's self-effacement and lack of ostentatiousness. His appellation is related to the fact that he "would at times betray a certain dreaminess of mood," and it was bestowed upon him at his return from his heroic West Indian cruise by a kinsman who had read these lines in Andrew Marvell's "Appleton House":

> This 'tis to have been from the first
> In a domestic heaven nursed,
> Under the discipline severe
> Of Fairfax and the starry Vere. [P. 61]

Vere's description thus adds an element that was absent in the portrait of Nelson as the Great Sailor. He is not only a man of courageous military spirit but also a man of a certain kind of distinguished intellect. His "starry" or celestial aspect, unlike Billy's and the "Handsome Sailor's," points not toward the figure of an animal, but toward the supposed height of humanity.

"Aside from his qualities as a sea officer Captain Vere was

an exceptional character." His exceptional quality was that of his mind:

> He had a marked leaning toward everything intellectual. He loved books, never going to sea without a newly replenished library, compact but of the best. . . . With nothing of that literary taste which less heeds the thing conveyed than the vehicle, his bias was toward those books to which every serious mind of superior order occupying any active post of authority in the world naturally inclines: books treating of actual men and events no matter of what era—history, biography, and unconventional writers like Montaigne, who, free from cant and convention, honestly and in the spirit of common sense philosophize upon realities.[11]

The fact that Vere is a "dry and bookish" man in the eyes of some officers adds to his natural aloofness. But the narrator's quotation of an "apt" remark about Vere shows that his officers are nevertheless aware of his abilities, and it also shows how Melville wants Vere to be understood in comparison to the Great Sailor: "Vere is a noble fellow, Starry Vere. 'Spite the gazettes, Sir Horatio is at bottom scarce a better seaman or fighter. But between you and me now, don't you think there is a queer streak of the pedantic running through him? Yes, like the King's yarn in a coil of navy rope?"[12] Captain Vere is thus a Great Sailor like Nelson, but his soul is laced by an education in practical wisdom. If Billy and the "Handsome Sailor" are "beauty and strength" and Nelson and the Great Sailor are glory and duty, Vere is honor and prudence. Vere is a certain version of Aristotle's magnanimous man, a man of great practical virtue; as his name suggests both *vir* and *veritas*, his is the soul of a man of practical or manly wisdom.

As a reader, Captain Vere does not have a purely philosophic interest in truth, for as a person of authority, he must *act*; in action, truth gives way to prudence. He is, in action, an analogue of Burke's statesman, whose thought and effort aim only at "the concrete and limited good of the particular community which he has to govern, and not the good of man in the abstract."[13] His historical studies serve as a ground for the political principle upon which he acts, and just as he stands above his fellow officers by reason of his "bookish" nature, he stands above his intellectual contemporaries by reason of his "disinterested" but practical convictions:

> In this line of reading he found confirmation of his own more reserved thoughts—confirmation which he had vainly sought in social converse, so that as touching most fundamental topics, there had got to be established in him some positive convictions which he forefelt would abide in him essentially unmodified so long as his intelligent part remained unimpaired. In view of the troubled period in which his lot was cast, this was well for him. His settled convictions were as a dike against those invading waters of novel opinion social, political, and otherwise, which carried away as in a torrent no few minds in those days, minds by nature not inferior to his own. While other members of that aristocracy to which by birth he belonged were incensed at the innovators mainly because their theories were inimical to the privileged classes, Captain Vere disinterestedly opposed them not alone because they seemed to him insusceptible of embodiment in lasting institutions, but at war with the peace of the world and the true welfare of mankind.[14]

As Vere is introduced, therefore, the reader meets a man who has arrived at a state of equilibrium: his political beliefs as a Burkean conservative have established a *modus vivendi* with his unconventional inclination to "philosophize upon realities." His "settled convictions" against novel theories derive from his practical belief in the human need for "lasting institutions" and his traditionalist notion of "the true welfare of mankind." He is distinguished from both the "innovators" and the self-interested "aristocrats," positioning himself, with practical truth, in the middle. As ruler of the *Bellipotent*, he seems to be the epitome of the Burkean politician, a "philosopher in action."[15] As captain and king of a ship of state, he seems to have achieved that coincidence of philosophy and rule which might promise to alleviate human or political ills. His ship is apparently ruled by practical wisdom as it prepares for war and victory.

At this point, it should be noted that there is a complex but well-structured frame which underlies the various comparisons and contrasts which have been made between the "Handsome Sailor" and Billy Budd, between the Great Sailor and Captain Vere, and among the four characters individually. The two introductory characters complement each other and combine to form a complete picture of political virtue: a natural king, god, and founder is portrayed beside a national nobleman, priest, and savior. Both the "Handsome Sailor" and the Great Sailor are presented as victims of advanced technology in the form, respectively, of steamships or ironclads, and both character types are drawn in contrast to enlightened philosophy as represented, respectively, by the atheistic and egalitarian French Assembly or the utilitarian Bentham. Since the "Handsome Sailor" is the more natural, original, or pure of the two, his fate has been the more pronounced in the face of adverse modernity. In recent times, the "Handsome Sailor" is but a shadow of his real, underlying nature as natural god-king, while the Great Sailor, who combined natural endowment with conventional rank, was able to survive in effective form even into modern times. But whatever distinctions exist between them, the "Handsome Sailor" and the Great Sailor both are placed in a scheme in which modern science and enlightened philosophy are called into question as principals in the destruction of political virtue.

Correspondingly, the differences between Billy Budd and Captain Vere exist beside parallel lines of development between each of them and his respective introductory character. Just as the nature of Billy Budd is a refracted image of the "Handsome Sailor" through the prism of Rousseauean philosophy, so also is the character of Captain Vere a refracted image of the Great Sailor through the prism of Burkean philosophy. That is, both Billy and Vere are modern versions of ancient archetypes, on the one hand the god-king of a Typean political "state of nature," and on the other, the magnanimous man of an Aristotelian ideal *polis*. The choice of the characters of both arational Billy Budd and conservative Captain Vere also duplicates the implied rejection of the Enlightenment contained in the very figures of the "Handsome Sailor" and the Great Sailor. Melville will test modern politics by testing the models of Rousseau and Burke, both of whom, though in different ways, also attacked enlightened philosophy. A character modeled directly on the philosophy of the Rights of Man is apparently not worth a major effort of criticism. Indeed, as will be seen, the ship's surgeon, who embodies modern natural science and is therefore closest to a model of enlightened modernity itself, is a caricature rather than a character.

In the end, the testing of modernity in *Billy Budd* will reveal the limitations of both Rousseau's hero and Burke's model in the man-of-war world. The peace which is the prerequisite for the noble savage is not to be expected, and the practical wisdom which presumably would ameliorate the man-of-war world is tragically inadequate to the task expected of it. Wisdom can actually *rule* only in the work of the self-conscious teacher-artist whose knowledge and art combine to reveal the limitations of human existence; such is the claim of the author of *White-Jacket*:

And I feel persuaded in my inmost soul, that it is to the fact of my having been a main-top-man; and especially my particular post being on the loftiest yard of the frigate, the main-royal-yard; that I am now enabled to give such a free, broad, off-hand, bird's-eye, and, more than all, impartial account of our man-of-war world; withholding nothing; inventing nothing; nor flattering, nor scandalizing any; but meting out to all—commodore and messenger-boy alike—their precise descriptions and deserts.[16]

Notes

¹ P. 55. The same considerations of pride and policy account for the authorized newspaper chronicle's reference to Billy's impressment in guarded terms: Billy was "one of those aliens . . . whom the present extraordinary necessities of the service have caused to be admitted into it in considerable numbers." (See p. 130 and *H&S*, p. 200.)

² See William York Tindall, "The Ceremony of Innocence," in R. M. MacIver, ed., *Great Moral Dilemmas in Literature, Past and Present* (New York: Harper & Brothers, 1956), p. 80.

³ Milton R. Stern, *The Fine Hammered Steel of Herman Melville* (Urbana, Ill.: University of Illinois Press, 1957), p. 207. See also Wendell Glick, "Expediency and Absolute Morality in *Billy Budd*," *PMLA* 68 (March 1953): 103; and Laurence Barret, "The Differences in Melville's Poetry," *PMLA* 70 (September 1955): 622–23.

⁴ P. 59. This is a historical episode in Nelson's career. (See *H&S*, pp. 151–52.) Melville reveled in the symbolic richness that could be gleaned from "actual reality." See especially his "Agatha Letter" to Nathaniel Hawthorne, 13 August 1852, in *The Letters of Herman Melville*, ed. Merrell R. Davis and William H. Gilman (New Haven: Yale University Press, 1960), pp. 153–61.

⁵ P. 56. But note that all these "naval magnates" are identified or easily identifiable with their countries.

⁶ On this point see Berthoff, " 'Certain Phenomenal Men': the Example of *Billy Budd*," *ELH* 27 (December 1960): 343–46, and passim. Compare Aristotle *Nicomachean Ethics* 1123a 34–1125a 35.

⁷ Pp. 59–60. Compare the state of affairs aboard the *Bellipotent* with the tyranny aboard the *Dolly* in *Typee* and the comedy induced by the incompetent Captain of the *Julia* in *Omoo*; see *Typee: A Peep at Polynesian Life* and *Omoo: A Narrative of Adventures in the South Seas*, in *The Writings of Herman Melville*, ed. Har-

NOTES

rison Hayford, Hershel Parker, and G. Thomas Tanselle, 15 vols.
(Evanston and Chicago: Northwestern University Press and The
Newberry Library, 1968–), 1:21 and 2:10, respectively. (The
former reference occurs during Tommo's argument in favor of
the right of revolt against a tyrant who imposes a long train of
abuses on his crew.)

8 Herman Melville, *White-Jacket: or The World in a Man-of-War*, in *The Writings of Herman Melville*, ed. Harrison Hayford,
Hershel Parker, and G. Thomas Tanselle, 15 vols. (Evanston and
Chicago: Northwestern University Press and The Newberry Library, 1968–), 5:23. For an account of Melville's view of the
"man-of-war" world, see Frederic I. Carpenter, "Melville: The
World in a Man-of-War," *University of Kansas City Review* 19
(Summer 1953): 257–64. Carpenter confuses authority with "authoritarianism" (for example, at pp. 258–59) and therefore concludes that *Billy Budd* is a work of "authoritarian philosophy" (p.
263). The present study agrees, however, with Carpenter's statement at p. 259 that Melville "believed war was the one constant
fact of human history." Cf., however, Joyce Sparer Adler, "*Billy Budd* and Melville's Philosophy of War," *PMLA* 91 (March
1976): 266–78.

9 *White-Jacket*, p. 9. Compare also the statement in *Omoo*, p.
14, concerning the need to subjugate riotous crews.
  Melville's view of the different place of discipline aboard a
merchantman (witness Captain Graveling's *Rights*) is corroborated
by Joseph Conrad. In *The Nigger of the Narcissus* (1897), Conrad
wrote, "Discipline is not ceremonious in merchant ships, where
the sense of hierarchy is weak, and where all feel themselves equal
before the unconcerned immensity of the sea and the exacting appeal of the work."

10 P. 60. Compare the deference of the officers here and in
White-Jacket, p. 23, with the natives' deference to Mehevi in
Typee, p. 77.

11 P. 62. Compare Vere's description with that of the captain
of the *Arcturion* in *Mardi*: "Could he talk sentiment or philosophy? Not a bit. His library was eight inches by four: Bowditch
and Hamilton Moore." (Bowditch and Moore wrote or edited
navigation manuals.) See *Mardi: and a Voyage Thither*, in *The*

Writings of Herman Melville, ed. Harrison Hayford, Hershel Parker, and G. Thomas Tanselle, 15 vols. (Evanston and Chicago: Northwestern University Press and The Newberry Library, 1968–   ), 3:5.

¹² P. 63. Compare the further remark on this page, that "in illustrating of any point touching the stirring personages and events of the time he would be as apt to cite some historic character or incident of antiquity as he would be to cite from the moderns," with Taji's remark about himself in *Mardi*, p. 14: "I have invariably been known by a sort of drawing-room title. . . . It was because of something in me that could not be hidden; stealing out in an occasional polysyllable . . . remote, unguarded allusions to Belles-Lettres affairs."

¹³ Francis P. Canavan, S.J., *The Political Reason of Edmund Burke* (Durham, N.C.: Duke University Press, 1960), p. 7.

¹⁴ Pp. 62–63. Burke is mentioned as Paine's opponent at p. 48, and the argument between the two is clearly evoked by this description of Vere's convictions.

¹⁵ Edmund Burke, *Thoughts on the Cause of the Present Discontents*, in *The Works of the Right Honorable Edmund Burke*, 12 vols. (Boston: Little, Brown, 1865–67), 1:530–31. Compare the whole description of Vere with Edmund Burke, *Reflections on the Revolution in France*, ed. Thomas H. D. Mahoney (Indianapolis: Library of Liberal Arts, 1955), pp. 34–35, 37–39, 42–45, 55–57, 60–73, 101–2.

For a view that relates Vere to Montaigne, see W. G. Kilbourne, Jr., "Montaigne and Captain Vere," *American Literature* 33 (January 1962): 514–17; and for another proposed model for Vere, see John C. Sherwood, "Vere as Collingwood: A Key to *Billy Budd*," *American Literature* 35 (January 1964): 476–84.

¹⁶ *White-Jacket*, p. 47.

4

Natural Depravity

THE NARRATOR'S ORIGINAL SKETCH of the "Handsome Sailor" left open the possibility that the purely natural authority which the "Handsome Sailor" embodied could also be lodged in the person of one who, at the same time, actually bore a commensurate rank of conventional authority. This possibility was subsequently realized in the narrator's introduction of the Great Sailor, Lord Nelson, whose full authority flowed from both his rank and a natural greatness and spiritedness of soul: his natural ability displayed itself in the defense of the conventional "founded law" of the British Empire. The particular instance of Captain Vere further emphasized the fact that the Great Sailor's "aristocratic virtue," while existing at times in the garb and with the shining "vouchers" of conventional rank and honor, nevertheless had its source in certain moral and, in Vere's case, intellectual qualities of soul, qualities which allowed the acceptance of conventional distinction as their due reward but which found their primary recognition in the great-souled man's pride in his own being.[1] Nevertheless, the detailed sketches of the Great Sailor and

Captain Vere, coupled with the narrator's introduction of the question of conventional rank, leave open another possibility, namely the possibility that conventional authority and rank may be borne by one whose soul is marked not by spiritedness and honor, but by baseness and vice.

The possibility of the coincidence of recognized authority and vice is apparently a problem only of advanced or "urbane" civilization. The source of the "Handsome Sailor's" distinction was Nature alone, and the fact that his distinguishing characteristics—strength, beauty, and a corresponding moral nature—were *natural* endowments meant that the one who embodied them was, for that very reason, also singled out as one of Nature's *noble* men. In the unexpectedly political state of nature that Melville presented in *Typee*, there was no possibility of ignobility in places of rank because proximity to nature guaranteed that political distinction could only flow from natural nobility. That is, in Melville's state of nature, natural and political distinctions are coincident. The introduction of John Claggart in *Billy Budd*, however, shows that modern, or earlier refined civilizations, have no such guarantee. The fact that in our complex civilization distinctions may flow from convention independently of nature means that the possibility of modern Great Sailors is purchased at the price of the possibility of vicious modern authorities. As the narrator says of Claggart's "natural depravity," "Civilization, especially if of the austerer sort, is auspicious to it" (p. 75). The worth of "urbane" civilization is at least limited by the fact that it thus offers to vice at least the promise of success.

The problem raised here is thus another facet of a theme which was introduced in the first sentence of the novel and which surfaced again during the discussion of Nelson. The theme is a variant of a Rousseauean one; the coming of prosaic, advanced civilization unfavorably affects the human condition. The god-kings, the "Handsome Sailors," the Great Sailors become extinct or progressively more rare, and the moral and political virtues which they embodied are no longer guaranteed actual political ascendancy. Indeed, John Claggart demonstrates that vice may find the home in advanced civilization which it did not have in the natural community of Melville's state of nature. This is not to say that Melville claims there is no vice by nature; Claggart's is a *natural* depravity, and as the narrator pointed out, when he admitted that sailors *do* have vices, such vices are "frank manifestations in accordance with *natural* law." What is at issue is *how* vices may be clothed, or whether they are clothed at all. On this issue, Melville sides with the sober Rousseau of the *Discourse on the Sciences and Arts*, who wrote:

> Before art had moulded our manners and taught our passions to speak an affected language, our customs were rustic but natural, and differences of conduct announced at first glance those of character. Human nature, basically, was no better, but men found their security in the ease of seeing through each other, and that advantage, which we no longer appreciate, spared them many vices.[2]

In *Typee*, Tommo found that the Typees paralleled Rousseau's description exactly:

> The lively countenances of these people are wonderfully indicative of the emotions of the soul, and the imperfections of their oral language are more than compensated for by the nervous eloquence of their looks and gestures. I could plainly trace, in every varying expression of their faces, all those passions which had been thus unexpectedly aroused in their bosoms.[3]

In contrast to the naked vices and passions in Melville's Typean state of nature, the viciousness and passions of John Claggart are clothed with "that manufacturable thing known as respectability," the artificial mantle of advanced civilization.

The introduction of Claggart completes Melville's picture
of human nature, a picture which includes the archetypes of
innocence, virtue, and vice. Melville apparently intends to
give an "impartial account" of human nature, an account which
avoids the extremes of both a Hobbes and a *philosophe*. In fact,
as early as *Typee*, Melville had shown his understanding that
man was naturally capable of both nobility and viciousness
and that the real, man-of-war world merely amplified the
human capability for evil which presumably was less pronounced or at least less effectual in man's pristine state. The
irresistible impressment of Billy Budd shows that Melville believed the man-of-war world was inevitable, and this was the
final stroke in the sober sketch of human nature he began in
Typee:

> [The Typees] seemed to be governed by that sort of tacit
> common-sense law which, say what they will of the inborn
> lawlessness of the human race, has its precepts graven on
> every breast. The grand principles of virtue and honor, how-
> ever they may be distorted by arbitrary codes, are the same
> all the world over. . . . It is to this indwelling, this universally
> diffused perception of what is *just* and *noble*, that the integ-
> rity of the Marquesans in their intercourse with each other
> is to be attributed.
>
> . . . .
>
> I will frankly declare, that after passing a few weeks in this
> valley of the Marquesas, I formed a higher estimate of hu-
> man nature than I had ever before entertained. But alas!
> since then I have been one of the crew of a man-of-war, and
> the pent-up wickedness of five hundred men has nearly
> overturned all my previous theories.[4]

In *Billy Budd* Melville no longer is seeking to embrace one of
these offsetting theories about human nature; he is presenting
the given facts of human affairs and impartially meting out to
the innocent, the virtuous, and the wicked their worldly fates.

[68]

Regarding human evil, impartiality does not produce specificity. The narrator opens his introduction of John Claggart by saying, "His portrait I essay, but shall never hit it," and the reader is thus presented a hint of the enigmatic quality of evil along with the person who will embody it.[5] On the other hand, the narrator does specify that Claggart's present position of authority owes its existence to the same scientific progress that threatened knightly valor with obsolescence and emasculated the "Handsome Sailor" archetype. The title "master-at-arms" seems "somewhat equivocal" to landsmen, and the reason is that the office has changed with time:

> Originally, doubtless, that petty officer's function was the instruction of the men in the use of arms, sword or cutlass. But very long ago, owing to the advance in gunnery making hand-to-hand encounters less frequent and giving to niter and sulphur the pre-eminence over steel, that function ceased; the master-at-arms of a great warship becoming a sort of chief of police charged among other matters with the duty of preserving order on the populous lower gun decks.[6]

The "advance in gunnery" eliminated the need for the courageous virtue necessary, as before, "to stand up crossing steel with steel in frank fight." Gone also was the need for the instructors who were artists at "hand-to-hand encounters" and who, presumably, shared in the courage needed therein. An office which thus previously assigned an authoritative place to the virtue of courage became instead merely an office for the preservation of order; it became an office, that is, which dealt only in the more austere aspects of an advanced and technologically complex civilization and its requisite discipline.

While John Claggart thus will bring evil into an office which provides fertile ground for evil, he is no mean figure:

> Claggart was a man about five-and-thirty, somewhat spare and tall, yet of no ill figure upon the whole. His hand was

too small and shapely to have been accustomed to hard toil. The face was a notable one, the features all except the chin cleanly cut as those on a Greek medallion; yet the chin, beardless as Tecumseh's, had something of strange protuberant broadness in its make that recalled the prints of the Reverend Dr. Titus Oates, the historic deponent with the clerical drawl in the time of Charles II and the fraud of the alleged Popish Plot. It served Claggart in his office that his eye could cast a tutoring glance. His brow was of the sort phrenologically associated with more than average intellect; silken jet curls partly clustering over it, making a foil to the pallor below, a pallor tinged with a faint shade of amber akin to the hue of time-tinted marbles of old. This complexion, singularly contrasting with the red or deeply bronzed visages of the sailors, and in part the result of his official seclusion from the sunlight, though it was not exactly displeasing, nevertheless seemed to hint of something defective or abnormal in the constitution and blood. But his general aspect and manner were so suggestive of an education and career incongruous with his naval function that when not actively engaged in it he looked like a man of high quality, social and moral, who for reasons of his own was keeping incog.[7]

In his own way, thus, Claggart appears as exceptional a character as Billy Budd and Captain Vere. He is at the same time socially incongruous in his naval office and well suited to it by his similarity to the accusing Titus Oates and his possession of a "tutoring glance." Like Billy, Claggart resembles a Greek figure, and somewhat like Vere, he has the marks of intellectuality, although there is no mention of Claggart's having a practical bent intellectually. The one thing amiss in his otherwise pleasing aspect is his amber hue, hinting of some abnormality. The hint of evil here well suits the subtlety with which his figure is portrayed.

Claggart shares a mysterious past with Billy, and both thus

contrast with Vere and his family heritage. The mystery surrounding Claggart's past—"Nothing was known of his former
life"—is used by the loyalist narrator both to cast doubt upon
the "patriotic" Claggart's English birth and to introduce the
ship's gossip about the master-at-arms:

> It might be that he was an Englishman; and yet there lurked
> a bit of accent in his speech suggesting that possibly he was
> not such by birth, but through naturalization in early child-
> hood. Among certain grizzled sea gossips of the gun decks
> and forecastle went a rumor perdue that the master-at-arms
> was a *chevalier* who had volunteered into the King's navy by
> way of compounding for some mysterious swindle where-
> of he had been arraigned at the King's Bench. The fact that
> nobody could substantiate this report was, of course, nothing
> against its secret currency. [P. 65]

The narrator goes on to remark that the ship's gossip had "a
vague plausibility" in "the period assigned to this narrative,"
and the reasons offered for the plausibility remind the reader
"of England's straits at the time confronted by those wars
which like a flight of harpies rose shrieking from the din and
dust of the fallen Bastille":

> . . . now for some period the British navy could so little
> afford to be squeamish in the matter of keeping up the muster
> rolls, that not only were press gangs notoriously abroad both
> afloat and ashore, but there was little or no secret about
> another matter, namely, that the London police were at
> liberty to capture any able-bodied suspect, any questionable
> fellow at large, and summarily ship him to the dockyard or
> fleet. . . . Such sanctioned irregularities . . . lend color to
> something for the truth whereof I do not vouch, and hence
> have some scruple in stating; . . . It was to this effect: In the
> case of a warship short of hands whose speedy sailing was
> imperative, the deficient quota, in lack of any other way of

making it good, would be eked out by drafts culled direct from the jails.[8]

But while the gossip is shown to be vaguely plausible, and while the reader is also reminded that the raging war in fact required "sanctioned irregularities" and did not allow legal fastidiousness in official practices, apparently the narrator's main purpose here is to emphasize by contrast his previous hint that Claggart's is not merely the prevalent, ordinary form of human evil. "The verdict of the sea quidnuncs has been cited only by way of showing what sort of moral impression the man made upon rude uncultivated natures whose conceptions of human wickedness were necessarily of the narrowest, limited to ideas of vulgar rascality—a thief among the swinging hammocks during a night watch, or the man-brokers and land-sharks of the seaports" (p. 67).

The narrator points out that the "field for unfavorable surmise" about tight-lipped Claggart was opened by his having joined the navy mysteriously "at mature life"; that the resulting gossip was kept alive by the sailors' propensity to indulge their suspicions with pedestrian notions of "rascality"; but also that the rumors about the master-at-arms were to be given "the less credence" because "no man holding his office in a man-of-war can ever hope to be popular with the crew" (pp. 65–67). The effect of these inconclusive facts is not only an enhancement of the mystery surrounding Claggart but also the suggestion that a proper understanding of Claggart will require one to dive beneath the "rude" and "uncultivated" view of evil for the more profound truth about evil. This requirement is dictated by the one fact that has emerged about Claggart, namely, that he is an exceptional man:

It was no gossip, however, but fact that though, as before hinted, Claggart upon his entrance into the navy was, as a novice, assigned to the least honorable section of a man-of-war's crew, embracing the drudgery, he did not long remain there. The superior capacity he immediately evinced, his constitutional sobriety, an ingratiating deference to superiors, together with a peculiar ferreting genius manifested on a singular occasion; all this, capped by a certain austere patriotism, abruptly advanced him to the position of master-at-arms. [P. 67]

The fact of Claggart's exceptionality and the mysteriousness given his character by the narrator's mentioning and then doubting the ship's gossip thus once again highlight the fact that the "Inside Narrative" addresses itself to a particular audience, an audience which seeks the "uncompromising truth" beneath the surface "truths."

At this point, then, the reader is alerted to Claggart's uncommon potential. The hints of Claggart's wickedness and the fact that his official direction of the ship's corporals puts "various converging wires of underground influence under [his] control" (p. 67) set up an air of anticipation about Claggart's actions. In the meantime, Billy has settled onto the *Bellipotent* and is "well content" in the society of topmen, who spend their leisurely moments lounging and "spinning yarns like the lazy gods." And while he was always efficient in his calling on the *Rights*, Billy is even more devoted to his duty upon the *Bellipotent*. "This heightened alacrity had its cause, namely, the impression made upon him by the first formal gangway-punishment he had ever witnessed, which befell the day following his impressment" (p. 68). Billy's dual reaction to this spectacle again reveals his conformity to Rousseau's principles, in this case to the two prerational principles of the Rousseauean natural soul, "of which one interests us ardently in our well-being and our self-preservation, and the other inspires in us a natural repugnance to see any sensitive being perish or suffer, principally our fellowmen."[9] But the resolutions that Billy makes as a result of this episode prove to be to no avail, and the reader's anticipation of trouble from Claggart is thus further stirred:

> When Billy saw the culprit's naked back under the scourge, gridironed with red welts and worse, when he marked the dire expression in the liberated man's face as with his woolen shirt flung over him by the executioner he rushed forward from the spot to bury himself in the crowd, Billy was horrified. He resolved that never through remissness would he make himself liable to such a visitation or do or omit aught that might merit even verbal reproof. What then was his surprise and concern when ultimately he found himself getting into petty trouble occasionally about such matters as the stowage of his bag or something amiss in his hammock, matters under the police oversight of the ship's corporals of the lower decks, and which brought down on him a vague threat from one of them.[10]

Billy's "unconcealed anxiety," which his "young topmates" find almost "comical," leads him to seek advice from a veteran old Dansker, who was "long anglicized in the service," who had been an "*Agamemnon* man . . . having served under Nelson," and who appears to Billy to be "the sort of person to go to for wise counsel." The Dansker's wisdom is that of experience, not only the experience of one man, but that of all the ages. His wisdom is thus "primitive in its kind," and his attitude towards Billy requires attention:

> Now the first time that his small weasel eyes happened to light on Billy Budd, a certain grim internal merriment set all his ancient wrinkles into antic play. Was it that his eccentric unsentimental old sapience, primitive in its kind, saw or thought it saw something which in contrast with the warship's environment looked oddly incongruous in the Handsome Sailor? But after slyly studying him at intervals, the old Merlin's equivocal merriment was modified; for now when the twain would meet, it would start in his face a

quizzing sort of look, but it would be but momentary and sometimes replaced by an expression of speculative query as to what might eventually befall a nature like that, dropped into a world not without some mantraps and against whose subtleties simple courage lacking experience and address, and without any touch of defensive ugliness, is of little avail; and where such innocence as man is capable of does yet in a moral emergency not always sharpen the faculties or enlighten the will.[11]

This is, of course, another "divergence" in which the narrator opens up the center of the "Inside Narrative." The Dansker's reactions to Billy Budd make explicit Melville's intention to demonstrate the fate of innocence in the man-of-war world. But it should be noted that the wisdom of this "salt seer," this "oracular . . . sea Chiron" is limited to an insight into the precariousness of Billy's fate. The Dansker will not attempt to save Billy Budd, and his primitive "sapience" thus, appropriately, is as quiescent as is Billy's primitive innocence. The Dansker's wisdom apparently allows him to keep himself out of trouble, but it is no defense against the occurrence of evil to others. This "Chiron's" wisdom will not in fact aid "his young Achilles" (p. 71) in the practical difficulties Billy will face, and the Dansker's wisdom is thus as "theoretical" as it is "primitive" and "oracular." In an odd way, the Dansker's wisdom is that of an onlooking and detached God rather than of an acting man.

Billy is puzzled to learn that in the Dansker's judgment, his troubles stem from the fact that "Jemmy Legs" (the term for the master-at-arms) is "down on" him. Billy's perplexity is due to his previous regard for Claggart, of whom he says, "I seldom pass him but there comes a pleasant word." In fact, the narrator indirectly provides grounds for Billy's incredulity by observing that the Dansker had developed a "pithy guarded cynicism that was his leading characteristic."[12] The very next day, also, Billy accidentally spills his soup in the path of Claggart and is greeted by the latter's words, "Handsomely done, my lad! And handsome is as handsome did it, too!" But while Billy innocently takes these words as proof of the Dansker's error, he does not notice "the involuntary smile, or rather grimace, that accompanied Claggart's equivocal words." Finally, the narrator sets the stage for the central treatment of Claggart by a further observation:

> Meantime that functionary, resuming his path, must have momentarily worn some expression less guarded than that of the bitter smile, usurping the face from the heart—some distorting expression perhaps, for a drummer-boy heedlessly frolicking along from the opposite direction and chancing to come into light collision with his person was strangely disconcerted by his aspect. Nor was the impression lessened when the official, impetuously giving him a sharp cut with the rattan, vehemently exclaimed, "Look where you go!" [Pp. 72–73]

There is thus no longer any doubt that the fruits of Claggart's malice will be realized, as the soup episode "may indicate to the discerning." The crucial issue is thus raised: "What was the matter with the master-at-arms?" Now the narrator observes that it would be "not so difficult" to explain Claggart's hatred for Billy by inventing some event in their pasts for which, unknown to Billy, Claggart bears Billy a grudge. "But in fact there was nothing of the sort." The necessary cause is mysterious: "For what can more partake of the mysterious than an antipathy spontaneous and profound such as is evoked in certain exceptional mortals by the mere aspect of some other mortal, however harmless he may be, if not called forth by this very harmlessness itself?" [13]

The close quarters aboard a warship causes the most "irritating juxtaposition of dissimilar personalities." The narrator invites the reader to "imagine how all this might eventually operate on some peculiar human creature the direct reverse of a saint!" But these hints are insufficient, and the approach to Claggart requires another divergence or "indirection." The divergence in this case is a recounting of the narrator's conversation with "an honest scholar, [his] senior" about the means necessary to dive beneath the façade of a certain "unimpeachably respectable" man. The scholar said he would require "some source other than what is known as 'knowledge of the world'," and the narrator was perplexed because, in his own opinion, "knowledge of the world assuredly implies the knowledge of human nature." The scholar's reply reaffirms the narrator's function of suggesting the path to more profound spiritual insights into his characters and events:

"Yes, but a superficial knowledge of it, serving ordinary purposes. But for anything deeper, I am not certain whether to know the world and to know human nature be not two distinct branches of knowledge, which while they may co-exist in the same heart, yet either may exist with little or nothing of the other. Nay, in an average man of the world, his constant rubbing with it blunts that finer spiritual insight indispensable to the understanding of the essential in certain exceptional characters, whether evil ones or good. . . . Coke and Blackstone hardly shed so much light into obscure spiritual places as the Hebrew prophets. And who were they? Mostly recluses." [Pp. 74–75]

Just as the lesser officers, "whose reading was mainly confined to the journals" (p. 63), could not understand Vere, and as mere shrewdness cannot lead to an understanding of Billy Budd, so too cannot any "knowledge of the world" comprehend Claggart. Such knowledge, whether scientific (as is the surgeon's) or legal (as is Coke's and Blackstone's), is not capable of the subtleties required of the task. Thus, as technological knowledge has made the office of master-at-arms more receptive to vice, more generally "knowledge of the world" has interfered with the proper comprehension of the vicious.

The narrator, who now sees "the drift" of the honest scholar's reply, would like to follow his suggestion that the requisite spiritual insight might be found in the prophets. But while "one might with less difficulty define and denominate certain phenomenal men" if the "lexicon which is based on Holy Writ were any longer popular," in his time "one must turn to some authority not liable to the charge of being tinctured with the biblical element." The authority he turns to is a lexicon attached to "the authentic translation of Plato," in which "occurs this: 'Natural Depravity: a depravity according to nature'."[14]

Before discussing this Platonic definition, it is necessary to take notice of the reintroduction of the narrator's criticism of the popular disregard for Holy Writ. Originally, he had remarked, in connection with Billy's description, that the present existence of "pristine and unadulterate" virtues suggested that they had been "exceptionally transmitted from a period prior to Cain's city"; this suggestion apparently tended "to corroborate the doctrine of man's Fall, *a doctrine now popularly ignored.*" While the attempt will be made below to show that this first observation and the added remarks on the unpopularity of Holy Writ immediately above do not necessarily imply that either the narrator or Melville offers Scripture as the long-sought source of truth, it is unmistakable that Holy Writ is being defended as possessing a "lexicon" more profound than that of the scientific rationalism or modern philosophy which have made its pages unpopular. This fact casts light upon the narrator's frequent biblical allusions in telling his story, and it suggests that all along he had offered these allusions for their great suggestive spiritual value and in deliberate opposition to their current unpopularity. Also, the suggestion that the biblical understanding of reality is in some way close to the understanding of the "Inside Narrative" will be crucial at the end of the novel when it becomes apparent that the "uncultivated" sailors will see Billy as a Christ-figure. In any case, the narrator gives this point great attention, and in fact, after discussing what *he* means by "natural depravity," he returns to it:

> Dark sayings are these, some will say. But why? Is it because they somewhat savor of Holy Writ in its phrase "mystery of iniquity"? If they do, such savor was far enough from being intended, for little will it commend these pages to many a reader of today. [P. 76]

The narrator observes, in reference to the Platonic defini-tion itself, that "though savoring of Calvinism, [it] by no means involves Calvin's dogma as to total mankind. Evidently its intent makes it applicable but to individuals" (p. 75). Clag-gart is thus an individual example of the natural existence of human depravity, and his portrait thus acts as both a clue to the narrator's understanding of the truth of Holy Writ and as a further correction of such liberal philosophers as Paine. Beginning with the former, it becomes apparent that the nar-rator views the doctrine of man's Fall, a doctrine taught in the extreme by Calvinism, as only adumbrating a truth about the human capability for evil. The error of the Calvinist dogma is apparently its simple condemnation of all men to a "fallen state"; the dogma ignores the human capacities for innocence and virtue just as the faith of liberal philosophy in man's per-fectibility ignores his inherent capacity for evil. The defense of Holy Writ is thus motivated by the narrator's desire to criticize the prevalent notions of modern philosophers like Paine, who held that man was naturally incapable of evil or, in other words, that man was "not the enemy of man, but through the medium of a false system of government."[15] The liberal philosophers underestimate the innate possibility of natural, noncivilizational evil, and Holy Writ does not. Claggart's evil is thus a curse upon civilization rather than a product of it; it is an evil born into a soul:

> Now something such an one was Claggart, in whom was the mania of an evil nature, not engendered by vicious training or corrupting books or licentious living, but born with him and innate, in short "a depravity according to nature." [P. 76]

The depravity is immense, but subtle, and it can thus insinuate itself, the opportunity being given, into high places. Its subtlety accounts for the facts that the ship's gossip cannot comprehend it and that the one who embodies it is able to use the requirements of civilizational order to his advantage:

> Not many are the examples of this depravity which the gallows and jail supply. At any rate, for notable instances, since these have no vulgar alloy of the brute in them, but invariably are dominated by intellectuality, one must go elsewhere. Civilization, especially if of the austerer sort, is auspicious to it. It folds itself in the mantle of respectability. It has its certain negative virtues serving as silent auxiliaries. It never allows wine to get within its guard. It is not going too far to say that it is without vices or small sins. There is a phenomenal pride in it that excludes them. It is never mercenary or avaricious. In short, the depravity here meant partakes nothing of the sordid or sensual. It is serious, but free from acerbity. Though no flatterer of mankind it never speaks ill of it. [Pp. 75–76]

In Claggart, thus, has been realized the possibility that civilization's artificial distinctions of rank, distinctions needed to order a complex, advanced society, may enfold an ignoble man. The apparently irresistible advance of civilization and the undeniable possibility of an innate capacity for human evil combine to limit the possibilities of political justice because the former necessarily provides an opportunity for the latter to operate from a position of strength.

While much of the narrator's description of Claggart is openly cloaked in mystery, there is one enigmatic part of that description which is far more subtle and which must be briefly noted here. The narrator has referred to Plato's notion of "natural depravity" to obtain authoritative support for the idea that there is an innate and individual human capacity for evil. This reference to Plato is certainly able to be supported: Book 10 of the *Republic* shows Socrates, in fact, fully describing "natural depravity" as that depravity is revealed within the soul of the tyrant. What must be noted, however, is that Socrates' description places the tyrannical man's depravity at the opposite pole of rationality and "the divine part" of our natures: Socrates' tyrant is the opposite of the philosopher. Nevertheless, in *Billy Budd*, the embodiment of "natural depravity" is said to be "dominated by intellectuality." This curious fact may tend to confirm our prior suspicions about the root cause of the destruction of human virtue: were the "Handsome Sailors" and Great Sailors opposed not only by *modern* science and *modern* philosophy, but by science and philosophy themselves? Is the ultimate depravity within man, contrary to Socrates, intellectuality itself? Is the possibility of real virtue destroyed by the same "apple of knowledge" which the celebrators of mere innocence blame for the destruction of natural simplicity? Such questions clearly point to the deepest parts of the lesson of *Billy Budd*, and they shall have to be returned to after the full story has unfolded.

In any case, the narrator has now rendered his subtle portrait of Claggart, and he notes that with "an added hint or two in connection with the incident at the mess, the resumed narrative must be left to vindicate, as it may, its own credibility." The hints deal with an explication of *why* the evil Claggart

directs himself against Billy in particular. As "the discerning"
may also have gathered from Claggart's soup-episode remark
to Billy, "he there let escape an ironic inkling . . . as to what
it was that had first moved him against Billy, namely, his significant personal beauty." Claggart is envious of Billy's beauty and
hates him for it, and since envy's "lodgment is in the heart not
the brain, no degree of intellect supplies a guarantee against
it. But Claggart's was no vulgar form of the passion."[16] Unlike
Saul's jealousy of David, "Claggart's envy struck deeper."
Claggart's envy stems from a deep insight into Billy's beauty:

> If askance he eyed the good looks, cheery health, and
> frank enjoyment of young life in Billy Budd, it was because
> these went along with a nature that, as Claggart magnetically
> felt, had in its simplicity never willed malice or experienced
> the reactionary bite of that serpent. To him, the spirit lodged
> within Billy . . . made him pre-eminently the Handsome
> Sailor. One person excepted, the master-at-arms was per-
> haps the only man in the ship intellectually capable of
> adequately appreciating the moral phenomenon presented
> in Billy Budd. And the insight but intensified his passion,
> which . . . at times assumed that of cynic disdain, disdain of
> innocence—to be nothing more than innocent! Yet in an
> aesthetic way he saw the charm of it . . . and fain would
> have shared it, but he despaired of it.
>
> With no power to annul the elemental evil in him, though
> readily enough he could hide it; apprehending the good, but
> powerless to be it; a nature like Claggart's, surcharged with
> energy as such natures almost invariably are, what recourse
> is left to it but to recoil upon itself and, like the scorpion for
> which the Creator alone is responsible, act out to the end
> the part allotted it.[17]

Unlike the detached Dansker, who apparently is satisfied with
mere knowledge of good, evil, and innocence, Claggart is led
by the same knowledge to hate innocence. That is, he hates the

lack of knowledge or the absence of sophistication: Claggart seeks to subvert the charming life of innocence.

In this atmosphere of antipathy, Claggart must have taken Billy's spilled soup "for the sly escape of a spontaneous feeling on Billy's part more or less answering . . . his own." Also, one of his corporals, "Squeak," whom he had used to cause the little trouble which so worried Billy, "made it his business, faithful understrapper that he was, to foment the ill blood by perverting to his chief certain innocent frolics of the good-natured foretopman, besides inventing for his mouth sundry contumelious epithets he claimed to have overheard him let fall." Thus Claggart's evil nature sets in motion evil events of which he himself loses control. His "subtler depravity" possesses an "uncommon prudence," which enables him to hide his maliciousness; but this very secretiveness cuts him off from "enlightenment" about suspected injuries, and he thus will act "upon surmise as upon certainty." His "conscience being but the lawyer to his will," Claggart makes "ogres of trifles," and thus his "retaliation is apt to be in monstrous disproportion to the supposed offense." In all, finally, "the occurrence at the mess, petty if it were, was a welcome one to that peculiar conscience assigned to be the private mentor of Claggart; and, for the rest, not improbably it put him upon new experiments" (pp. 79–80).

The portrait of Claggart reveals that the flaw in modern philosophy, whether that of Paine, the *philosophes*, or the radical Rousseau of the *Second Discourse*, is failure to appreciate the possibility of an innate human capacity for evil. It is this capacity that makes futile any conjecturing upon human innocence, like the radical Rousseauean innocence embodied by Billy Budd. Billy's fate is threatened by the existence of the unavoidable human evil, War, but Billy is finally undone by human evil in an individual form, the evil of John Claggart. As the external war with France threatens England and Billy with political evil from the left, so Claggart, the "chief of police" and austere patriot, internally threatens Billy with political evil on the right. Combined, the war and Claggart will show that Billy's ability to live an apolitical existence—whether in animal happiness on the tolerant *Rights* or in divine lounging in the topmasts of the *Bellipotent*—is merely illusory. The fact of human history is political existence, and it is given to man to act politically in the face of natural evil. The dialectic of the story thus appears to move toward locating the only possibile true heroism in the politically virtuous Captain Vere. The difficulty will remain, however, that such heroism is imperfect, and its corresponding political decisions will not always induce one's acceptance.

Notes

1 The sketch of Vere shows, that is, that the honor he embodies is not merely the philosophically "false" or "whimsical" honor that Montesquieu found in monarchies. See Baron De Montesquieu, *The Spirit of the Laws*, trans. Thomas Nugent, Hafner Library of Classics, no. 9 (New York: Hafner, 1949), pp. 25, 29–32.

2 Jean-Jacques Rousseau, *Discourse on the Sciences and Arts*, in *The First and Second Discourses*, ed. Roger D. Masters and trans. Roger D. and Judith R. Masters (New York: St. Martin's, 1964), p. 37. Of course, Melville opposed the more radical Rousseau of the *Second Discourse* who apparently denied that there was any "depravity" by nature.

3 *Typee: A Peep at Polynesian Life*, in *The Writings of Herman Melville*, ed. Harrison Hayford, Hershel Parker, and G. Thomas Tanselle, 15 vols. (Evanston and Chicago: Northwestern University Press and The Newberry Library, 1968–   ), 1:142.

4 Ibid. pp. 201, 203. The Typees *do* have wars or battles with the Happars, but proximity to nature also alters the face of this human evil. Of his experience of Marquesan warfare, Tommo says, "I felt in some sort like a 'prentice-boy who, going to the play in the expectation of being delighted with a cut-and-thrust tragedy, is almost moved to tears of disappointment at the exhibition of a genteel comedy." (See ibid., p. 128.)

5 The enigma of evil extends to its source and to the reasons for its actual occurrence, but it is apparently clear that evil *will* occur, as confirmed by the scroll quoted in *Mardi*: "And though all evils may be assuaged; all evils can not be done away. For evil is the chronic malady of the universe; and checked in one place, breaks forth in another." See *Mardi: and a Voyage Thither*, in *The Writings of Herman Melville*, ed. Harrison Hayford, Hershel Parker, and G. Thomas Tanselle, 15 vols. (Evanston and Chicago: Northwestern University Press and The Newberry Library, 1968–   ), 3:529.

6 P. 64. Compare this description of the office of master-at-arms with that in *White-Jacket*: "The master-at-arms is a sort of high constable and schoolmaster, wearing citizen's clothes, and known by his official rattan. He it is whom all sailors hate. His is the universal duty of a universal informer and hunter-up of delinquents. On the berth-deck he reigns supreme; . . . But as it is a heartless, so it is a thankless office. Of dark nights, most masters-at-arms keep themselves in readiness to dodge forty-two pound balls, dropped down the hatchways near them." See *White-Jacket: or, The World in a Man-of-War*, in *The Writings of Herman Melville*, ed. Harrison Hayford, Hershel Parker, and G. Thomas Tanselle, 15 vols. (Evanston and Chicago: Northwestern University Press and The Newberry Library, 1968–   ), 5:26–27.

7 P. 64. In view of the part played by "the authentic translation of Plato" below, compare Claggart's beardless chin with the ill-covered chin of Socrates' accuser, Meletos, in the *Euthyphro* 2b 10–11. Is Claggart more like Socrates or Meletos? (Hayford and Sealts suggest insightful parallels between other parts of Claggart's description and passages in *Redburn* and *White-Jacket* at *H&S*, pp. 154–55.)

8 Pp. 65–66. The narrator also points out that even "patriotic" or "voluntary" enlistees were sometimes really only refugees from debts and moral promiscuity. Also, the narrator's recollection of a conversation with "an old pensioner" in Greenwich "now more than forty years ago" about drafting recruits from the jails is of the same character as his recollection of the Liverpool Negro Handsome Sailor. (See *H&S*, pp. 135–36, 156, and the discussion at fn. 1 in chap. 2 of the present study.)

9 Rousseau, *Discourse on the Origin and Foundations of Inequality Among Men*, in *The First and Second Discourses*, p. 95.

10 Pp. 68–69. In a note to the text of *Omoo*, Melville wrote, "I do not wish to be understood as applauding the flogging system practiced in men-of-war. As long, however, as navies are needed, there is no substitute for it. War being the greatest of evils, all its accessories necessarily partake of the same character; and this is about all that can be said in defense of flogging." See *Omoo: A Narrative of Adventures in the South Seas*, in *The Writings of Herman Melville*, ed. Harrison Hayford, Hershel Parker, and G. Thomas

Tanselle, 15 vols. (Evanston and Chicago: Northwestern University Press and The Newberry Library, 1968–   ), 2:108. Hayford and Sealts remark that this sentiment "may be closer to Melville's position at the time of [writing] *Billy Budd* than is the . . . assault on flogging in Ch. 33–36 of *White-Jacket*, with which *Billy Budd* is usually compared." (See *H&S*, p. 157.)

¹¹ Pp. 69–70. On the Dansker, see James Baird, *Ishmael* (Baltimore: Johns Hopkins University Press, 1956), pp. 249–51. Also, note that the Dansker is the originator of Billy's nickname, "Baby."

¹² P. 71. Also, the Dansker's judgment is called a "smoky idea" at p. 73.

¹³ Pp. 73–74. Claggart's "spontaneous" antipathy contrasts with the "spontaneous homage" won by the "Handsome Sailor" (p. 43).

¹⁴ P. 75. The translation is evidently the Bohn edition of 1848–54. "Natural depravity" is defined (p. 143) in vol. 6 of that edition as "a badness by nature, and a sinning in that, which is according to nature." (See *H&S*, pp. 162–63.)

¹⁵ Thomas Paine, *The Rights of Man*, in *Complete Writings of Thomas Paine*, ed. Philip S. Foner, 2 vols. (New York: Citadel, 1945), 1:343. Again, it goes without saying that the disagreement with Paine also applies to those aspects of Rousseau which absolutize natural man's innocence rather than grant, as before, that in the state of nature, "human nature, basically, was no better." Rousseau had criticized Hobbes's view "that because man has no idea of goodness he is naturally evil." The implication that natural man is too innocent to display *either* virtue *or* vice is, of course, the explicit theme of the *Discourse on Inequality*, Rousseau's more "modern" discourse. (See the *Discourse on Inequality*, p. 128.) The disagreement with Rousseau on this score parallels the disagreement on the existence of political virtue and rank in the state of nature.

¹⁶ P. 77. The facts that Claggart's passion is not "vulgar" in form and that his depravity "partakes nothing of the sordid or sensual" would seem to suggest that those critics err who read frustrated homosexual desire as Claggart's motive. See E. L. Grant Watson, "Melville's Testament of Acceptance," *New England Quarterly* 6 (June 1933): 324–25; W. H. Auden, *The Enchafèd*

Flood: or the Romantic Iconography of the Sea (New York: Random House, 1950), pp. 147–49; and Geoffrey Stone, *Melville* (New York: Sheed & Ward, 1949), pp. 312–13.

[17] P. 78. Compare Claggart's judgment that Billy had not "experienced the reactionary bite of that serpent" with the narrator's earlier remark (p. 53) that Billy's hesitancy in speech "was a striking instance that the arch interferer, the envious marplot of Eden, still has more or less to do with every human consignment to this planet of Earth." Claggart's apparent error in seeing Billy as "pre-eminently the Handsome Sailor" is the first indication that his cunning is not based on full or *true* knowledge. Does true knowledge flow from a source other than "intellectuality"?

5

A Deplorable Occurrence

AS THE "INSIDE NARRATIVE" moves from the presentation of the characters of its "phenomenal men" to the
presentation of their actions, it moves also into its more specifically, and perhaps more narrowly, *political* dimension. Since
the sphere of politics is the sphere of action, the action of the
narrative primarily will reveal the strictly political lessons of
the novel. On one level, these lessons are more or less coincident with the acknowledged political bias of the narrator;
"inside" the narrative, however, are the lessons of the author,
whose agreements or disagreements with the narrator derive
from his claimed poetic knowledge, rather than from mere
partisan prejudice. Moreover, the action of the narrative always
assumes the character sketches themselves, and "inside" the
narrator's matter-of-fact presentation of the characters, the
author has already revealed the ultimate frame of reference
within which the specifically political lessons of the novel are
taught. That frame, again, is one which brings *all* of modern
politics into question by contrasting "phenomenal" modern
political types with their natural counterparts. In the end,

thus, the action of the narrative will present not only modern political lessons and a lesson about the limits of modern politics as a whole, but also, by extension, a lesson about the true character of political life per se.

The French war and John Claggart are the two evils that will show that human innocence cannot defend itself and thus cannot be the basis for the conduct of human affairs. These two evils will also show the limitations of modern conservative statesmanship. As the external disruption of the war was related earlier to the internal disruption of the Great Mutiny, so too now will the evil represented by John Claggart be related to the evil represented by the war with revolutionary France. The war results from the opposition of "founded law" to the lawlessness of "unbridled and unbounded revolt"; it results, that is, from a confrontation between political lawfulness and political lawlessness. That Britain is "constitutionally sound" does not mean, however, that all its laws or practices are just; the practice of impressment alone reveals that lawfulness is not proof of absolute justice. Lawfulness is, however, the mark of a regime that prizes continuity and established procedure: the continuity of custom and the procedure of legal adjudication, both of which unfortunately had sanctioned impressment. The constitutionally sound regime thus accepts a tolerance for specific or temporary injustices as the price of its preference for the working of established political processes. In like manner, on the personal rather than political level, the evil of John Claggart results from personal lawlessness which is opposed to the good order of the "sea commonalty," an order which can survive only insofar as social relationships partake of procedures founded in the "law of reason." Rational relationships are not necessarily good ones; indeed they may be a mere façade, concealing hatred and more violent antipathy. But the social order accepts a tolerance for hidden animosities as the price of its preference for surface relations which are amiable and easy. Social order demands at least the semblance of personal lawfulness in preference to "unbridled" personal lawlessness.

It is the measure of Claggart's cunning that he uses his "mantle of respectability" not merely to conceal his hatred but to cultivate it and prepare it for its lawless fruition. That is to say, Claggart is able to appear as if he were conforming to the demands of social order by the same means he uses to prepare to violate the social order. The narrator says of him:

> But the thing which in eminent instances signalizes so exceptional a nature is this: Though the man's even temper and discreet bearing would seem to intimate a mind peculiarly subject to the law of reason, not the less in heart he would seem to riot in complete exemption from that law, having apparently little to do with reason further than to employ it as an ambidexter implement for effecting the irrational. That is to say: Toward the accomplishment of an aim which in wantonness of atrocity would seem to partake of the insane, he will direct a cool judgment sagacious and sound. These men are madmen, and of the most dangerous sort, for their lunacy is not continuous, but occasional, evoked by some special object; it is protectively secretive, which is as much as to say it is self-contained, so that when, moreover, most active it is to the average mind not distinguishable from sanity, and for the reason above suggested: that whatever its aims may be—and the aim is never declared—the method and the outward proceeding are always perfectly rational.[1]

Thus, Claggart, at heart rioting "in exemption from" the rational law of society, will appear rational as he prepares for the socially irrational. His sagacity has already been revealed in his careful setting of those "mantraps" for Billy Budd which give a vague justification for his spontaneous hatred of the beautiful sailor. But events will reveal that this sagacity is not true wisdom and that the knowledge possessed by the politically vicious is as necessarily limited as the knowledge possessed by the politically virtuous.

The narrator says, "Probably the master-at-arms' clandestine persecution of Billy was started to try the temper of the man; but it had not developed any quality in him that enmity could make official use of or even pervert into plausible self-justification; so that the occurrence at the mess, . . . was a welcome one . . . ; and, for the rest, not improbably it put him upon new experiments" (p. 80). Billy's accidental spilling of his soup thus stirred Claggart's antipathy and gave justification for his hatred to seek further nourishment. After the narrator has set up this atmosphere of dark forebodings, he relates a scene in which the reader senses Claggart's "clandestine persecution" at work in a deadly "new experiment." On a warm, dark night Billy is sleeping peacefully in the open air "on the uppermost deck," presumably as he would have done aboard the *Rights*. "Presently he was stirred into semiconsciousness by somebody, who must have previously sounded the sleep of the others, touching his shoulder." As Billy raises his head, a voice quickly whispers, "Slip into the lee forechains, Billy; there is something in the wind. Don't speak. Quick, I will meet you there." Because of his essential good nature, Billy has "a reluctance, almost an incapacity of plumply saying *no* to an abrupt proposition not obviously absurd on the face of it, nor obviously unfriendly, nor iniquitous." While the mysteriousness of the stranger's actions and words might have given another person some cause for apprehension, Billy is unsuspecting: "Like his sense of fear, his apprehension as to aught outside of the honest and natural was seldom very quick." Billy "mechanically" and "sleepily" goes to the appointed place, where he discerns, despite the fact that the night is yet moonless and hazy, the figure of "one of the afterguard."[2]

Billy's interview with the afterguardsman highlights his naiveté and hints at the fact that his speech impediment, that is, his essential, apolitical characteristic, will be this Achilles' flaw:

"Hist! Billy," said the man, in the same quick cautionary whisper as before. "You were impressed, weren't you? Well, so was I"; and he paused, as to mark the effect. But Billy, not knowing exactly what to make of this, said nothing. Then the other: "We are not the only impressed ones, Billy. There's a gang of us.—Couldn't you—help—at a pinch?"

"What do you mean?" demanded Billy, here thoroughly shaking off his drowse.

"Hist, hist!" the hurried whisper now growing husky. "See here," and the man held up two small objects faintly twinkling in the night-light; "see, they are yours, Billy, if you'll only—"

But Billy broke in, and in his resentful eagerness to deliver himself his vocal infirmity somewhat intruded. "D—— d——damme, I don't know what you are d——d——driving at, or what you mean, but you had better g——g——go where you belong!" For the moment the fellow, as confounded, did not stir; and Billy, springing to his feet, said, "If you d——don't start, I'll t——t——toss you back over the r——rail!" There was no mistaking this, and the mysterious emissary decamped, disappearing in the direction of the mainmast in the shadow of the booms. [P. 82]

Because of his own intellectual haziness, Billy is unable to discern the stranger's meaning, but more importantly, his speech impediment does not allow him to cope with the proposition made. Placed in a corner, Billy simply resorts to a threat of brute force, despite the fact that he says he doesn't know what the afterguardsman means. In contrast, "the discerning" reader senses a plot to implicate Billy in a supposed mutiny, an implication which indeed "enmity could make official use of."

Billy is able to satisfy the query made by an awakened forecastleman by telling him that his "raised voice" was due to his chasing an afterguardsman from the forecastle area. The reader might imagine that Billy's explanation is not far from the truth, that in his confusion he merely fell back upon one of those "sea prejudices" which forebad "territorial encroachments." Billy is "puzzled" by the episode: "It was an entirely new experience, the first time in his life that he had ever been personally approached in underhand intriguing fashion." His reaction befits his nature, and the narrator's description of it recurs to the animal imagery with which Billy was introduced:

> In his disgustful recoil from an overture which, though he but ill comprehended, he instinctively knew must involve evil of some sort, Billy Budd was like a young horse fresh from the pasture suddenly inhaling a vile whiff from some chemical factory, and by repeated snortings trying to get it out of his nostrils and lungs. This frame of mind barred all desire of holding further parley with the fellow, even were it but for the purpose of gaining some enlightenment as to his design in approaching him. [Pp. 82–84]

Billy's sensing of evil is thus devoid of any practical comprehension; it lacks, that is, the one thing necessary for action to protect himself. He will not front evil: evil will engulf him.

The following day when Billy spots the afterguardsman, he is surprised to see him "chatting and laughing in free-hearted way, . . . the last man in the world, one would think, to be overburdened with thoughts, especially those perilous thoughts that must needs belong to a conspirator in any serious project, or even to the underling of such a conspirator." The afterguardsman nods to Billy in a "friendly recognition as to an old acquaintance," and some days afterwards he offers Billy "a flying word of good-fellowship" as he passes Billy on a gun deck. Billy was now "more at a loss than before." He smothers the "speculations" which are so "alien" to him.

> It never entered his mind that here was a matter which, from its extreme questionableness, it was his duty as a loyal blue-

jacket to report in the proper quarter. And, probably, had such a step been suggested to him, he would have been deterred from taking it by the thought, one of novice magnanimity, that it would savor overmuch of the dirty work of a telltale. He kept the thing to himself. [Pp. 84–85]

Thus, Billy is rendered impotent by his inability to "speculate" and by his novice form of "magnanimity," which in fact overrides his sense of self-preservation. He differs from the Great Sailor in that his "greatness" of soul renders him a pawn in events, whereas the Great Sailor's magnanimity allows *him* to confront events.

The reader's suspicion of Claggart's influence in the mysterious episode is confirmed in an oblique way through the person of the Dansker. The reader knows that the Dansker's "cynical" opinion about Billy's former petty troubles was proved correct by the narrator's subsequent revelation of Claggart's demonic "depravity." Now, when Billy relates the incident with the afterguardsman to the Dansker in a "partial and anonymous account," the latter, who "seemed to divine more than he was told," says, "Didn't I say so, Baby Budd? ... Why, *Jemmy Legs* is *down* on you." When Billy demands to know what Claggart has "to do with that cracked afterguardsman?" the Dansker responds briefly and characteristically:

"Ho, it was an afterguardsman, then. A cat's-paw, a cat's-paw!" And with that exclamation, whether it had reference to a light puff of air just then coming over the calm sea, or a subtler relation to the afterguardsman, there is no telling, the old Merlin gave a twisting wrench with his black teeth at his plug of tobacco, vouchsafing no reply to Billy's impetuous question, though now repeated, for it was his wont to relapse into grim silence when interrogated in skeptical sort as to any of his sententious oracles, not always very clear ones, rather partaking of that obscurity which invests most Delphic deliverances from any quarter.

Long experience had very likely brought this old man
to that bitter prudence which never interferes in aught and
never gives advice. [Pp. 85–86]

The Dansker confirms Claggart's clandestine machinations
and reaffirms his own standing as a quiescent Delphic "sage"
whose "prudence" lets both good and evil alone. His is not
the "uncommon prudence" which allows Claggart to conceal
his own evil nor the "prudence" by which Captain Graveling
seeks to insure his peaceful pipe.[3] Nor will the Dansker's "bitter prudence" be the same thing as the prudence of Captain
Vere, who *acts* in terms of his view of good and evil. The
prudence of the Dansker, unlike the innocence of Billy Budd,
is not the mark of an essential impuissance, but rather the mark
of deliberate nonintervention. The Dansker is like an unrespon-
sive God, unwilling to sacrifice himself to save an endangered
soul, even one whom he himself has christened "baby" and thus
has acknowledged as his "child." Apparently, the only true
redeemers and saviors are the Great Sailors of *this* world, who
are willing to sacrifice themselves to save others.

In his innocence, Billy is completely confounded by the
Dansker's opinion. The narrator observes that this is "not so
much to be wondered at." Billy is, as the title of the novel suggests, preeminently a Sailor, and in certain things, "some sailors
even in mature life remain unsophisticated enough." Young
Billy is "much of a child-man" even among sailors who themselves, "as a class, . . . are in character a juvenile race." Billy's
is an enduring child's innocence, a sailor's extreme "frankness"
in contrast to the landsman's "finesse":

... a child's utter innocence is but its blank ignorance, and
the innocence more or less wanes as intelligence waxes. But
in Billy Budd intelligence, such as it was, had advanced while
yet his simple-mindedness remained for the most part unaffected. Experience is a teacher indeed; yet did Billy's years

make his experience small. Besides, he had none of that in-
tuitive knowledge of the bad which in natures not good or
incompletely so foreruns experience, and therefore may pertain, as in some instances it too clearly does pertain, even to
youth.[4]

Again, Billy's sense of evil does not include any practical
knowledge of evil, and his childlike innocence is thus the reason for his inability to protect himself. Since Claggart's malice
is not obvious, Billy is unable to see any sense in the Dansker's
opinion.

   Billy no longer finds himself in petty difficulties after the
episode of the spilled soup. As for Claggart's smile and "pleasant passing word, these were, if not more frequent, yet if anything more pronounced than before." Claggart's reactions to
Billy Budd reveal that his hatred is building up to a final frenzy:

When Claggart's unobserved glance happened to light on
belted Billy rolling along the upper gun deck in the leisure
of the second dogwatch, exchanging passing broadsides of
fun with other young promenaders in the crowd, that glance
would follow the cheerful sea Hyperion with a settled medi-
tative and melancholy expression, his eyes strangely suffused
with incipient feverish tears. Then would Claggart look like
the man of sorrows. Yes, and sometimes the melancholy expression would have in it a touch of soft yearning, as if Claggart could even have loved Billy but for fate and ban. But
this was an evanescence, and quickly repented of, as it were,
by an immitigable look, pinching and shriveling the visage
into the momentary semblance of a wrinkled walnut. But
sometimes catching sight in advance of the foretopman coming in his direction, he would, upon their nearing, step aside
a little to let him pass, dwelling upon Billy for the moment
with the glittering dental satire of a Guise. But upon any
abrupt unforeseen encounter a red light would flash forth
from his eye like a spark from an anvil in a dusk smithy. That

quick, fierce light was a strange one, darted from orbs which in repose were of a color nearest approaching a deeper violet, the softest of shades.[5]

While Billy necessarily notices Claggart's glances, they were "beyond the construing of [his] nature." The narrator unnecessarily but pointedly reminds the reader that Billy did not have the "sensitive spiritual organization which in some cases instinctively conveys to ignorant innocence an admonition of the proximity of the malign." Billy had done nothing unfriendly to Claggart, and his "innocence was his blinder." Nor does he notice the strange glance of two of Claggart's messmates, the glance which shows "that the man from whom it comes has been some way tampered with." Billy's "general popularity" gives him no cause for concern, and if "shrewd" readers cannot believe Billy's complacency, it shows only that mere shrewdness cannot comprehend Billy's nature (pp. 88–90).

The tension of the novel is now at its decisive point, and the animosity created by Claggart's confrontation with a nature like Billy Budd gives way to action. The narrator's character sketches are thus the source from which the events of *Billy Budd* necessarily flow, and the artist's control of his characters and events allows him to reveal the truth which the contingencies of real life would obscure.

The *Bellipotent* is dispatched on a mission away from the fleet, and the stage is set for the decisive act of the novel. The *Bellipotent*'s availability for "detached service" was mentioned earlier, but the narrator indicated then that this fact was extraneous to the story. Now, as this detail is pointedly raised again, the narrator reveals that the use of the *Bellipotent* as a "scout" or for "more important" service has a previously unmentioned justification: the *Bellipotent* is relied upon "not alone because of her sailing qualities, not common in a ship of her rate, but quite as much, probably, that the character of her commander, it was thought, specially adapted him for any duty where under unforeseen difficulties a prompt initiative might have to be taken in some matter demanding knowledge and ability in addition to those qualities implied in good seamanship" (p. 90). Vere's standing in the eyes of his superiors is thus the crucial element in the special assignments given the *Bellipotent*, and the reader is told directly that Vere is thought to possess the special prudential "knowledge and ability" necessary for "a prompt initiative" in "unforeseen difficulties." Vere is, in other words, the best representative of the political order which he serves.

The *Bellipotent* sights and chases an enemy frigate on a distant mission, but in the end, the frigate manages to escape. Significantly, the malicious Claggart approaches Captain Vere soon "after the pursuit had been given up, and ere the excitement incident thereto had altogether waned away." Claggart capitalizes on the chase of the enemy frigate for his own purposes; since he will accuse Billy of mutinous activities, he knows that the time which most favors his accusation's success is the time when the danger of war is most clearly apprehended, that is, the time when the enemy has been sighted. Climbing up into the light "from his cavernous sphere," Claggart stands "respectfully" before Captain Vere in a spot from which a petty officer would "seek a hearing" only if "warranted" by "some exceptional cause." [6]

Vere senses Claggart's presence, and although the captain's knowledge of the master-at-arms "had only begun at the time of the ship's last sailing from home" (when Claggart first joined the *Bellipotent*), the sight of the master-at-arms provokes in the captain "a vaguely repellent distaste." Vere then asks Claggart what his business is, and Claggart begins his accusation:

With the air of a subordinate grieved at the necessity of being a messenger of ill tidings, and while conscientiously determined to be frank yet equally resolved upon shunning overstatement, Claggart at this invitation, or rather summons to disburden, spoke up. What he said, conveyed in the language of no uneducated man, was to the effect following, if not altogether in these words, namely, that during the chase and preparations for the possible encounter he had seen enough to convince him that at least one sailor aboard was a dangerous character in a ship mustering some who not only had taken a guilty part in the late serious troubles, but others also who, like the man in question, had entered His Majesty's service under another form than enlistment. [Pp. 91–92]

Claggart's guarded reference to the practice of impressment, which is similar to the oblique reference in the authorized journal's account of the story, does not sit well with Captain Vere. Previously, the narrator said of men like Vere: "Their honesty prescribes to them directness, sometimes far-reaching like that of a migratory fowl that in its flight never heeds when it crosses a frontier" (p. 63). Thus Vere does not heed here the fastidiousness of an "austere patriot" and interrupts Claggart, saying, "Be direct, man; say *impressed men*" (p. 92). Vere's own patriotism, like that of the narrator, does not entail a conscious attempt, wherever possible, to avoid undisguised mention of "officially sanctioned irregularities."

Making "a gesture of subservience," Claggart proceeds, telling Vere that he had suspected something amiss lately but thought he should not report anything while his suspicion "remained indistinct." But his observations that day had moved his suspicion closer to certainty. "He deeply felt, he added, the serious responsibility assumed in making a report involving such possible consequences to the individual mainly concerned, besides tending to augment those natural anxieties which every naval commander must feel in view of extraordinary outbreaks so recent as those which, he sorrowfully said it, it needed not to name" (p. 92). Claggart thus not only reveals his intention to cause dire "consequences" for Billy Budd, but he also openly suggests the thinking which has made him act at this time, namely, his understanding of the fear of mutiny at the time of war. When Claggart continues and attempts to remind Vere of one particular ship's fate at the time of the Nore Mutiny, Vere is angered and orders him to be silent. To Vere's "quick sense of self-respect it even looked under the circumstances something like an attempt to alarm him"; that is to say, Vere sees through Claggart's purpose as well as he sees the master-at-arms' attempt here as "a most immodest presumption." But despite his anger at Claggart's allusion, "Captain Vere did not permit himself to be unduly disturbed by the general tenor of his subordinate's report" (p. 93).

Vere's calm exists side by side with his determination that "prompt action should be taken at the first palpable sign of recurring insubordination." In addition, he sees far enough to realize that it would also "keep the idea of lingering disaffection alive" if he were to show "undue forwardness in crediting an informer," even his "chief of police." Besides, Vere had also seen a display of what the authorized journal will call Claggart's "strong patriotic impulse," and it had "irritated him as appearing rather supersensible and strained." Finally, Claggart's very "self-possessed and somewhat ostentatious manner in making his specifications" reminds Vere of a "perjurous witness" in a court-martial of which he had been a member.[7] In all, Vere demonstrates a subtle understanding of the complex situation in which he is forced to act, and he also shows that his own moral palate is such that he senses Claggart's wickedness and sees through his self-aggrandizing patriotic and subservient gestures.

Asked to name the accused, Claggart startles Vere by naming "William Budd." Vere asks if he could possibly mean the popular "Handsome Sailor," and Claggart's response evi-

dences his ability to pervert innocence into guilt and hints at
his envy of Billy Budd:

> "The same, your honor; but for all his youth and good
> looks, a deep one. Not for nothing does he insinuate himself
> into the good will of his shipmates, since at the least they
> will at a pinch say—all hands will—a good word for him, and
> at all hazards. Did Lieutenant Ratcliffe happen to tell your
> honor of that adroit fling of Budd's, jumping up in the cut-
> ter's bow under the merchantman's stern when he was being
> taken off? It is even masked by that sort of good-humored
> air that at heart he resents his impressment. You have but
> noted his fair cheek. A mantrap may be under the ruddy-
> tipped daisies." [P. 94]

Claggart's assumption that Billy's farewell to the *Rights-of-
Man* would have adversely moved Vere is shown to be ill-
founded. Lieutenant Ratcliffe had indeed reported Billy's
"adieu" to Vere, but the latter, "though *mistakenly understanding* it as a satiric sally, had but thought so much the better
of the impressed man for it; as a military sailor, admiring the
spirit that could take an arbitrary enlistment so merrily and
sensibly." The envy which Claggart feels for Billy's physical
beauty and moral innocence caused the master-at-arms to re-
sent Billy's farewell to the *Rights*; Vere does not experience
that envy—indeed, he *admires* Billy for these same characteristics: Vere "had congratulated Lieutenant Ratcliffe upon his
good fortune in lighting on such a fine specimen of the *genus
homo*, who in the nude might have posed for a statue of young
Adam before the Fall."[8]

Captain Vere is thus the one other person in the ship who,
as the narrator said, was "intellectually capable of adequately
appreciating the moral phenomenon presented in Billy Budd."
This fact, and the corresponding one that Vere *likes* Billy for
his nature, as Vere understands it, are often overlooked by

critics who would make Vere into a villain. Although Vere is a strict disciplinarian, he apparently welcomes the sight of Billy Budd on his ship. Vere sees Billy's popularity in the best light; it is a private matter which is to the credit of the "Handsome Sailor." On the other hand, Claggart resents Billy's private popularity and sees it only as a threat to the ship's order, or at least as a usable "proof" of such a threat. Claggart also ignores Billy's proficiency, while Vere regards it well, so well, in fact, that "he had thought of recommending [Billy] to the executive officer for promotion to a place that would more frequently bring him under his own observation."⁹

Also unnoticed by many critics of Vere is that the captain explicitly establishes himself as the only potential source of real justice in the matter of John Claggart. He asks the master-at-arms to cite "an act or spoken word" to substantiate his "foggy" accusation but warns the accuser, "Stay, . . . heed what you speak. Just now, and in a case like this, there is a yardarm-end for the false witness." Also, Vere here reveals that he is judging events in the light of present circumstances, circumstances that might require actions other than those he might take in the most favorable situations. Vere's appreciation of the complexity of the present situation is further evidenced after Claggart, "in virtuous self-assertion," cites Billy's supposedly incriminating "words and acts" and offers to produce "proof" of his specifications. Vere opts for caution in the face of his doubt of "the informer's good faith":

Though something exceptional in the moral quality of Captain Vere made him, in earnest encounter with a fellow man, a veritable touchstone of that man's essential nature, yet now as to Claggart and what was really going on in him his feeling partook less of intuitional conviction than of strong suspicion clogged by strange dubieties. The perplexity he evinced proceeded less from aught touching the man informed against—as Claggart doubtless opined—than from considerations how best to act in regard to the informer. At first, indeed, he was naturally for summoning that substantiation of his allegations which Claggart said was at hand. But such a proceeding would result in the matter at once getting abroad, which in the present stage of it, he thought, might undesirably affect the ship's company. If Claggart was a false witness—that closed the affair. And therefore, before trying the accusation, he would first practically test the accuser; and he thought this could be done in a quiet, undemonstrative way.

The way Vere decides upon is to have Billy summoned by the captain's valet and have him confront his accuser in the captain's cabin, out of sight of the now-curious topmen and sailors.[10] Vere decides, that is, to face the "dubieties" of the situation by an appeal to a procedure modelled on common law practice.

When Billy finds himself in the captain's cabin, he is surprised, but his surprise is without "apprehension or distrust." To a nature like his own, "essentially honest and humane, forewarning intimations of subtler danger from one's kind come tardily if at all." In fact, Billy's only thought is that he is about to be promoted by the captain, who has always looked "kindly upon" him. But then Vere orders Claggart to repeat his allegations, and the latter stands close to Billy, "mesmerically looking him in the eye," and accuses Billy to his face of mutiny. The power of Melville's art is shown in the confrontation:

Not at first did Billy take it in. When he did, the rose-tan of his cheek looked struck as by white leprosy. He stood like one impaled and gagged. Meanwhile the accuser's eyes, removing not as yet from the blue dilated ones, underwent a phenomenal change, their wonted rich violet color blurring into a muddy purple. Those lights of human intelligence, losing human expression, were gelidly protruding like the

alien eyes of certain uncatalogued creatures of the deep. The
first mesmeristic glance was one of serpent fascination; the
last was as the paralyzing lurch of the torpedo fish.

Captain Vere orders "transfixed" Billy: "Speak! Defend your-
self!" But the captain's order, Billy's amazement at the accusation, and his "horror of the accuser's eyes," force his "lurking
defect" to the surface, and Billy is thrown "into a convulsed
tongue-tie." Billy's face is "like that of a condemned vestal
priestess in the moment of being buried alive, and in the first
struggle against suffocation." The narrator observes that although "at the time Captain Vere was *quite ignorant* of Billy's
liability to vocal impediment, he now immediately divined it,"
being reminded of a schoolmate of his who was subject to the
same defect. Vere, in a fatherly tone, tries to soothe Billy by
telling him to take his time, but this only adds to Billy's effort
to speak, placing him in a "paralysis."[11]

At this point, Billy is about to strike out at Claggart, but it
is necessary to pause and to note not only that Billy's speech
impediment undermines Vere's purpose in having the master-
at-arms confront the accused but also that Vere's emphasized
ignorance of that impediment is a necessary ingredient in the
tragedy that immediately follows. At his trial, Billy significantly says, "Could I have used my tongue I would not have struck
him" (p. 106). Mistakenly, Captain Vere fully expects Billy
to "use his tongue," at least to respond to, if not to refute,
Claggart's charges. That is to say, Vere mistakenly expects
Billy to respond politically and rationally, or to be an adequate
"spokesman" for himself, or to act as a true "Handsome Sailor."
Captain Vere, who is relying upon a rational and quasi-legal
preliminary proceeding to "test the accuser," does not make
provision for the irrational. Until it is too late, Vere, who is
"capable" of an adequate understanding of Billy Budd, mistakenly understands Billy as a true "Handsome Sailor," and

his reflexive reliance upon an apparently reasonable legal convention leaves his original judgment of Billy undisturbed and allows a merely personal misunderstanding to lead to political tragedy.

On the one hand, Vere's unavoidable ignorance of Billy's defect indicates the imperfection of political prudence and goes on to suggest the limits of political life itself. Vere's inclinations and intentions are blameless, and yet the circumstance in which he acts simply denies him the kind of knowledge that would allow him to protect innocence from disaster. By extension, thus, the natural and aggressive evil of Claggart, combined with the unavoidable bounds upon virtuous Vere's vision, suggest the pessimistic view that calamity is endemic to political life. On the other hand, however, there is at least a hint here that there are additional limitations to be noticed by the reader, limitations which are attached specifically to Vere's *particular* variety of political prudence. Ironically, a perfect, conventionally reasonable Burkean statesman, a "philosopher in action," contributes to the occurrence of political tragedy by acting *exactly* according to his "settled convictions"! Vere's instant reliance upon conventional procedure is a manifestation of his Burkean equation of the right or the rational with the historically approved, and yet this very procedure not only allows but perhaps even invites the reaction that will lead to Billy's eventual destruction. In a way, just as innocence is Billy's blinder and limitation, Burkean conventionalism is Vere's.[12] In fact, what must remain here as merely a hint becomes an explicit lesson at Billy's trial: there we shall see that Vere's "settled convictions" heighten the tragedy in *Billy Budd* by eliminating the possibility of defending as natural the political authority which must act in the midst of human calamity.

Billy's face, at the moment of the above digression, is a "crucifixion to behold," and then:

The next instant, quick as the flame from a discharged cannon at night, his right arm shot out, and Claggart dropped to the deck. Whether intentionally or but owing to the young athlete's superior height, the blow had taken effect full upon the forehead, so shapely and intellectual-looking a feature in the master-at-arms; so that the body fell over lengthwise, like a heavy plank tilted from erectness. A gasp or two, and he lay motionless. [P. 99]

The narrator's comparison of Billy's arm to a discharging cannon recalls the episode related by Captain Graveling of the *Rights* to Lieutenant Ratcliffe at the time of Billy's impressment. The episode reveals the dialectic movement of *Billy Budd* and demonstrates the limitations placed upon the title character:

"[My crew] took to [Billy] like hornets to treacle; all but the buffer of the gang, the big shaggy chap with the fire-red whiskers. He indeed, out of envy, perhaps, of the newcomer, and thinking such a 'sweet and pleasant fellow,' as he mockingly designated him to the others, could hardly have the spirit of a gamecock, must needs bestir himself in trying to get up an ugly row with him. Billy forebore with him and reasoned with him in a pleasant way—he is something like myself, Lieutenant, to whom aught like a quarrel is hateful—but nothing served. So, in the second dogwatch one day, the Red Whiskers in presence of the others, under pretense of showing Billy just whence a sirloin steak was cut—for the fellow had once been a butcher—insultingly gave him a dig under the ribs. Quick as lightning Billy let fly his arm. I dare say he never meant to do quite as much as he did, but anyhow he gave the burly fool a terrible drubbing. It took about half a minute, I should think. And, lord bless you, the lubber was astonished at the celerity. And will you believe it, Lieutenant, the Red Whiskers now really loves Billy—loves him, or is the biggest hypocrite that ever I heard of. But they all love him. . . . You are going to take away my peacemaker!"

"Well," said the lieutenant, . . . "well, blessed are the peacemakers, especially the fighting peacemakers. And such are the seventy-four beauties some of which you see poking their noses out of the portholes of yonder warship lying to for me," pointing through the cabin window at the *Bellipotent*.[13]

The narrator's description of Billy at Claggart's murder thus shows that Claggart's evil plan has indeed turned Billy into an ignoble "peacemaker" like one of the *Bellipotent*'s cannons. Billy becomes merely an instrument of destruction because he is unable to use his tongue to defend himself against evil. Had Billy been a *true* "Handsome Sailor," he would nevertheless have had to face the power of natural evil, but the implication is that the past's *true* "Handsome Sailors" dealt with evil politically and nobly, as the Great Sailor dealt with the natural evil of war politically and nobly. Where the Great Sailor earned eternal glory and national redemption in *his* confrontation with unavoidable evil, the imperfect "Handsome Sailor," Billy Budd, will earn official infamy and personal tragedy in his own confrontation with evil. For Melville, it seems, real tragedy lies not in man's inability to conquer evil, for that is his given limitation; tragedy lies rather in facing evil without the possibility of achieving recognizable and demonstrable glory. Indeed, the tragedy of modernity is apparently that it lessens, or perhaps even eliminates, this very possibility.

While Billy's "virtues" are his ability to bring an effortless peace and his desire *for* peace, it is now shown that his ability is limited and his desire is frustrated by the presence of evil. Confronted with evil, whether in the comical form of Red Whiskers or in the tragic forms of the afterguardsman or Claggart, the "child-man" has no recourse to speech or conventional procedures, and he must thus ignobly breach the peace in an effort to preserve it. That is to say, in the presence of evil, Rousseau's natural man is forced to violence in a manner which precludes the attainment of political glory. If the case of Captain Vere shows that political reason is not a sufficient condition for peace, the case of Billy Budd shows that speech or *politics* is a necessary condition for nobly dealing with natural evil. In the peaceful world of the *Rights-of-Man*, the "crime" which results from the presence of evil and the absence of speech was a comical affair. But in the man-of-war world, the corresponding crime brings about the tragedy of Billy Budd.[14]

The last limitation revealed is, of course, that peculiar one placed upon the wicked Claggart. The master-at-arms is killed at the moment his cunning is about to reap its reward, and the murder thus reveals that Claggart's "intellectuality" is ultimately restricted and cannot really guarantee its own success, or more precisely, cannot live to see its success. Claggart's "self-contained" depravity is the mark of a contracted soul, and such a soul is limited and cut "off from enlightenment" about the real world. Up until Billy's arm flashes out at him, Claggart appeared to have reversed the Socratic dictum and to have demonstrated that *vice* is knowledge. But Billy's reaction to the charges shows that Claggart's knowledge of the so-called "Handsome Sailor" did not in fact include an adequate understanding of Billy's own limitations. Claggart did not understand that Billy's very innocence rendered him unable to meet the accusations with denials. Claggart, cleverly prepared to refute Billy's denials with "substantiating proof," is struck dead by a blow, significantly, to his "intellectual-looking" forehead. It should also perhaps be noted that, although Claggart's limitation is, in a way, the same as Captain Vere's—that is, a limitation on his knowledge—Claggart's actions at the time of the murder are directed at an "atrocity" while Vere's are directed at eliciting the truth.[15] The peculiarity of Claggart's limitation is that he nevertheless succeeds in his evil design: Billy will be destroyed. Also, there is more than a hint of some authorial revenge in the revelation of the exact point of impact of Billy's blow. This matter will require further treatment later.

The "deplorable occurrence" within the captain's cabin is thus the climax of *Billy Budd*. Here are revealed the flaws in the perfectly drawn sketches of the novel's "phenomenal men." Because these characters exist as archetypes of the available human possibilities in modern dress, the murder of John Claggart by Billy Budd in the presence of Captain Vere is a stark revelation of the limits placed upon modern human activity. Modernity grants respectability to vice; those moderns who celebrate innocence are refuted by the natural character and power of evil; and those moderns who place their faith in the prudence of traditionalist statesmen will see their heroes fail to protect innocence against vice. But the occurrence within the small cabin does not suggest only the limits of modern political life: evil, innocence, and prudence are perennial problems, and the truths first suggested in the "closeted" space aboard H.M.S. *Bellipotent* in 1797 ironically are all too relevant to other places and other times.

Notes

1 P. 76. The same point is made at p. 90.

2 Pp. 81–82. Compare the description of the limitations due to Billy's good nature with those of the also good-natured Captain Delano of "Benito Cereno," in Herman Melville, *Piazza Tales*, ed. Egbert S. Oliver (New York: Hendricks House, 1962), p. 55.

3 Cf. p. 80 and p. 45; see also *H&S*, p. 151.

4 Pp. 86–87. Note that "innocence" is distinguished from "goodness," and compare this with Auden's poem, "Herman Melville," in *Collected Poetry of W. H. Auden* (New York: Random House, 1945), pp. 146–47.
Note also that the comparison of sailors and landsmen here (in chap. 16 of *Billy Budd*) reinforces the earlier disparaging remarks on "men of the world": see especially p. 87. On sailors, see *Redburn: His First Voyage*, in *The Writings of Herman Melville*, ed. Harrison Hayford, Hershel Parker, and G. Thomas Tanselle, 15 vols. (Evanston and Chicago: Northwestern University Press and The Newberry Library, 1968–   ), 4:94, 136–40.

5 Pp. 87–88. The statement that "Claggart could even have loved Billy" should be read in relation to the earlier statement that the master-at-arms "fain would have shared" Billy's innocence, "but he despaired of it" (p. 78). Hayford and Sealts show that "ban" is not a quiet reference to the forbidden nature of homosexuality at *H&S*, p. 172.

6 P. 91. At p. 88, Claggart's various glances are called "caprices of the pit," which, as "cavernous sphere" does here, suggests his Satanic character.

7 Pp. 93–94. Note that the narrator directly supports Vere's superiors' view that he is capable of "prompt action" in the event of "difficulties."

8 Pp. 94, 95 (italics added). In reality, of course, Billy is incapable of satire, "sinister dexterity," or "double meanings and

insinuations of any sort" (p. 49). It goes without saying, of course, that the same incapacity does not necessarily characterize the narrator or the author of *Billy Budd*. Also, on Billy as Adam, cf. pp. 52, 94.

⁹ P. 95 On the same page, the narrator sums up Vere's reaction to Billy: "Captain Vere had *from the beginning* deemed Billy Budd to be what in the naval parlance of the time was called a 'King's bargain': that is to say, for His Britannic Majesty's navy a capital investment at small outlay or none at all" (italics added). Compare this with Claggart's "spontaneous antipathy" (p. 74). Also, note that the impressing officer, Lieutenant Ratcliffe, also regards Billy spontaneously as a good find for the king (pp. 45, 48).

¹⁰ Pp. 95–97. See Leonard Casper, "The Case against Captain Vere," *Perspective* 5 (Summer 1952): 150, where Casper mentions Vere's threat to Claggart only to "contrast" it with Vere's actions after the crime; see also Phil Withim, "*Billy Budd*: Testament of Resistance," *Modern Language Quarterly* 20 (June 1959): 118, where the entire rationale given by the narrator for Vere's decision here is disregarded: Withim says, "There seems to be no relevant reason for Vere's decision." (I have deliberately presented this scene in detail to suggest the extent to which the ironist critics have simply dispensed with the text of the novel.)
Note also the biblical allusion to describe Claggart here (*Billy Budd*, p. 96): his look before Vere is like "that of the spokesman of the envious children of Jacob deceptively imposing upon the troubled patriarch the blood-dyed coat of young Joseph."

¹¹ Pp. 97–99. The added italics mark the second indication of Vere's misunderstanding of Billy's true nature. See note 8 above.

¹² The novel's "deplorable occurrence" is Billy's killing of Claggart in the presence of Captain Vere, and that occurrence has *three* ingredients: Claggart's naturally evil antipathy, Billy's ironically explosive natural innocence, and Vere's characteristically traditionalist decision to arrange a quasi-legal confrontation between accuser and accused. The depiction of the last ingredient *might* indicate that Melville misunderstood the Burkean position as promising to *eliminate* political ills: Melville's portrayal of a surprised Vere would then be aimed at the utopian expectations of an erroneously optimistic Burke. I believe, however, that Melville's

understanding of Burke was generally more accurate. By having Vere's procedure provide the arena in which Billy changes from an innocent target of evil to an observed killer, Melville suggests that tradition is simply not the best available guide for the Burkean statesman's sober and nonutopian effort to contain or to mitigate political injustice. Vere's procedure, in fact, represents a disastrously unsuccessful attempt to impose tradition upon the contest between natural evil and innocence. And does the failure of that attempt suggest that unstudied Great Sailors are more attuned to the *nature* of political things?

[13] Pp. 47–48. Note that, like Claggart, Red Whiskers was moved "perhaps" by "envy" and refers to Billy as a "sweet and pleasant" fellow. (Compare pp. 47–48, 71, 77–78.) Also, compare Graveling's comparison of Billy to "treacle" with the description of Lycurgus in Plutarch, *The Lives of the Noble Grecians and Romans*, trans. John Dryden and rev. by Arthur Hugh Clough (New York: Random House, Modern Library, n.d.), p. 69.

[14] On the comic aspects of the Red Whiskers affair, see Leonard Nathanson, "Melville's *Billy Budd*, Chapter 1," *Explicator* 22 (May 1964), item 75.
Compare the present view of Billy's "tragic flaw" with Rollo May, *Power and Innocence: A Search for the Sources of Violence* (New York: Norton, 1972), pp. 205–11.

[15] This point is conceded by Withim in *"Billy Budd*: Testament of Resistance," p. 118; Withim also notes there the agreement of Lawrance Thompson on the purpose of Vere's actions at the time his knowledge is shown to be limited.

6

A Drumhead Court

"INSIDE" THE NARRATOR'S DESCRIPTIONS of Billy
Budd, Captain Vere, and John Claggart, there lay the
authorial frame which set the novel's "phenomenal men" in the
context of an analysis of modernity's effect upon the character,
status, and strength of political virtue and natural vice. Then,
"inside" the narrator's account of the "deplorable occurrence"
in Captain Vere's cabin, there lay Melville's revelation of the
limitations both of the proposed modern heroes, Billy Budd and
Captain Vere, and of the modern villain, John Claggart. The
novel's character sketches and its decisive event thus combine
to construct the vehicle which conveys Melville's central lessons, the lessons of the "Inside Narrative." From this point of
view, the trial and execution of Billy Budd are ancillary events,
the sad final outcomes of the central "deplorable occurrence."
And yet, the trial and execution scenes are important in themselves, for they will add to our understanding of modern political reality. In particular, the trial scene will add decisively to
our understanding of the modern character of Captain Vere's
thought, actions, and limitations. In other words, while the trial

scene constitutes, in effect, the narrator's defense of Vere's political character and Vere's consistent devotion to duty, *within* that defense lies more readily visible evidence of the limitations of the Burkean conservatism upon which Vere acted when confronted with Claggart's charges and upon which he will now act with respect to Billy's crime.

A return to the narrator's treatment of Vere before Billy's crime shows that the narrative emphasizes Vere's political character, that is, his ability to act in a political way. When John Claggart's malice toward Billy Budd becomes manifest, Billy is thrown into a paralysis, and he finally responds with an ignoble act of brute force. Billy, the embodiment of moral innocence, commits a crime, and he does so because he has no recourse to other, more political, measures.[1] In the man-of-war world, manifest evil causes the Rousseauean natural man to become violent and criminal and robs him of his peaceful nature. While Billy, however, is thus forced to *mere* violence by Claggart's accusations, Captain Vere's response to them is entirely different. Having heard Claggart's charges, Vere determines upon a legal or procedural method of eliciting the truth: he will have accuser face the accused. Apparently, he believes the confrontation will establish a more or less definite ground upon which he might act; although Vere's plan fails, its *intent* is to make an initial determination of the likelihood of his having to deal legally and politically with a case of either incipient mutiny or "false witness."

It is clear how Vere would handle the former case, but there is an ambiguity concerning his intentions in the latter case. He had threatened Claggart with "a yardarm-end" if Claggart could not substantiate his charges against Billy, but when Claggart *did* specify the grounds for his charges, Vere had opted for a private confrontation, one which would allow the affair to be "closed" if Claggart proved to be a "false witness." The ambiguity can be resolved and Vere's intentions can be shown to be consistent if one notes that *what* he will do in either case apparently will depend upon how much of a *public* or political problem is revealed to him. Vere will thus act swiftly against public "false witness" or any *"palpable sign* of recurring insubordination," but he will allow the affair to be "closed" if Claggart's charges turn out to be lies confined to the quarter-deck. The dangerous times dictate caution, but the cautious method Captain Vere chooses is a politic way of preparing himself for a specific legal action, the particular action being dependent upon the result of the confrontation in his cabin: Vere *may* have to try either a mutineer or a "false witness" whose lies have gotten "abroad." The point is that while Captain Vere, the civilized man, is forced into a state of war by political evil outside his own society, he has quasi-legal procedure and convention as potential resources for confronting suspected or demonstrated evil within his society. In fact, since his position in the French war makes him a defender of "founded law" against "unbridled revolt," Vere's actual foreign and domestic policies are totally consistent: as he militarily defends the law of Britain against revolutionary France, he attempts politically to pave a path for the implementation of that law in the suspicious matter of John Claggart's accusations against Billy Budd.

The failure of Vere's plan is caused by Billy's action, and the futility of the plan itself is due to Billy's nature, a nature which Vere first inadequately had comprehended and which Vere's devotion to legal procedure then sadly had obscured. But if Vere's prudence is thus shown to be only an imperfect wisdom, his reliance upon legal procedure is clearly not meant to be seen as simply reprehensible. In terms of the story itself, Vere's arrangement of the confrontation between Billy and Claggart is not only a reasonable act, but it also stems, in fact, from his perceptive distrust of the accuser rather than from any alarm at the accusations made. The confrontation might possibly lead to legal action against a suspected mutineer or a public "false witness," and Vere's warning to Claggart about the yardarm-end clearly shows that Vere first anticipated having to deal with the master-at-arms rather than with Billy. In the face of suspected evil on Claggart's part, Vere resorts to a preliminary quasi-legal proceeding; the fact that the proceeding is foredoomed does not impugn the *sensibility* of his intention, although, as noted, it *does* ultimately raise questions about the adequacy of the "settled convictions" that dictate Vere's chosen procedure.

It must be noted, also in regard to the actions and intentions that precede Billy's crime, that Captain Vere's warning to Claggart about the danger of "false witness" reveals another important thing about Vere's thinking. The captain apparently sensed that Claggart was lying; he knew he could not ignore Claggart's "false witness" if the crew learned of it, and he anticipated the possibility that the appropriate punishment for "false witness" might necessarily and automatically have to follow. If, as Vere suspected, Claggart was lying, and the lie did *not* get "abroad," that "closed the affair"; but if Claggart's false witness became public and therefore incited the crew, Claggart would face the yardarm-end. Thus, Captain Vere believes that once legal guilt is publicly established as fact, the formal procedures of the law are left only the task of vindication. It is not clear whether Vere believes that, on its own, formal legal procedure is simply unable to elicit the *fact* of guilt; this may be doubted because the court-martial Vere once participated in apparently managed at least to single out a "perjurous witness." What *can* be concluded, however, is this: Vere acts on the assumption that, in certain times, when guilt *is* clearly assignable, and when criminality has become a public fact, the full punishment of the law must automatically follow the legal proceeding convened to try the proven criminal. If this position seems unyielding, it is because "just now, and in a case like this," circumstances demand strict discipline and militate against leniency.

The implications of Vere's warning to Claggart must be kept in mind as the reader proceeds to Billy's trial itself. Vere has witnessed a killing, a crime in which there is no doubt concerning Billy's technical guilt. Vere's reaction is thus not an automatic "authoritarian" condemnation of Billy Budd, but rather a sad revelation of what he believes necessarily must follow. Just as Vere would have had Claggart quickly tried and executed if the master-at-arms' accusations had proved false and had gotten "abroad," he will have Billy Budd quickly tried and executed for the unconcealable crime the foretop-man has committed. Without yet having to consider the reasons for Vere's apparent determination, the reader witnesses the narrator's display of Captain Vere's consistent devotion to discipline at the time of Claggart's murder:

> "Fated boy," breathed Captain Vere in tone so low as to be almost a whisper, "what have you done! But here, help me."
>
> The twain raised the felled one from the loins up into a sitting position. The spare form flexibly acquiesced, but inertly. It was like handling a dead snake. They lowered it back. Regaining erectness, Captain Vere with one hand covering his face stood to all appearance as impassive as the object at his feet. Was he absorbed in taking in all the bearings of the event and what was best not only now at once to be done, but also in the sequel? Slowly he uncovered his face; and the effect was as if the moon emerging from eclipse should reappear with quite another aspect than that which had gone into hiding. The father in him, manifested towards Billy thus far in the scene, was replaced by the military disciplinarian.

. . . .

But Captain Vere was now again motionless, standing absorbed in thought. Again starting, he vehemently exclaimed, "Struck dead by an angel of God! Yet the angel must hang!" [Pp. 99–100, 101]

The narrator emphasizes Vere's thoughtful pondering of the situation and the emergence of Vere's disciplinary nature. The narrator's question concerning the subject of Vere's thought is later answered affirmatively: Vere decides Billy "must hang" as "the sequel" to the event. In the meantime, Vere orders his valet to fetch the ship's surgeon in order to confirm Claggart's death.

The entrance of the surgeon into the story forces a delay in the consideration of the reasons for Vere's decision to see Billy hanged. The surgeon's reactions to the scene in the cabin and to his captain's manner, however, serve to introduce Vere's justifications and to establish another plane from which the captain's words and deeds may be judged. The surgeon is, of course, a man of scientific knowledge, and his viewpoint will thus be a scientific, "knowledgable" one. But it also must be noted that the initial introduction of the surgeon emphasizes the fact that he enters upon the scene with no knowledge of the events that led up to the crime:

When the surgeon entered—a self-poised character of that grave sense and experience that hardly anything could take him aback—Captain Vere advanced to meet him, thus unconsciously intercepting his view of Claggart, and, interrupting the other's wonted ceremonious salutation, said, "Nay. Tell me how it is with yonder man," directing his attention to the prostrate one.

The surgeon looked, and for all his self-command somewhat started at the abrupt revelation. On Claggart's always pallid complexion, thick black blood was now oozing from nostril and ear. To the gazer's professional eye it was unmistakably no living man that he saw.

"Is it so, then?" said Captain Vere, intently watching him. "I thought it. But verify it." Whereupon the customary tests confirmed the surgeon's first glance, who now, looking up in unfeigned concern, cast a look of intense inquisitiveness upon his superior. But Captain Vere, with one hand to his brow, was standing motionless. Suddenly, catching the surgeon's arm convulsively, he exclaimed, pointing down to the body, "It is the divine judgment on Ananias! Look!"

Disturbed by the excited manner he had never before observed in the *Bellipotent*'s captain, and *as yet wholly ignorant of the affair*, the prudent surgeon nevertheless held his peace, only again looking an earnest interrogatory as to what it was that had resulted in such a tragedy.

. . . .

At [Vere's] passionate interjections, mere incoherences to the listener *as yet unapprised of the antecedents*, the surgeon was profoundly discomposed. [Pp. 100–101, italics added]

The "self-poised," scientific surgeon is thus confused by the "tragedy" and wears an expression of "intense inquisitiveness" as to the cause of the event. In marked contrast to his immediate, "professional" certainty that Claggart is dead, the surgeon is thoroughly taken aback by the question of the "antecedents" of the death. He does not know what brought the scene about, and in large part it is this ignorance which makes Captain Vere's reactions seem so strange. The surgeon is "disturbed" by Vere's "excited manner" and "discomposed" at the captain's "passionate interjections"; Vere's manner and words are meaningless to the surgeon especially *because* he is ignorant of what actually happened. (In fact, the surgeon at this point does not even know *who* is involved since, previous to the surgeon's entry into the cabin, Vere ordered Billy to stay in an aft stateroom.) The final element is added to the surgeon's inquisitive perplexity when Vere asks him to help remove Claggart's body into another compartment; the surgeon is "anew disturbed by a request that, as implying a desire for secrecy, seemed unaccountably strange to him" (p. 101).

What the surgeon confronts, then, is first, a completely enigmatic scene, and second, the captain's apparently incoherent actions and words. Now, Vere presumably then tells the surgeon at least the bare facts of the crime because he sends the surgeon off to tell the lieutenants and the captain of marines what has happened and that he "presently" would convene a drumhead court. The surgeon's reactions to all this are related but are separable into two areas: his continued perplexity about Vere (which was initially born of his ignorance of the antecedent events), and his doubts about Vere's proposed course of action. The surgeon's continuing misgivings about Vere himself must be due to one of two facts: either he still does not know enough about the events that led up to the murder to see the meaning of Vere's exclamations, or, although now knowing the whole story, he still does not see any sense in those exclamations. In either case, the surgeon's doubt about Vere's personal bearing is the basis for his "disquietude" about Vere's proposal:

> Full of disquietude and misgiving, the surgeon left the cabin. Was Captain Vere suddenly affected in his mind, or was it but a transient excitement, brought about by so strange and extraordinary a tragedy? As to the drumhead court, it struck the surgeon as impolitic, if nothing more. The thing to do, he thought, was to place Billy Budd in confinement, and in a way dictated by usage, and postpone further action in so extraordinary a case to such time as they should rejoin the squadron, and then refer it to the admiral. He recalled the unwonted agitation of Captain Vere and his excited . . . manner. Was he unhinged? [Pp. 101–2]

Faced with Captain Vere's "unwonted agitation" and unusual exclamations, the surgeon can only attribute them to traumatic insanity.

The entire tenor of the novel to this point, that is, the narrator's constant emphasis on the unusual character of the personages and events of the story, would suggest that the surgeon's response simply disqualifies him as one who might understand the exceptional characters and events within such a narrative. To the surgeon, what is unusual is insane, while to the "discerning" reader, what is unusual is morally phenomenal and ultimately reveals the truth. Moreover, the narrator's above description of the surgeon's ignorance of the prior events would seem to suggest that his reactions may owe their existence to his understandable confusion and lack of factual information. And beyond all this, there is the point that Melville, the author of the narrator's comments, held that "science and sophistry, if taken as 'the whole truth,' are both crass and stultifying approaches to reality."[2] Thus, even *if* the surgeon is now reacting on the basis of full information received from Vere, his judgment about events would ultimately be called into question. But the most important light thrown upon the surgeon's opinions is that of *Billy Budd* itself. After Billy's death, the reader is explicitly given reason to doubt the surgeon's profundity, but here it will suffice to note both the narrator's implied critique of "professional" psychological opinion and his explicit warning that the surgeon's opinions must be seen in the larger context of the whole narrative:

Who in the rainbow can draw the line where the violet tint ends and the orange tint begins? Distinctly we see the difference of the colors, but where exactly does the one first blendingly enter into the other? So with sanity and insanity. In pronounced cases, there is no question about them. But in some supposed cases, in various degrees supposedly less pronounced, to draw the exact line of demarcation few will undertake, though for a fee becoming considerate some professional experts will. There is nothing namable but that some men will, or undertake to, do it for pay.

Whether Captain Vere, as the surgeon professionally
and privately surmised, was really the sudden victim of any
degree of aberration, every one must determine for himself
by such light as this narrative may afford. [P. 102]

Judging the "sanity" of Vere's mind means, of course, directly confronting the reasons he gives for his determination
to have Billy quickly tried and executed. So far it has been
seen that Vere is politic and consistent, that he would have
had the publicly lying Claggart punished as quickly and as
severely. But it is necessary to weigh Vere's judgments, however consistent, on their own merits. Moreover, this necessity
is the more acute because the lieutenants, to whom the surgeon said "nothing as to the captain's state," nevertheless also
"seemed to think that such a matter should be referred to the
admiral" (p. 102). Whatever value the surgeon's scientific
opinion may or may not possess, the lieutenants' opinion, ostensibly sober and military, calls Vere's proposal into question.
Significantly, the treatment of Vere's justification is presented as part of the straight narrative, and the dramatization
which surrounded the crime itself is temporarily halted. The
narrator begins by corroborating the judgment Vere implied
when he warned Claggart to be wary of what the latter
charged "just now, and in a case like this":

That the unhappy event which has been narrated could not
have happened at a worse juncture was but too true. For it
was close on the heel of the suppressed insurrections, an
aftertime very critical to naval authority, demanding from
every English sea commander two qualities not readily in-
terfusable—prudence and rigor. Moreover, there was something crucial in the case.

Vere's view of the present situation, a view which concluded
that discipline must be rigorous "just now," is thus "too true."

The reason it is "too true" is that Vere realizes that Billy had been innocently led into the crime:

In the jugglery of circumstances preceding and attending the event on board the *Bellipotent*, and in the light of that martial code whereby it was formally to be judged, innocence and guilt personified in Claggart and Budd in effect changed places. In a legal view the apparent victim of the tragedy was he who had sought to victimize a man blameless; and the indisputable deed of the latter, navally regarded, constituted the most heinous of military crimes. Yet more. The essential right and wrong involved in the matter, the clearer that might be, so much the worse for the responsibility of a loyal sea commander, inasmuch as he was not authorized to determine the matter on that primitive basis. [Pp. 102–3]

These facts are thus "too true" for Vere, who, despite his desire to "philosophize upon realities," must come to act upon "indisputable" appearances.

In the face of these ambivalent demands, Vere decides that this case requires "circumspectness not less than promptitude," and he thus seeks "to guard as much as possible against publicity" until such time as all his decisions have been made and are about to be carried out. (Again, the public or political dimension of events is a crucial point in Vere's deliberations.) The narrator says of Vere's method: "Here he may or may not have erred." The reason for this observation is that "some officers" subsequently criticized Vere's secrecy, and, says the narrator, there was "some imaginative ground" for the criticism. Vere's "maintenance of secrecy in the matter, the confining all knowledge of it for a time to the place where the homicide occurred, the quarter-deck cabin; in these particulars lurked some resemblance to the policy adopted in those tragedies of the palace which have occurred more than once in the capital founded by Peter the Barbarian."[3] While Hayford and

Sealts claimed that "this sentence is nearer than any other in *Billy Budd* to indicating disapproval of Vere's course of action" (*H&S*, p. 177), the sentence actually refers only to one of Vere's auxiliary decisions, that is, to his decision to maintain initial secrecy. What the "imaginative" criticism reveals is not Vere's hidden tyrannical nature but his real liability to a form of criticism which caricatures his actual motives and seizes upon unsightly "particulars" to condemn *all* his actions. This would suggest that the narrator here intends not to induce criticism of Vere, but rather to indicate a rather obvious shortcoming of Vere's political action: Vere is forced by his view of circumstances to take particular kinds of actions; however justifiable those actions might be, they may be construed so as to breed discontent and induce the kind of criticism which undermines his ruling authority.

This suggestion is strengthened by the narrator's matter-of-fact support of Vere's rationale and the very favorable picture of Vere contained therein:

> The case indeed was such that fain would the *Bellipotent*'s captain have deferred taking any action whatever respecting it further than to keep the foretopman a close prisoner till the ship rejoined the squadron and then submitting the matter to the judgment of his admiral.
>
> But a true military officer is in one particular like a true monk. Not with more self-abnegation will the latter keep his vows of monastic obedience than the former his vows of allegiance to martial duty.
>
> Feeling that unless quick action was taken on it, the deed of the foretopman, so soon as it should be known on the gun decks, would tend to awaken any slumbering embers of the Nore among the crew, a sense of the urgency of the case overruled in Captain Vere every other consideration. But though a conscientious disciplinarian, he was no lover of authority for mere authority's sake. Very far was he from embracing opportunities for monopolizing to himself the

perils of moral responsibility, none at least that could prop-
erly be referred to an official superior or shared with him by
his official equals or even subordinates. So thinking, he was
glad it would not be at variance with usage to turn the matter
over to a summary court of his officers, reserving to himself,
as the one on whom the ultimate accountability would rest,
the right of maintaining a supervision of it, or formally or
informally interposing at need. Accordingly a drumhead
court was summarily convened, he electing the individuals
composing it: the first lieutenant, the captain of marines, and
the sailing master.[4]

Thus, Vere's inclination is to delay any action, but his "allegiance to martial duty" and his judgment that Billy's crime was
liable to reawaken the spirit of the Nore Mutiny combine to
demand quick action. It also should be noted that Vere again
embraces a legal method of action, the convening of a court
which will act with the authority of the "sea commonalty."
Although his quasi-legal preliminary proceeding has ended in
tragedy, he turns again to the law and "usage." Also, Vere's
reservation of a supervisory position in the court is the corol-
lary of the fact that "the ultimate accountability would rest"
on himself.

Since the division in *Billy Budd* criticism revolves largely
around the critics' disagreements concerning Vere's disciplinary actions, the captain's judgments after Billy's crime are
crucial elements in the story. The ironist case against Vere
must sooner or later arrive at the argument that Vere *should*
not have proceeded with Billy's trial. But in terms of the story
itself, what Vere *might* have done is "but boggy ground to
build on"; the narrator himself presents Vere's rationale as
reasonable and, in fact, "too true." Vere's judgment is the only
really authoritative one offered; since he considers but dis-
misses the lieutenants' more cautious proposed policy, he can
only be said to have erred *if* his fears of rekindled mutiny can

be shown to be ill-founded. In light of both the narrator's own remarks concerning the critical "aftertime" of the mutinies and his explicit warning that the era, as it was lived, presented itself as "mysterious and prodigious," it would seem impossible to fault the sense of Vere's judgment without appeals beyond the universe of the story. Vere's critics so much as admit this by having to rely either on a selective "ironic" reading of some of the narrator's remarks or on the surgeon's perplexed surmises. As far as the plain words of the narrator's story are concerned, Captain Vere's prudential decision, to paraphrase Richard Chase, "is impeccable, irrefutable, and fully conscious of the pathetic irony *of the situation*." In other words, as Warner Berthoff noted, in *Billy Budd*, "Melville does not choose, as he did in *White-Jacket*, to judge the martial discipline by a higher moral law."[5]

Since the ironist reading was a reaction to the "testament of acceptance" criticism, it should be pointed out that the above is not meant to suggest agreement with the "acceptance" critics. Both readings err in that they both claim that the novel's meaning depends upon the ideological "acceptability" of Billy's trial and execution. It has been argued here that the really determining scene is that of Billy's crime itself. It is this scene that reveals the limits of the phenomenal characters of the story, and what follows the scene is the denouement, the stark revelation of what the limitations have wrought. To claim Melville uses *Billy Budd* to signal his "acceptance" of the legal tragedy of Billy Budd actually obscures the significance of Billy's crime. It would be more correct to say that *Billy Budd* is meant to reveal the truth about human affairs through a revelation of the tragic consequences of the modern project. The introduction of the question of whether the trial and execution are to be "accepted" or "resisted" is thus, in reality, the grafting of the readers' response to the secondary events onto the real heart of the story. If the light which the "narrative may afford" is such that its readers may discern opposite or confusing outlines, the narrative's own integrity is not impaired. The narrative's lights are purposely dim because, as the narrator of *Mardi* says, "Some revelations show best in a twilight."[6]

In a related concern, other critics have argued that, contrary to Vere's statements, he *could* have acted otherwise or, with particular reference to the laws involved, that he was not legally *compelled* to act as he did toward Billy. This type of criticism must be distinguished from the previously discussed form because the argument concerning the legal necessity of Vere's action centers upon parts of Vere's trial argument and not upon his antecedent judgments. For instance, when C. B. Ives studied Vere's appeals to the Articles of War at Billy's trial, he concluded that "Vere, contrary to some of his statements to his officers, had, as a matter of fact, the broadest powers in dealing with Billy. He could let him off, he could impose a minor punishment, he could refer the case to a general court-martial, or he could hang him."[7] The reason Ives is both correct in this statement and incorrect in believing he had thereby pulled the rug from under Vere is that, as will be seen, Vere's trial arguments are partially *rhetorical*; they are meant to convince men of inferior minds to endorse the course of action which Vere has judged must be followed. In other words, Vere's rhetoric makes it possible to present his chosen policy as the only permissible one. Vere had retained the powers of "supervision" and "interposing" to allow for this very possibility, and thus, when his trial arguments are distinguished from his prior judgments, the criticism of the former collapses into a criticism of the latter. Again, the above observations concerning what Vere *should* have done would then apply.[8]

Nevertheless, the trial scene is important because the particular arguments which Vere chooses to persuade the officers cast added light upon the foundations of Vere's modern conservatism, the form of conservatism that is *behind* what the narrator sees as Vere's consistent and sensible appeals to law.[9] When Vere's arguments are closely examined, the reader begins to sense that, within the narrator's positive presentation of Vere's political character and his legal and disciplinary consistency, there lurks a more profound criticism of Vere than the ironist critics have supposed. The ironists want to condemn Vere for his condemnation of Billy Budd: for them, Vere's disciplinary action is an authoritarian violation of Billy Budd's equal natural rights. In other words, the ironists' standard of justice must ultimately derive from an attainable "higher moral law" which is grounded in the very egalitarianism which the "Inside Narrative" consistently rejects. Once this fact is appreciated, the reader will seek in Vere's trial conduct not his failings in the eyes of certain modern partisans but his standing in the eyes of a profound critic of modernity as a whole. It might be suggested then, in this vein, that Melville does not intend Vere's actions either to arouse the reader's moral indignation or to affirm the reader's allegiance to modern egalitarian notions. Rather, it is Melville's intention to have Vere's sadly "irrefutable" consistency contribute to the reader's understanding of the limitations of the modern conservative statesman and hero.

The court is held in the captain's cabin, the aft staterooms of which house the prisoner and the dead victim. Vere appears "necessarily" as the sole witness, but in doing so, he carefully maintains an outward sign of his reservation of ultimate responsibility, "namely . . . he testified from the ship's weather side." Vere relates "all that had led up to the catastrophe, omitting nothing in Claggart's accusation and deposing as to the manner in which the prisoner had received it." Despite the fact that they were apparently already informed of the basic facts of "the unfortunate affair" by the surgeon, the three officers "glanced with no little surprise at Billy Budd, the last man they

would have suspected either of the mutinous design alleged
by Claggart or the undeniable deed he himself had done." But
in response to the first lieutenant, Billy confirms Vere's testimony, and in Billy's words and Vere's own response, the
reader witnesses the transcendent feeling that now exists between the two:

> "Captain Vere tells the truth. It is just as Captain Vere
> says, but it is not as the master-at-arms said. I have eaten the
> King's bread and I am true to the King."
> "I believe you my man," said the witness, his voice in-
> dicating a suppressed emotion not otherwise betrayed.
> "God will bless you for that, your honor!" not without
> stammering said Billy, and all but broke down. [Pp. 105–6]

Vere thus explicitly states his faith in Billy's innocence of
mutiny, and his affection for Billy surfaces beside his determination to meet the requirements of "martial duty." Also, note
that Billy's sense of loyalty is expressed in the lowest terms:
like an animal, he is loyal to the hand that feeds him, perhaps
simply *because* it feeds him.

The court officers are perplexed at this exchange because
it suggests that Claggart acted without a motive. Asked about
his relationship to the master-at-arms, Billy responds:

> "No, there was no malice between us. I never bore malice
> against the master-at-arms. I am sorry that he is dead. I did
> not mean to kill him. Could I have used my tongue I would
> not have struck him. But he foully lied to my face and in
> presence of my captain, and I had to say something, and I
> could only say it with a blow, God help me!" [P. 106]

To Billy, Claggart's maliciousness remains a closed book, but
he apparently has realized that his inability to speak and defend
himself politically has been shown to be his tragic flaw. The
further implications of his naiveté are raised when Billy is
asked if he was aware of "aught savoring of incipient trouble"

in "any section of the ship's company." Billy lies and answers
negatively because his "same erring sense of uninstructed hon-
or" once again prohibits him from "playing a part at all approaching that of an informer" against the afterguardsman.
Thus, Billy's "uninstructed" innocence, an adjunct of his
apolitical speechlessness, actually protects the afterguardsman
from justice and destroys any possibility of bringing added
light to Claggart's maneuverings.[10]

The problem of Claggart's motive hence remains, and so
the marine officer directly asks what could have led the master-
at-arms to have lied. The question touches "on a spiritual sphere
wholly obscure to Billy's thoughts," and he is "nonplussed" by
it and exhibits a confusion which some might "have construed
into involuntary evidence of hidden guilt." Turning to Vere
as "his best helper and friend," Billy seeks the captain's aid.
Vere's response begins his initial effort to have the trial exclude
all matters that might interfere with the outcome he believes
is necessary:

> "The question you put to him comes naturally enough. But
> how can he rightly answer it?—or anybody else, unless in-
> deed it be he who lies within there," designating the com-
> partment where lay the corpse. "But the prone one there
> will not rise to our summons. In effect, though, as it seems
> to me, the point you make is hardly material. Quite aside
> from any conceivable motive actuating the master-at-arms,
> and irrespective of the provocation to the blow, a martial
> court must needs in the present case confine its attention to
> the blow's consequence, which consequence justly is to be
> deemed not otherwise than as the striker's deed." [P. 107]

Vere's argument here could be the first step in the realization
of his own prior decision; hence, at this point, he has introduced
a crucial argument for his case; he must here believe that the
outcome of the trial will depend upon the acceptance or re-

jection of his insistence that the court's attention must be confined only to Billy's "blow."

Billy's reaction to Vere's argument recurs to his earlier comparison to a St. Bernard dog: he gives Vere "a look in its dumb expressiveness not unlike that which a dog of generous breed might turn upon his master." But the officers comprehend the implications of Vere's words: those words bear an "unanticipated" import, "involving a prejudgment on the speaker's part." The "mental disturbance" of the officers is hence augmented as they sense the direction Vere would have them follow. Their disturbance is further accentuated by the fact that Claggart's motivation "remains mysterious in this matter"; the officers would like to know Claggart's motives, but, fooled by Billy's lie, they believe that there is "nobody . . . none of the ship's company, . . . —who might shed lateral light, if any is to be had, upon" the affair. At this, Vere reiterates his earlier point and, significantly, does so in the same biblical terms the narrator first used:

> "Ay, there is a mystery; but to use a scriptural phrase, it is a 'mystery of iniquity,' a matter for psychologic theologians to discuss. But what has a military court to do with it? Not to add that for us any possible investigation of it is cut off by the lasting tongue-tie of—him—in yonder," again designating the mortuary stateroom. "The prisoner's deed—with that alone we have to do."[11]

Vere's twice-made point ends the testimony portion of the trial because the captain's first-hand account is clearly irrefutable and unchallengeable. In order to end the marine's continued assertive discussion of Claggart's motives, Vere gives "a glance more effective than words" to the first lieutenant, and the latter officer "resumed . . . primacy" in the court. With this and a final ascertainment that Billy had "said all," the formal trial ends, and Billy leaves the scene. Vere has given his testimony, tried to steer the court away from the "psycho-logic" mystery of Claggart's iniquity, and twice made a crucial argument by which he sought to win the officers' consent to his prior judgment that Billy must hang. What stands between Vere's argument and the realization of his judgment is the natural hesitancy of the officers to embrace the terrible con-clusion that Billy must die. Sensing the court's "troubled in-decision," Vere paces "the cabin athwart; in the returning ascent to windward climbing the slant deck in the ship's lee roll, without knowing it symbolizing thus in his action a mind resolute to surmount difficulties even if against primitive in-stincts strong as the wind and the sea." Vere must apparently argue against the officers' inclination to judge the events on the basis of what they instinctively believe is the "essential right and wrong involved." Vere may believe, as the narrator earlier said, that "he was not authorized to determine the mat-ter on that primitive basis."[12] In any case, the crucial implica-tion is that, for at least the narrator, questions of "essential" or natural "right and wrong" touch "primitive instincts" as un-certain and formless as "the wind and the sea." Vere's own upcoming defense of conventional law thus might also be the other side of the coin of a rejection of nature as a usable stan-dard for conduct.

Vere's problem is largely a rhetorical one. He must tailor an argument so that the officers will accept what he sees as incumbent upon them to accept. His prudential judgment that the present dangerous situation dictates "rigor" and strict discipline must be made to prevail. Hence, the narrator says, "After scanning their faces [Vere] stood less as mustering his thoughts for expression than as one inly deliberating *how best to put them* to well-meaning men not intellectually mature, men with whom it was necessary to demonstrate certain prin-ciples that were axioms to himself" (p. 109, italics added).

Vere believes that the general good of the "sea commonalty" and its very survival demand rigorous attachment to the law in a time of war and internal danger. The lieutenants, who would rather refer the case to the admiral, need to be convinced that Vere's proposed course of action must be followed, whether or not they may come to share Vere's ultimate understanding of the requirements of the present situation. Vere's rhetoric, thus, will seek to convey his "axioms" and "principles" in language which will lead his officers to accept the way he has decided to apply those principles in the immediate case. Vere's rhetorical way is, in fact, to argue that his chosen application follows directly and automatically from his first principles. And the manifest advantage of this rhetorical argument is that it excuses the officers in advance for any responsibility for Billy's execution.

When Vere speaks, he demonstrates "the influence of unshared studies" upon his "practical training," and he suggests the grounds for the "pedantry" imputed to him by his fellow-officers, "who nevertheless would frankly concede that His Majesty's navy mustered no more efficient officer of their grade than Starry Vere." Vere begins by noting the officers' "moral scruple" in a favorable light but arguing that, nonetheless, the case is a practical one:

"Hitherto I have been but the witness, little more; and I should hardly think now to take another tone, that of your coadjutor for the time, did I not perceive in you—at the crisis too—a troubled hesitancy, proceeding, I doubt not, from the clash of military duty with moral scruple—scruple vitalized by compassion. For the compassion, how can I otherwise than share it? But, mindful of paramount obligations, I strive against scruples that may tend to enervate decision. Not, gentlemen, that I hide from myself that the case is an exceptional one. Speculatively regarded, it well might be referred to a jury of casuists. But for us here, acting not as casuists or moralists, it is a case practical, and under martial law practically to be dealt with." [Pp. 109–10]

Vere's purpose is to bring the officers' critical hesitancy out into the open and then to discredit the natural compassion and moral scruples behind that hesitancy.[13]

Vere then takes it upon himself to state the officers' scruples and to contrast those scruples with his settled principles:

"If, mindless of palliating circumstances, we are bound to regard the death of the master-at-arms as the prisoner's deed, then does that deed constitute a capital crime whereof the penalty is a mortal one. But in natural justice is nothing but the prisoner's overt act to be considered? How can we adjudge to summary and shameful death a fellow creature innocent before God, and whom we feel to be so?—Does that state it aright? You sign sad assent. . . . It is Nature. But do these buttons that we wear attest that our allegiance is to Nature? No, to the King. Though the ocean, which is inviolate Nature primeval, though this be the element where we move and have our being as sailors, yet as the King's officers lies our duty in a sphere correspondingly natural? So little is that true, that in receiving our commissions we in the most important regards ceased to be natural free agents. . . . For suppose condemnation to follow these present proceedings. Would it be so much we ourselves that would condemn as it would be martial law operating through us? For that law and the rigor of it, we are not responsible. Our vowed responsibility is this: That however pitilessly that law may operate in any instances, we nevertheless adhere to it and administer it." [Pp. 110–11]

Now the elements of Vere's rhetoric should be clear in the above speech. In fact, Vere himself emphatically does not act out of *mere* allegiance to the king. He opposes the "novel" political opinions based on the natural rights of man because he "disinterestedly" judges them to be "at war with . . . the true welfare of mankind." Also, Vere himself clearly recognizes his own "ultimate accountability" for the trial's outcome: he knows that *he* has decided how "pitilessly" the law is to operate in the case of Billy Budd. Vere knows, that is, that he is no mere administrator of the *king's* law and judgment. The reader who is aware of Vere's rhetoric, however, must also note that the rhetoric nevertheless packages Vere's actual political "axioms." Most crucial to note is that Vere's speech repeats the narrator's earlier imagery: for Vere too, "natural justice" is as formless as the ocean, which he calls "inviolate Nature primeval." Vere's argument for a pitiless application of the law, however rhetorical, is thus premised upon a radical distinction between convention and nature. For Vere, the law alone is certain; his "Nature" is unpredictable, orderless, a mass of unknowable crosscurrents. While Vere's argument attempts to get the officers now to adhere to the law blindly and mechanically, his own general adherence to the law is based upon thought-out "settled convictions" which deny that nature is a knowable guide for human conduct. Vere's allegiance to convention, like the narrator's, is thus dependent upon his prior rejection of nature. However clearly it must be conceded to Vere, as in fact it must, that standards of "natural justice" cannot in fact be applied directly to actual cases, it still remains true that Vere's "positive convictions" deny that there is any natural guide or measure for the statesman's prudence. Indeed, taken to its extreme, Vere's portrait of nature both subverts the real authority of the, by implication, merely conventional king whom he serves and, perhaps more importantly here, denies that one can ultimately defend the "natural regality" that the "Inside Narrative" affirms.

The most obvious indication of the problem of Vere's "axioms" is perhaps the fact that Vere's rhetorically presented principles still fail to persuade the court. Although Vere goes on to warn against following the natural dictates of the heart and "private conscience," repeating and reemphasizing all his previous arguments,[14] he has still to convince the officers to condemn Billy Budd. Perhaps they sense sophistry within his arguments that they have no real choice in the matter and that they will not be responsible for their decision. In any case, they resist and remain hesitant until Vere's rhetoric finally avoids principles and appeals to a combination of their sense of duty and their fears.

Vere brings about this resolution himself by recurring to the facts of the crime: "In wartime at sea a man-of-war's man strikes his superior in grade, and the blow kills. Apart from its effect the blow itself is, according to the Articles of War, a capital crime." War demands the strictest punishment. But the captain of marines breaks in here, conceding Vere's observation, but adding that "surely Budd purposed neither mutiny nor homicide." Vere counters by showing that the Mutiny Act, the child of War, shares with its father a concern only for appearances. Mutual enemies do not distinguish between reluctant conscripts and volunteers, or between the loyal and the disloyal, or between war supporters and war opponents. Of Billy's lack of malicious intent Vere thus says:

". . . . before a court less arbitrary and more merciful than a martial one, that plea would largely extenuate. At the Last Assizes it shall acquit. But how here? . . . War looks but to the frontage, the appearance. And the Mutiny Act, War's child, takes after the father. Budd's intent or non-intent is nothing to the purpose." [Pp. 111–12]

While this argument again results in a concentration upon Billy's "deed alone," it arrives at that point through a legal question, and that question opens up other legal questions by alerting the officers to the points of law in the case. The officers now realize, that is, that they may be able to concede Vere's insistence that they restrict themselves solely to Billy's indisputable deed and yet be able to prevent the realization of Vere's tragic objective. Thus, when Vere rhetorically asserts that "the enemy may be sighted and an engagement [may] result" and that "one of two things must we do—condemn or let go," the officers again object; the sailing master asks, "Can we not convict and yet mitigate the penalty?" This is the legal objection that forces Vere to alter his rhetorical line.

Vere's response repeats the narrator's previous description of Vere's thinking, but in the captain's own words:

"Gentlemen, were that clearly lawful for us under the circumstances, consider the consequences of such clemency. The people" (meaning the ship's company) "have native sense; most of them are familiar with our naval usage and tradition; and how would they take it? Even could you explain to them—which our official position forbids—they, long molded by arbitrary discipline, have not that kind of intelligent responsiveness that might qualify them to comprehend and discriminate. No, to the people the foretopman's deed, however it be worded in the announcement, will be plain homicide committed in a flagrant act of mutiny. What penalty for that should follow, they know. But it does not follow. *Why*? they will ruminate. You know what sailors are. Will they not revert to the recent outbreak at the Nore? Ay. They know the well-founded alarm—the panic it struck throughout England. Your clement sentence they would account pusillanimous. They would think that we flinch, that we are afraid of them—afraid of practicing a lawful rigor singularly demanded at this juncture, lest it should provoke new troubles. What shame to us such a conjecture on their part, and how deadly to discipline. You see then, whither, prompted by duty and the law, I steadfastly drive. But I beseech you, my friends, do not take me amiss. I feel as you do for this unfortunate boy. But did he know our hearts, I take him to be of that generous nature that he would feel even for us on whom in this military necessity so heavy a compulsion is laid."[15]

Vere thus finally admits that what the law specifically *requires* is not really clear; thus, if he is "prompted by duty and the law," it is because *he* sees it as his present duty to *preserve* the law in the most "pitiless" way. Vere's law does not admit subtle distinctions because to the "uncultivated" people for whom the law is made Billy's act is "plain homicide" and "a flagrant act of mutiny." According to Vere, for its own preservation and because of the character of its "people," the law demands plain applications, without casuistic subtleties. Vere's entire prudential position thus also presupposes an anti-Enlightenment view of the status of "the people" and of their "true welfare," a view which is similar to the authorial view found "inside" the narrator's descriptions of the "Handsome Sailor" and Lord Nelson, although that authorial view proceeded from an understanding of a given *natural*, and not merely "official," human hierarchy.

With this argument, Vere's participation in the trial ends. Significantly, it is his appeal to duty and fear that finally wins the officers' consent, that is, his argument "as to the practical consequences to discipline, considering the unconfirmed tone of the fleet at the time, should a man-of-war's man's violent killing at sea of a superior in grade be allowed to pass for aught else than a capital crime demanding prompt infliction of the penalty" (p. 113). Thus, while Vere first attempted to steer the officers toward consent to his prior judgment by having them exclude *everything* but Billy's deed from consideration, he now has succeeded in his plan by appealing rhetorically to the very political circumstances which his own prudential judgment has weighed so heavily. The revelation of his judgment concerning the danger of the times succeeds in having the officers agree that they must act on the "frontage" of Billy's deed. Only now has Vere succeeded in preventing any further hesitancy due to the murder's mystery, the officers' natural instincts of compassion, or their strictly private consciences. It might be added, thus, that the failure of Vere's first rhetorical arguments points out another limitation upon his ruling ability: he could not convey his "axiomatic" principles in a persuasive way. And the reason for this failure, in the author's eyes, may be that those principles are simply unpersuasive.

It is here that the narrator raises his story's similarity to the *Somers* affair. The reference is to "history, and here cited without comment." But the narrator cautions that the similarity lies in "the urgency felt" and not in the actual circumstances of the case. The narrator's purpose appears to be to stress the difficulty of judging the events of the *Somers* case or those of the affair aboard H.M.S. *Bellipotent*. In an oblique citation of Melville himself, the narrator notes:

> Says a writer whom few know, "Forty years after a battle it is easy for a noncombatant to reason about how it ought to have been fought. It is another thing personally and under fire to have to direct the fighting while involved in the obscuring smoke of it. Much so with . . . other emergencies involving considerations both practical and moral, and when it is imperative promptly to act." [P. 114]

Thus, it is idle to presume to criticize Vere's prudential judgment-on-the-spot and to argue that he "should have" judged otherwise. The long trial has ended in the officers' confirmation of the captain's initial determination that the dangers of war and mutiny prohibit the moral and legal discriminations that otherwise might have saved Billy Budd. When it has been seen that the trial amounts to Vere's struggle to obtain consent to his prior judgment, it becomes obvious that *Billy Budd* is not intended as a vehicle for suggesting practical alternatives to Vere's trial decisions. Rather, the trial and the execution to follow are revealed as the terribly direct and successive consequences of an action which demonstrated the fragility of innocence, the unavoidable existence of evil, and the inadequacy of practical wisdom. Again, the core of *Billy Budd* is the "deplorable occurrence" which sets the subsequent, "irrefutable" chain of events and decisions into motion. The reader is not asked to accept or resist those later events and decisions, but rather to see in Billy's crime the inherently tragic nature of political life and to see in Vere's modern "axioms" the tragic undermining of those natural standards by which the virtuous can be measured as truly glorious.

Notes

1 The fact that Billy has indeed committed a *criminal* action is often lost behind the critic's concern for Billy's natural innocence. Billy's crime is emphasized, however, in two essays which are substantially at odds with the present study: C. B. Ives, "*Billy Budd* and the Articles of War," *American Literature* 34 (March 1962): 32; and Charles A. Reich, "The Tragedy of Justice in *Billy Budd*," *Yale Review* 56, New Series (Spring 1967): 377.

2 Darrel Abel, " 'Laurel Twined with Thorn': The Theme of Melville's *Timoleon*," *The Personalist* 41 (Summer 1960): 337; see also *H&S*, p. 35.

3 P. 103. Note that the "resemblance" to tyranny applies only to Vere's "maintenance of secrecy" in the case, and compare this with the comparison of Ahab and Czar Nicholas in Herman Melville, *Moby-Dick; or, the Whale*, ed. Harrison Hayford and Hershel Parker (New York: Norton, 1967), pp. 129–30.

Also compare Vere with the ungentlemanly and implicitly Czarist Captain Riga in *Redburn: His First Voyage*, in *The Writings of Herman Melville*, ed. Harrison Hayford, Hershel Parker, and G. Thomas Tanselle, 15 vols. (Evanston and Chicago: Northwestern University Press and The Newberry Library, 1968–), 4:67–71, 263.

For a negative view of Vere based on the passage in question, however, see Alice Chandler, "Captain Vere and the 'Tragedies of the Palace,' " *Modern Fiction Studies* 13 (Summer 1967): 259–61.

4 P. 104. Note that at Billy's trial, the officers carefully refrain from even mentioning the word "mutiny" (p. 106), showing that they too are aware of the "embers of the Nore."

5 Richard Chase, "Dissent on *Billy Budd*," *Partisan Review* 15 (November 1948): 1215 (italics added); Warner Berthoff, " 'Certain Phenomenal Men': The Example of *Billy Budd*," *ELH* 27 (December 1960): 340.

⁶ *Mardi: and A Voyage Thither*, in *The Writings of Herman Melville*, ed. Harrison Hayford, Hershel Parker, and G. Thomas Tanselle, 15 vols. (Evanston and Chicago: Northwestern University Press and The Newberry Library, 1968–   ), 3:56.

⁷ Ives, *"Billy Budd* and the Articles of War," p. 35. The relevance of the real Articles to the story's own universe is being conceded for the sake of the argument. Ives's essay has a positive effect in counterbalancing the impression left by Hayford and Sealts that Melville's use of the Articles was improper and misinformed. (See *H&S*, p. 176.)

⁸ In Ives's own case, his argument with what Vere in fact chose to do seems to depend on a torturous portrayal of Vere's character. See *"Billy Budd* and the Articles of War," pp. 37–39.

Also, Ives claims (p. 36) that "there is no reason for the reader to suppose that these officers of Vere's were foolish men." The officers may not be "foolish," but they are of conventional and practical minds. The naval officers' "intelligence was mostly confined to the matter of active seamanship and the fighting demands of their profession." (*Billy Budd*, p. 105.)

⁹ The narrator also suggests that the trial shows another instance of Vere's political prudence. The inclusion of the captain of marines in the trial of a sailor "deviated from general custom." Apparently, Vere is motivated by a desire to place the marines on his side in the event of "difficulties"; note that the suppression of the Nore was made possible in part by "the unswerving loyalty of the marine corps." (See pp. 55, 104.)

¹⁰ P. 106. On p. 107, the narrator also notes that Billy realized he had committed a serious crime by not reporting the afterguardsman in the first place. His negative answer to the question about "incipient trouble" is self-defensive perjury. The "innocent" Billy is thus multiplying his crimes, perhaps because he believes no purpose would be served if he told the story of the afterguardsman's proposition. (Note his "feeling . . . that nothing really was being hatched.")

¹¹ Pp. 107–8. Notice the added ironic reversal of the story: now it is Claggart who is "tongue-tied."

¹² Cf. pp. 103, 108–9.

¹³ Note that Vere hesitated to include the "extremely good-natured" captain of marines on the court because he "might not prove altogether reliable in a moral dilemma involving aught of the tragic" (pp. 104–5).

¹⁴ P. 111. Vere might say that it is the heart, in fact, that often blinds literary critics to Billy's real guilt and perjury. Also, Vere's opposition to the notion that man ought to be guided by his heart or by compassion places him in conservative opposition to the celebration of compassion by Rousseau and his followers.

¹⁵ Pp. 112–13. According to *Omoo*, established "sea usages . . . know no exceptions." See *Omoo: A Narrative of Adventures in the South Seas*, in *The Writings of Herman Melville*, ed. Harrison Hayford, Hershel Parker, and G. Thomas Tanselle, 15 vols. (Evanston and Chicago: Northwestern University Press and The Newberry Library, 1968–   ), 2:71.

7

An Execution at Sea

THE *reasonableness* OF VERE'S JUDGMENT that Billy must hang is supported by the narrator's portrait of Vere's character, the narrator's own confirmation of the dangerous situation in 1797, and the eventual agreement of the court's officers in Vere's prior judgment. Moreover, one of the great ironies of the novel is that *Claggart's* judgment that the times would dictate dire consequences for a mutineer is confirmed. The officers finally agree that guilty Billy will be regarded as a mutineer by "the people," while Claggart had attempted to make innocent Billy a mutineer in the eyes of the captain; in either case, all agree that the penalty for the identified mutineer is a capital one. The tragedy of Billy's crime is thus the fact that it creates a situation in which Vere might ironically affirm Claggart's "uncommon prudence." Melville's intent in the novel is not to criticize what follows upon the "deplorable occurrence" but to seek in those tragic subsequent events further insight into the modern assumptions that allow man's confrontation with natural evil to issue in tragedy rather than in glorious "exaltations of sentiment."

It is in this same regard that the execution of Billy Budd, otherwise merely the full and final realization of Vere's initial decision, also assumes significance in its own right. Together, the execution scene and its aftermath round out the narrative's tragic portrayal of modern political reality, a reality which seems to deny any place to true glory. Indeed, the difficulty in approaching the execution scene is that the very tragedy of it appeals to the heart and tends to obscure the truth intended to be conveyed. Billy's conviction is and is meant to be a stark event, and Billy's execution will only add to the stark reality of the trial's outcome:

> In brief, Billy Budd was formally convicted and sentenced to be hung at the yardarm in the early morning watch, it being now night. Otherwise, as is customary in such cases, the sentence would forthwith have been carried out. In wartime on the field or in the fleet, a mortal punishment decreed by a drumhead court—on the field sometimes decreed by but a nod from the general—follows without delay on the heel of conviction, without appeal. [P. 114]

The difficulty of seeing beyond this starkness presents the essential challenge of *Billy Budd*.

The tragic strength of the execution scene is accentuated by the narrator's "conjectures" about Vere's communication to Billy of the sentence of the court. Vere takes on this task "of his own motion," and the narrator's observations are meant to emphasize again the exceptional characters of both Vere and Billy, "each radically sharing in the rarer qualities of our nature —so rare indeed as to be all but incredible to average minds however much cultivated." The narrator's conjectures thus hint that, just as Vere and Billy rise above the roles fate has allotted to them, the reader of more than "average mind" must rise above the tragedy of the events of the "Inside Narrative." Those who find the feeling that exists between Vere and Billy "incredible" will also never understand that a merely passionate reaction to Billy's fate only obscures a "truth uncompromisingly told." For these, it might be well to note that the narrator shows, after his conjectures, that Vere did in fact tell the truth when he said that he also felt for "unfortunate" Billy Budd:

It would have been in consonance with the spirit of Captain Vere should he on this occasion have concealed nothing from the condemned one—should he indeed have frankly disclosed to him the part he himself had played in bringing about the decision, at the same time revealing his actuating motives. On Billy's side it is not improbable that such a confession would have been received in much the same spirit that prompted it. Not without a sort of joy, indeed, he might have appreciated the brave opinion of him implied in his captain's making such a confidant of him. Nor, as to the sentence itself, could he have been insensible that it was imparted to him as to one not afraid to die. Even more may have been. Captain Vere in end may have developed the passion sometimes latent under an exterior stoical or indifferent. He was old enough to have been Billy's father. The austere devotee of military duty, letting himself melt back into what remains primeval in our formalized humanity, may in end have caught Billy to his heart, even as Abraham may have caught young Isaac on the brink of resolutely offering him up in obedience to the exacting behest. But there is no telling the sacrament, seldom if in any case revealed to the gadding world, wherever under circumstances at all akin to those here attempted to be set forth two of great Nature's nobler order embrace. There is privacy at the time, inviolable to the survivor; and holy oblivion, the sequel to each diviner magnanimity, providentially covers all at last.

The first to encounter Captain Vere in act of leaving the compartment was the senior lieutenant. The face he beheld, for the moment one expressive of the agony of the strong, was to that officer, though a man of fifty, a startling revelation. That the condemned one suffered less than he who mainly had effected the condemnation was apparently indicated by the former's exclamation in the scene soon perforce to be touched upon.[1]

The narrator's observations reveal that the existence of Billy and Vere as two of "Nature's nobler order" transcends the fact that they embody opposite forms of nobility: whereas the one possesses such nobility as is to be had in apolitical innocence, the other possesses a form of the nobility of political virtue. The reader sees, thus, both that Billy's "novice magnanimity" hinted at a real nobility which could exist without any actual political ramifications and again that Vere's conventionally exemplary characteristics nevertheless derived from certain natural endowments. The narrator also reveals another instance of Vere's honesty and directness, and the narrator gives the first indication that Billy Budd has come to comprehend the subtle facts of his situation. Through this comprehension, Vere and Billy are able to share their experiences; Vere is able to indulge in "primeval" human sentiments, and Billy, the reader is promised, will make an exclamation that will indicate a new awareness of the nature of Vere's "exacting behest."

"The people" of the *Bellipotent* are now told of Billy's deed, trial, and sentence. In the brief hour and a half in which Billy and Claggart had been closeted in the captain's cabin, the crew, "like villagers," had indulged in speculations and rumors, and so they are prepared for some "extraordinary" announcement as they are unusually assembled in the second dogwatch. Vere addresses his men as they stand before him, his officers, and "the marine guard under arms." Clearly and concisely, Vere tells "the people" what has happened, but he carefully avoids both using the word "mutiny" and preaching on discipline, "thinking perhaps that under existing circumstances in the navy the consequence of violating discipline should be made to speak for itself." The crew's reaction is the important element in the scene: "Their captain's announcement was listened to by the throng of standing sailors in a dumbness like that of a seated congregation of believers in hell listening to the clergyman's announcement of his Calvinistic text" (pp. 116–17). Here, in the narrator's second reference to Calvinism, is revealed another vital fact about "the people," and this fact leads directly into the subject of their character. "The people" are "believers," and they hear Vere's announcement of the condemnation of one man as if it were merely a part of the announcement of the "natural depravity" of "total mankind."

When the narrator first spoke of Calvinism and its relationship to the Platonic concept of "natural depravity," he argued that the Calvinist dogma wrongly applied the concept of individual depravity to the whole human race. Still, in comparison to the reigning philosophy of the day, which saw men as naturally perfectible or naturally incapable of evil, Calvinism retained an important degree of truth. In the particular instance of John Claggart's "irrational" hatred for Billy Budd, Calvinism would have no difficulty in accounting for the phenomenon of Claggart, while the faith of the Enlightenment philosophers is thrown into disarray by the possibility of natural, inborn, human evil. Despite its extremism, Calvinism possesses the virtue of reminding "the people" of the philosophically unpopular doctrine of man's Fall, thereby countering the modern doctrine of man's perfectibility.

"The people" of the *Bellipotent* thus are somewhat behind their own times, and they understand Vere's announcement in a Calvinistic way. More important than the particular denominational form their response takes is the fact that their response is religious and not secular. The crew understands the affair aboard H.M.S. *Bellipotent* in terms of the lexicon of Christianity and Holy Writ, the Calvinist form of their response serving to highlight, by its extremity, the totally religious character of that response. Thus, after Billy's execution, the narrator points out that the sailors of the British fleet venerated Billy as a Christ-figure. What is important to note is that the sailors' religious view of Billy Budd achieves for them a glimpse of the exceptionality of the *Bellipotent*'s affair, an exceptionality which they cannot come to know fully:

> Everything is for a term venerated in navies. Any tangible object associated with some striking incident of the service is converted into a monument. The spar from which the foretopman was suspended was for some few years kept trace of by the bluejackets. Their knowledges followed it from ship to dockyard and again from dockyard to ship, still pursuing it even when at last reduced to a mere dockyard boom. To them a chip of it was as a piece of the Cross. Ignorant though they were of the secret facts of the tragedy, and not thinking but that the penalty was somehow unavoidably inflicted from the naval point of view, for all that, they instinctively felt that Billy was a sort of man as incapable of mutiny as of wilful murder. They recalled the fresh young image of the Handsome Sailor, that face never deformed by a sneer or subtler vile freak of the heart within. This impression of him was doubtless deepened by the fact that he was gone, and in a measure mysteriously gone.[2]

In their ignorance of the subtler psychic "facts of the tragedy," the sailors are confronted with a potentially meaningless execution, but the event is given spiritual meaning through their religiosity. They accept the execution of Billy Budd as simply unavoidable "from the naval point of view," but they are still able to see Billy in terms of his original moral innocence by viewing him as a redemptive Christ. In other words, *Billy Budd* lends some support to the Christian version of the "testament of acceptance" reading of some critics, but the novel does so with the proviso that the Christian understanding is *not* to be understood as the whole truth: it is that reflection of the truth that is visible to the "uncultivated" or "average" eye.

The peculiar ability of the religious version of the events aboard H.M.S. *Bellipotent* to achieve a partial, unrefined glimpse of the significance of those events is further witnessed by the chaplain's visit to the manacled Billy Budd. The chaplain comes upon Billy in a moment of repose, and he withdraws "for the time, peradventure feeling that even he, the minister of Christ though receiving his stipend from Mars, had no consolation to proffer which could result in a peace transcending that which he beheld" (p. 120). The chaplain thus immediately senses Billy's spiritual tranquility, and he is able finally to accept Billy's incapacity to embrace the Christian message because he, the chaplain, feels that "innocence was even a better thing than religion wherewith to go to Judgment" (p. 121). In this way, the chaplain is able to include Billy in the salvation of Christ, an inclusion predicated upon his belief in Billy's "innocence." Again, the chaplain's Christian view merely touches the surface of Billy's real moral state. The "Inside Narrative" reveals that Billy's peace does not flow from any "godly understanding that he must die," but rather from his proximity to the state of nature. Faced with death, Billy "was wholly without irrational fear of it, a fear more prevalent in highly civilized communities than in those so-called barbarous ones which in all respects stand nearer to unadulterate Nature. And, as elsewhere said, a barbarian Billy radically was."[3] Similarly, Billy is unable to understand the chaplain's "efforts to bring home to him the thought of salvation and a Savior." Billy listens to the chaplain out of "a certain natural politeness," regarding the chaplain's words in the same way as he would "any discourse abstract or out of the common tone of the workaday world." Billy's "sailor way of taking clerical discourse in not wholly unlike the way in which the primer of Christianity, full of transcendent miracles, was received long ago on tropic isles by any superior *savage*, so called—a Tahitian, say, of Captain Cook's time or shortly after that time."[4] Despite the fact that the Christian message is thus lost on Billy Budd, the chaplain is able to see Billy in Christian terms; confident in the foretopman's moral innocence of murder, the chaplain grants a spiritual significance to Billy's death and accepts the fact of Billy's punishment: "Stooping over, he kissed on the fair cheek his fellow man, a felon in martial law, one whom though on the confines of death he felt he could never convert to a dogma; nor for all that did he fear for his future" (p. 121). The chaplain's faith rises above his inability to convert Billy and expresses itself in a corresponding faith in Billy's salvation.

Just as the "Inside Narrative" saw a truth hidden within the doctrine of man's Fall, it sees a truth hidden within the religious faith that Billy will be saved in the afterlife. In both cases, the religious dogmas recognize a spiritual dimension of human life which gives transcendent significance to merely "historical" events and characters. The similarity of the "Inside Narrative" and the religious viewpoint need not be made any more specific than this: they both perceive a more crucial, spiritual dimension to merely mundane realities. But the significance of their similarity is perhaps best seen in comparison to the surgeon's scientific view, a view which in fact reduces the mundane to something even lower. Thus, after Billy's hanging, when the purser (who is "more accurate as an accountant than profound as a philosopher") remarks to the surgeon that the phenomenal stillness of Billy's suspended body was a remarkable "testimony to the force lodged in will power," the surgeon objects to seeing any psychic significance in the fact:

"Your pardon, Mr. Purser. In a hanging scientifically conducted—and under special orders I myself directed how Budd's was to be effected—any movement following the completed suspension and originating in the body suspended, such movement indicates mechanical spasm in the muscular system. Hence the absence of that is no more attributable to will power, as you call it, than to horsepower—begging your pardon."

When the purser then observes that such "spasm" is, however, usually invariable, the surgeon is put upon to explain its absence in Billy's case:

> "Mr. Purser, it is clear that your sense of the singularity in this matter equals not mine. You account for it by what you call will power—a term not yet included in the lexicon of science. For me, I do not, with my present knowledge, pretend to account for it at all."

. . . .

> "It was phenomenal, Mr. Purser, in the sense that it was an appearance the cause of which is not immediately to be assigned."

The persistent purser then asks if Billy's death was caused "by the halter" or "was it a species of euthanasia?" The surgeon's response completes the picture of his reduction of both the Christian and Platonic spiritual realities:

> "*Euthanasia*, Mr. Purser, is something like your *will power*: I doubt its authenticity as a scientific term—begging your pardon again. It is at once imaginative and metaphysical—in short, Greek.—But," abruptly changing his tone, "there is a case in the sick bay that I do not care to leave to my assistants. Beg your pardon, but excuse me." And rising from the mess he formally withdrew.[5]

The scientific surgeon thus refuses to admit any transcendent significance into his "lexicon." The "imaginative and metaphysical" religious and "Greek" views of reality are simply dismissed. For him, the man of science, Billy's death was merely a "scientifically conducted" curiosity, its phenomenal character only awaiting scientific explanation. For the surgeon, what is phenomenal needs only to be explained away in terms of underlying physical functions, while for the "Inside Narrative," what is phenomenal adumbrates the perennial and universal moral truth. It goes without saying that the surgeon's opinion about Vere's insanity is correspondingly shown to be both "crass and stultifying." And it should be noted that the scientific view of the events aboard H.M.S. *Bellipotent* obscures even more of the true character of those events than does the official, historical view of the authorized naval journal. While the journal's account sees only "vulgar rascality" and simply puts Billy down as a mutinous, depraved criminal and Claggart down as a glorious patriot, it nevertheless sees in the events, in a slanted way, the purpose of Vere's action. Thus, the journal notes: "The promptitude of the punishment has proved salutary. Nothing amiss is now apprehended aboard H.M.S. *Bellipotent*." On the other hand, for the surgeon, no appreciation of the entire question of purpose is even indicated, and everything falls before his labeling of what is sane and insane, or scientific and unscientific. The purser's potentially insightful observation concerning the painless and merciful aspect of Billy's death is met only with the surgeon's departure. His dedication to the *newest* scientific information blinds him to "the *essential* in certain exceptional characters."

The fact that "the people" see events in a religious way not only highlights the spiritual obscurantism of science and official history but also underlines the previously raised implicit authorial claim that human endeavors require some indication of divine approbation. Nelson's "priestly" sacrifice was seen as the great example of winning in modern times the "plenary absolution" god-kings or archetypical "Handsome Sailors" once granted by their very existence as the points of confluence between the human and the divine. In this regard, the chaplain's anomalous position as "the minister of Christ though receiving his stipend from Mars" is also significant. The narrator goes on to show that the apparent incongruity of the chaplain's position is tied directly to the purpose of winning religious sanction for the *Bellipotent*'s military endeavors:

> Marvel not that having been made acquainted with the young sailor's essential innocence the [chaplain] lifted not a finger to avert the doom of such a martyr to martial discipline. So to do would not only have been as idle as invoking the desert, but would also have been an audacious transgression of the bounds of his function, one as exactly prescribed to him by military law as that of the boatswain or any other naval officer. Bluntly put, a chaplain is the minister of the Prince of Peace serving in the host of the God of War—Mars. As such, he is as incongruous as a musket would be on the altar at Christmas. Why, then, is he there? Because he indirectly subserves the purpose attested by the cannon; because too he lends the sanction of the religion of the meek to that which practically is the abrogation of everything but brute Force.[6]

Thus, Christianity is seen as playing essentially the same role in regard to "the people" (who, again, have "native sense") as any primitive religion played in regard to the native "savages." That role is, however, an absolutely necessary one, and those who would attempt to rule without some kind of gods are shown to be ignorant of the true nature of "the people." Hence, the regime defended by Captain Vere is the regime in the present hostilities which is the more attuned to the true nature of "the people." Significantly, thus, Vere is fatally wounded in a battle with the French ship, the *Athée*, a name which proclaimed "the infidel audacity" of the Directory. The *Athée* was formerly the *St. Louis* and had been rechristened, or rather *dechristened* the "Atheist." The narrator observes that this name, "though not so intended to be," was "the aptest name, if one consider it, ever given to a warship." One may speculate that the reason for this observation is that the narrator, and perhaps the author, regards war, "the abrogation of everything but brute Force," as a direct proof of the absence of the Christian God.[7]

In the "Inside Narrative," thus, the English regime, which assigns a chaplain to its warship, is defended against the revolutionary regime of France, and *Billy Budd* shows that this defense of England is predicated in part upon an understanding of both "the people's" need for religion and the ability of religion to adumbrate the spiritual truth of human life. But England is also defended for another reason, namely, because its espousal of "founded law" against "unbridled revolt" also reflects a true picture of the nature of "the people." As has already been seen, Vere's worry about the result of clemency in Billy's case stems from his appreciation of the crew's familiarity with and concern for naval usage, and this facet of "the people's" character now demands attention.

Returning to the scene of Vere's announcement of Billy's fate, the reader finds that the crew's uncertain "murmur" in response to the announcement is cut off by the "shrill whistles of the boatswain and his mates" and an order "to about ship." That is, the murmur is stopped by a call to duty and a return to business as usual. The crew's response to the call is automatic because "the people" are accustomed to following orders without question.[8] But it is not the case that the sailors are diabolically molded in this way by the officers. Rather, "the people" themselves *demand* adherence to accepted procedure:

> In . . . every public [proceeding] growing out of the tragedy strict adherence to usage was observed. Nor in any point could it have been at all deviated from, either with respect to Claggart or Billy Budd, without begetting undesirable speculations in the ship's company, sailors, and more particularly men-of-war's men, being of all men the greatest sticklers for usage.[9]

Later, after Billy's execution, Captain Vere is able to make use of "the people's" natural susceptibility to discipline in order to guarantee that the order of the ship is not disrupted. Following the silence attendant upon the moment of Billy's death, a strange murmur arises from the crew:

> Being inarticulate, it was dubious in significance further than it seemed to indicate some capricious revulsion of thought or feeling such as mobs ashore are liable to, in the present instance possibly implying a sullen revocation on the men's part of their involuntary echoing of Billy's benediction. But ere the murmur had time to wax into clamor it was met by a strategic command, the more telling that it came with abrupt unexpectedness: "Pipe down the starboard watch, Boatswain, and see that they go."
>
> Shrill as the shriek of the sea hawk, the silver whistles of the boatswain and his mates pierced that ominous low sound, dissipating it; and yielding to the mechanism of discipline the throng was thinned by one-half. For the remainder, most of them were set to temporary employments connected with trimming the yards and so forth, business readily to be got up to serve occasion by any officer of the deck. [P. 126]

Critics of an ironist turn usually read these lines as proof of Captain Vere's tyrannical subjection of the crew. What these critics forget, however, is that all Vere's actions are directed toward the preservation of order at a time in which his country, one of "founded law and freedom defined," is at war. Vere has already observed that the enemy will not make fine distinctions in battle and will slay "the people" of the *Bellipotent* without regard to their political beliefs. Vere's purpose, thus, is to maintain the crew as an organized fighting force for their own protection as well as for the protection of the empire. Moreover, Vere's maintenance of internal order is based upon "the people's" demonstrated need for that order. Thus, to argue that "the people" should be freed from the yoke of usage and discipline is actually to argue in favor of the ideology of the French enemy; such an argument is, according to the "Inside Narrative," as out of keeping with the true nature of "the people" as the argument that they can or should be freed from the yoke of religion was in fact shown to be. Indeed, the connection between the maintenance of internal order and the opposition to revolutionary France is based upon this view of "the people's" dependence upon usage; after Billy's burial at sea, the narrator reveals that Vere explicitly makes the connection:

An uncertain movement began among [the crew], in which some encroachment was made. It was tolerated but for a moment. For suddenly the drum beat to quarters, which familiar sound happening at least twice every day, had upon the present occasion a signal peremptoriness in it. True martial discipline long continued superinduces in average man a sort of impulse whose operation at the official word of command much resembles in its promptitude the effect of an instinct.

. . . .

All this occupied time, which in the present case was the object in beating to quarters at an hour prior to the customary one. That such variance from usage was authorized by . . . Captain Vere, a martinet as some deemed him, was evidence of the necessity for unusual action implied in what he deemed to be temporarily the mood of his men. "With mankind," he would say, "forms, measured forms, are everything; and that is the import couched in the story of Orpheus with his lyre spellbinding the wild denizens of the wood." And this he once applied to the disruption of forms going on across the Channel and the consequences thereof.[10]

Like Nelson, Vere is able to vary his procedure to suit his purposes, and he is no mere "martinet" to usage. But the crucial point to be made is that *Billy Budd* endorses the regime of "measured forms" because it is more attuned to the needs of mankind. Although it is certainly imperfect, England is chosen as the superior regime *in the present conflict*; the choice does not indicate that the "uncompromising" truth is possessed by the *politics* of the "free conservative" regime, but rather that the ultimate truth is suggested there rather than in the revolutionary regime. The English regime, and not the French, retains something of the pre-Enlightenment political understanding which Melville placed "inside" the narrator's earlier character sketches: in the English conventions, nature finds an echo.

These somewhat labyrinthine considerations concerning the varying accounts of both the events aboard H.M.S. *Bellipotent* and the nature of "the people" are not meant to detract from the artistic force of the execution scene itself. The scene is prepared for by a vision of Billy after he had been turned over to the routine preceding execution. Billy lies on the upper gun deck amid the black armaments of the *Bellipotent*. "In contrast with the funereal hue of these surroundings, the prone sailor's exterior apparel, white jumper and white duck trousers, each more or less soiled, dimly glimmered in the obscure light of the bay." Billy's white innocence is thus appropriately soiled, marking not only his real crime but also his inner disruption. Billy's face is thinning, and this hints at his suffering from the experience of Claggart:

> In fervid hearts self-contained, some brief experiences devour our human tissue as secret fire in a ship's hold consumes cotton in the bale.
>
> But now lying between the two guns, as nipped in the vice of fate, Billy's agony, mainly proceeding from a generous young heart's virgin experience of the diabolical incarnate and effective in some men—the tension of that agony was over now. It survived not the something healing in the closeted interview with Captain Vere. [Pp. 118–19]

It is this repose that the chaplain witnesses, and its relationship to the interview with Vere reminds the reader of the importance of Billy's upcoming exclamation. Billy will reveal that, although he has been made a "peacemaker" like the cannons he lies among, he has achieved a new inner peace and reconciliation.

At eight bells, "the people" are summoned to witness Billy's punishment. All the strands of the story converge on the scene:

At sea in the old time, the execution by halter of a military sailor was generally from the foreyard. In the present instance, for special reasons the mainyard was assigned. Under an arm of that yard the prisoner was presently brought up, the chaplain attending him. It was noted at the time, and remarked upon afterwards, that in this final scene the good man evinced little or nothing of the perfunctory. Brief speech indeed he had with the condemned one, but the genuine Gospel was less on his tongue than in his aspect and manner towards him. The final preparations personal to the latter being speedily brought to an end by two boatswain's mates, the consummation impended. Billy stood facing aft. At the penultimate moment, his words, his only ones, words wholly unobstructed in the utterance, were these: "God bless Captain Vere!" Syllables so unanticipated coming from one with the ignominious hemp about his neck—a conventional felon's benediction directed aft towards the quarters of honor; syllables too delivered in the clear melody of a singing bird on the point of launching from the twig—had a phenomenal effect, not unenhanced by the rare personal beauty of the young sailor, spiritualized now through late experiences so poignantly profound.[11]

Achieving a final harmony without the message of the Gospel, Billy is able to turn a "conventional felon's benediction" into a "spiritualized" blessing. Ironically, it is Billy's unimpaired exclamation that grants to Vere the divine approbation and

natural legitimacy which his own trial arguments had undermined:

> Without volition, as it were, as if indeed the ship's populace
> were but the vehicles of some vocal current electric, with
> one voice from alow and aloft came a resonant sympathetic
> echo: "God bless Captain Vere!" And yet at that instant
> Billy alone must have been in their hearts, even as in their
> eyes.[12]

The spiritual dimension of Billy's death is marked by an
appropriately ambiguous symbol of the transcendent significance of the event. Unlike the Christian Gospel's "transcendent miracles," the "miracle" at Billy's death points to an un-
specified, brooding presence of something transhistorical. It is
compared to a Christian vision as another reminder that only a
spiritual lexicon can do justice to man's spirit:

> The hull, deliberately recovering from the periodic roll to
> leeward, was just regaining an even keel when the last signal,
> a preconcerted dumb one, was given. At the same moment it
> chanced that the vapory fleece hanging low in the East was
> shot through with a soft glory as of the fleece of the Lamb of
> God seen in mystical vision, and simultaneously therewith,
> watched by the wedged mass of upturned faces, Billy as-
> cended; and, ascending, took the full rose of the dawn.[13]

The exceptionality of this final scene caps the exceptionality of the characters and events of the "Inside Narrative." It
is the spirituality of the scene which the surgeon's observations
ignore, and it is the moving tragedy of the scene against which
Vere orders his men back to duty. While the "Inside Narrative" does not share the Christian faith in Billy's spiritual
salvation, it nevertheless sees Billy as a "martyr to martial
discipline." Also, Vere's "exacting behest" does not create this
tragedy for Billy Budd, but rather confirms the tragedy inherent in the limitations of innocence and prudential wisdom.
The agony Billy suffers is due to his experience of the "incar-

nate and effective" evil of Claggart, and the agony Vere suffers
is due to his experience of the necessary tragedy of political
life. At his death, Vere reacts accordingly, neither "accepting"
nor "resisting" the tragedy, but rather recognizing it for the
unresolvable tension it creates. Vere dies at Gibraltar, the
strategic and symbolic bastion of the empire he defended to the
death, but even the exemplary character of his career could
not obscure the fact that the crime and death of Billy Budd had
revealed both the limits of politics and the limits of his most
cherished principles:

> Not long before death, while lying under the influence of
> that magical drug which, soothing the physical frame, mys-
> teriously operates on the subtler element in man, he was
> heard to murmur words inexplicable to his attendant: "Billy
> Budd, Billy Budd." That these were not the accents of re-
> morse would seem clear from what the attendant said to the
> *Bellipotent*'s senior officer of marines, who, as the most re-
> luctant to condemn of the members of the drumhead court,
> too well knew, though here he kept the knowledge to him-
> self, who Billy Budd was. [P. 129]

What was the real character of Vere's words of longing, if not
remorseful, would, but for the "Inside Narrative," have been
forever covered by the captain's passage into "holy oblivion."
The "discerning" reader knows that Vere's last words name
the young man whose crime and death revealed to him the
tragic nature of the time in which it was allotted him to act.
Perhaps such a reader will also suspect that Vere, at death
drugged and so not in perfect control of his faculties, finally
came to doubt some of those "positive convictions which he
[had] forefelt would abide in him essentially unmodified so
long as his intelligent part remained unimpaired." Or, in other
words, perhaps at his death, Vere came to suspect that nature,
not man-made "measured forms," should ultimately guide
"everything."

[164]

Notes

¹ Pp. 114–15. The fact that Vere is "old enough" to be "Billy's father" suggests that their relationship approximates the kind necessary for true tragedy. (See Aristotle *Poetics* 1453b.) Note again, also, that, for the narrator, the natural or "primeval" part of man is as uncertain as is sentiment.

² P. 131. The religion of sailors is not necessarily one of strict morality, of course. *White-Jacket* pictures the sailors' devotion to relics and their moral laxity as part and parcel of their popularized form of Christianity: White-Jacket says that the veterans of the navy "carry about their persons bits of 'Old Ironsides', as Catholics do the wood of the true cross," and that "sailors, as a class, entertain the most liberal notions concerning morality and the Decalogue; or rather, they take their own views of such matters, caring little for the theological or ethical definitions of others concerning what may be criminal, or wrong." See *White-Jacket: or, The World in a Man-of-War*, in *The Writings of Herman Melville*, ed. Harrison Hayford, Hershel Parker, and G. Thomas Tanselle, 15 vols. (Evanston and Chicago: Northwestern University Press and The Newberry Library, 1968–   ), 5:9, 38.

³ P. 120. Compare Billy's lack of any fear of death with that of Rousseau's savage man in the *Discourse on the Origin and Foundations of Inequality Among Men*, in *The First and Second Discourses*, ed. Roger D. Masters and trans. Roger D. and Judith R. Masters (New York: St. Martin's, 1964), p. 116.

⁴ P. 121. Note that Vere said that sailors "have native sense" (p. 112). The time "shortly" after Cook's is roughly the time of *Omoo*, wherein "Typee" found only two real Christians despite all the missionary work in Polynesia. See *Omoo: A Narrative of Adventures in the South Seas*, in *The Writings of Herman Melville*, ed. Harrison Hayford, Hershel Parker, and G. Thomas Tanselle, 15 vols. (Evanston and Chicago: Northwestern University Press and The Newberry Library, 1968–   ), 2:280. The reference here to the South Seas also indirectly supports the references to *Typee*

in chapter 2 of the present study, where the "Handsome Sailor" type was contrasted with Billy and related to King Mehevi of the Typees.

[5] Pp. 124–25. Compare the surgeon's sudden departure with that of Euthyphro in Plato *Euthyphro* 15e 3–4.

[6] Pp. 121–22. The superiority of the cannon over the canon is itself indicative of the fact that war is an unavoidable human evil. Note also that the narrator can speak of Billy's "essential innocence" without condemning Vere.

[7] Pp. 128–29. The war against French atheism is also a war in defense of the English monarchy. On the other side was the slogan which summarized the French revolutionaries' opposition to both theism and monarchy: "God is dead, the King must die!" See Albert Camus, *The Rebel: An Essay on Man in Revolt*, trans. Anthony Bower (New York: Random House, Vintage Books, 1956), p. 114.

[8] For a humorous account of this phenomenon as it exists even on a merchantman, see *Redburn: His First Voyage*, in *The Writings of Herman Melville*, ed. Harrison Hayford, Hershel Parker, and G. Thomas Tanselle, 15 vols. (Evanston and Chicago: Northwestern University Press and The Newberry Library, 1968–   ), 4:29. The same point is made seriously at p. 87 of *Billy Budd* and here at p. 117.

[9] P. 117. Thus, the Typees also live by unvarying procedures despite their ostensibly complete freedom. See *Typee: A Peep at Polynesian Life*, in *The Writings of Herman Melville*, ed. Harrison Hayford, Hershel Parker, and G. Thomas Tanselle, 15 vols. (Evanston and Chicago: Northwestern University Press and The Newberry Library, 1968–   ), 1:149. On discipline's effect, see also *Billy Budd*, pp. 50, 112.

[10] Pp. 127–28. What is "superinduced" onto the sailor by discipline is his automatic obedience to *direct commands*. In contrast, the Typee "people," while *no less susceptible* to "forms," obey apparently by *pure* instinct, as in following the unpublished dictates of the Taboo. (See *Typee*, pp. 221–24.)

[11] P. 123. For the ironists' interpretation of Billy's exclamation, see Joseph Schiffman, "Melville's Final Stage, Irony: A Re-

examination of *Billy Budd* Criticism," *American Literature* 22 (May 1950): 133; and Lawrance Thompson, *Melville's Quarrel with God* (Princeton: Princeton University Press, 1952), pp. 406–9. The chief obstacles to seeing irony in Billy's words are Billy's own lack of the "sinister dexterity" to deal in "double meanings" and the narrator's promise that Billy's exclamation would reveal a *lack* of bitter suffering and agony on his part. Note also that the bird imagery surrounding Billy's benediction makes the benediction the one song composed by Billy in the novel: Billy's one artistic moment serves the interests of the political regime. (See *Billy Budd*, p. 52.)

[12] P. 123. Later, Vere acts to preserve this "sympathetic echo" against the murmur which "possibly" might mean a desire to revoke it (p. 126).

[13] P. 124. For the controversy concerning the Christian significance of Billy's "ascension," see Harry Modean Campbell, "The Hanging Scene in Melville's *Billy Budd, Foretopman*," *Modern Language Notes* 66 (June 1951): 378–81, and "The Hanging Scene in Melville's *Billy Budd*: A Reply to Mr. Giovannini," *Modern Language Notes* 70 (November 1955): 497–500; G. Giovannini, "The Hanging Scene in Melville's *Billy Budd*," *Modern Language Notes* 70 (November 1955): 491–97; and Nathalia Wright, "Biblical Allusion in Melville's Prose," *American Literature* 12 (May 1940): 194n.

8

Ragged Edges

AFTER CONCLUDING THE EXECUTION SCENE, the narrator makes the observation which has been seen here as
the key to understanding the noval as "An Inside Narrative":

> The symmetry of form attainable in pure fiction cannot so
> readily be achieved in a narration essentially having less to
> do with fable than with fact. Truth uncompromisingly told
> will always have its ragged edges; hence the conclusion of
> such a narration is apt to be less finished than an architectural
> finial. [P. 128]

The narrator then goes on to relate the story of Vere's death,
to reveal the existence of the authorized journal's account of
the story, and to reproduce the sailor's ballad, "Billy in the
Darbies." In these last three chapters, the narrator thus actually
does "finish" his narrative; the chapters reveal conservative
Vere's unsettled mind, the obscurantism of mere history, and
the sailors' poetic-religious acceptance of Billy's fate. In all,
these chapters do in fact complete a picture of the unsettling
"uncompromising truth" beyond both history and revelatory

religion. This would suggest that the story's "ragged edges" or loose ends do not reveal simply that the narration is substantively "incomplete," but rather that the very substance of the narrative is such that its message is "ragged" or rough. This suggestion especially undermines the reading of the novel which holds that its final attitude is one of Christian "acceptance" because the suggestion hints that the real message of the story is not so easily acceptable.

The method of the narration was appropriately suited to the "raggedness" of its content: the interplay between the straightforward, quasi-historical narrative and the narrator's "conjectures," "bypaths," and dramatizations throws "unequal cross-lights" upon the characters and events of the story and subtly points to the author's own "inside" intentions. The result was that, as in the case of the similarly illumined painting at "The Spouter-Inn" in *Moby-Dick*, "it was only by diligent study and a series of systematic visits to it . . . that you could any way arrive at an understanding of its purpose."[1] Such an understanding, it is argued here, reveals not only that the "Inside Narrative" deliberately supports various interpretations, but also that it does so only in order to distinguish the author's own interpretation from the others, thus ultimately revealing the true picture of political reality. The *purpose* of the narrative is to reveal the truth, and such a purpose would suggest that the message of the story is as "unacceptable" to most readers as is the truth itself. That is, the narrative's "raggedness" also marks Melville's concealed but intentional effort to abrade modern political, religious, and scientific opinions.

Melville placed his story in the setting of the Wars of the French Revolution, in 1797, nearly the end of the century of the Enlightenment. The time was that of *the* political event of the modern age, an event in which the opposing parties each embodied in clearest form the contrary principles of conventional civilization and the natural rights of man. On the one side was

Burke's conception of the true rights of men, rights which are real only insofar as they are understood to be impure, that is, woven into the fabric of historically developed social convention. "Men cannot enjoy the rights of an uncivil and of a civil state together," wrote Burke. "That [man] may obtain justice, he gives up his right of determining what it is in points the most essential to him. That he may secure some liberty, he makes a surrender in trust of the whole of it."[2] On the other side, Paine challenged the authority of conventional law and defined freedom according to the pure and abstract natural rights of man, rejecting Burke's notion that rights and liberty need to be "given up" or "surrendered in trust" to others. It was before these rights that convention was to be called in judgment, and it was Paine's prayer that the various national forms of convention would give way to the universal justice of the rights of man. Paine hoped, as he wrote to George Washington, "that the Rights of Man may become as universal as your benevolence can wish, and . . . regenerate the Old [World]."[3] While England had her revolutionaries and France her loyalists, the external opposition of England and France placed these political opinions in higher relief than would be possible in any delineation of internal divisions. The stark juxtaposition of political regimes in *Billy Budd* is thus the crucial background of the events aboard H.M.S. *Bellipotent*.

Whatever may have been the result of the French and British War, the intellectual result of the French Revolution was that "invading waters of novel opinion social, political, and otherwise, . . . carried away as in a torrent no few minds in those days," and this intellectual situation still prevailed in Melville's own time, complicated too by the addition of romanticism as yet another form of "novel opinion." This suggests that the first and most obvious reason why *Billy Budd* might be abrasive to modern readers is that the narrator of the story is so clearly "old-fashioned" and politically conservative.

In a modern world in which atheism is fashionable, the narrator speaks favorably of "that lexicon which is based on Holy Writ," and to readers who are imbued with egalitarian notions, the narrator praises the existence of a "virtue aristocratic in kind" in Nelson and in Vere. In all, for the conservative and old-fashioned narrator, the French Revolution, the ideas behind it, and its aftermath represent an "unbridled and unbounded revolt" against the "constitutionally sound" regime of "founded law and freedom defined." Thus, Melville could not but expect that his use of such a narrator in a world which was in love with "novel opinion" would "little . . . commend [his] pages to many a reader" of his day.

But *Billy Budd* is more abrasive yet because beneath the narrator's Burkean conservatism there lie certain opinions of the author which are similarly opposed to modern opinion, especially also radical atheistic and egalitarian opinion. Melville placed, for instance, "inside" the narrator's description of the "Handsome Sailor" a picture of "natural regality" which asserted the natural legitimacy of human god-kings, and "inside" the description of Nelson, Melville revealed the necessity of the "priestly" and sacrificial in a political milieu which sometimes demands "plenary absolution." And whatever may be the precisely religious or theological implications of these points, the very notions of "regality" and "nobility" involved in Melville's "inside" story placed him in aristocratic opposition to the enlightened egalitarianism of both Anacharsis Cloots and of his own time. While the context of Melville's last novel is the French and British War, it should thus not be surprising that the events of the novel take place totally within one British vessel, totally on the British side. Hence, the suggestion is made that Melville intended to make the unpopular point that the strictly *political* choices to be made in modern times must be made within the horizon of the conservative British regime.

At this point, however, Melville may have been directly abrasive only to the modern liberal's political opinions. But below the author's more profound agreement with some of the narrator's "illiberal" opinions, one saw Melville's critique of both the modern conservative and the romantic alternatives to modern liberalism. Captain Vere, Burke's statesman, not only cannot contain the evil attendant upon political tragedy, but he actually contributes to political tragedy's dimensions by his merely traditionalist principles; and Billy Budd, Rousseau's natural man, is turned into a cannon-like instrument of destruction in the face of unavoidable, inherent, "natural depravity." Burkean prudence is inadequate to the task expected of it, and peaceful, natural innocence is either doomed to destruction or is forced to become, like the *Bellipotent*, tragically "capable of war." In all, thus, *Billy Budd* amounts to an abrasive critique of all of modern politics. Tragedy is endemic to modern politics because attractive romantic innocence is too fragile in a man-of-war world, because modern conservative conventionalism is too limited in vision and scope, and because natural evil is too effective in the complex civilizations of modernity.

This critique of modern politics occurred within a more general critique of the whole of modernity. The composite picture of political virtue which was formed by the "inside" description of the archetypical "Handsome Sailor" and Great Sailor also called into question modern science and its technology, as represented by steamships and ironclads, and modern philosophy, as represented by the enlightened French Assembly and the utilitarian Bentham. Moreover, "natural depravity" was given a more "auspicious" prospect in modern times by modern technology, which replaced "sword or cutlass" with "niter and sulphur" (thereby opening the office of master-at-arms to those who were not virtuously courageous) and by such modern jurisprudential philosophies as those of "Coke

and Blackstone," which obscured the spiritual insight necessary to comprehend the "elemental evil" of men like John
Claggart. Modernity itself, then, in all its political, scientific,
and philosophic dimensions, is the subject of an attack in
Billy Budd. Put bluntly, modernity induced in Melville a feeling of deep pessimism.[4]

One is entitled at this point to ask precisely what it is about
modernity that led Melville to reject and even to attack it.
More precisely, one is entitled to ask what Melville regarded as
the essential characteristic of modernity; what is its informing
theme; or what is the modern characteristic that proved to be
so destructive of political virtue and human greatness. And
here then one shall see, beneath the narrator's conservatism,
beneath the author's hierarchic and aristocratic opinions, and
beneath Melville's criticism of the whole of modern politics,
the most abrasive of all of the lessons of *Billy Budd.*

The difficulty for the reader is that, at the time of the narrative, the pure "Handsome Sailor" and Great Sailor types are
already extinct or on the road to extinction. The reader thus is
not shown the effects of modernity upon the unproblematic
instances of human and political virtue. Nevertheless, the reader does witness the physical or psychological destruction of
the Rousseauean and Burkean variants of these ancient archetypes, and therein perhaps may be seen the true nature of destructive modernity. Since the psychological destruction of
Vere is actually ancillary to the physical destruction of Billy
Budd, this would mean that the essence of modernity might
be revealed in Claggart's hatred for and subsequent attack upon
Billy Budd; and it is this hatred and this attack that is most
clearly viewed by the reader. Thus, just as Billy's fate as Rousseau's savage man exposed the errors of Rousseau, so too may
Billy's fate as a "Handsome Sailor," whom Billy was "something [like] in nature," expose the actual destruction of political virtue by the essence of modernity.

It will be recalled that Billy's similarity in nature to the true "Handsome Sailor" lay in his lack of knowledge and in his essentially prephilosophic character. This facet of Billy's nature was revealed in terms of biblical allusions to "the doctrine of man's Fall." Hence, Billy had no "trace of the wisdom of the serpent"; he had not yet been "proferred the questionable apple of knowledge"; and he was like Adam "ere the urbane Serpent wriggled himself into his company." These biblical allusions occurred within a framework which actually related a secular version of the Fall of man as a result of the "apple of knowledge," that is, a variant of Rousseau's hypothesis that man evolves from a happy, natural savage into a reflecting, reasoning, and therefore "depraved" animal.[5] Nevertheless, the biblical allusions are themselves important, for they point to the ultimate abrasive point of the novel which is being sought. Hence, it is significant that John Claggart is explicitly given the role of the proud and destructive Serpent in *Billy Budd*. Claggart's nature will "recoil upon itself" like Milton's Satan and "like the scorpion for which the Creator alone is responsible"; Claggart ascends "from his cavernous sphere" to accuse Billy of mutiny; his glance into stunned Billy's eyes is "one of serpent fascination"; and moving his corpse is "like handling a dead snake." Thus, Claggart's antipathy toward Billy Budd actually results in the reenactment of the original destruction of the unsophisticated "Handsome Sailor" by the proud purveyor of the apple of wisdom, knowledge, or science.

This satanic Claggart has one trait that distinguishes him from Melville's important earlier villains, Jackson in *Redburn* and Bland in *White-Jacket*: his intellectuality.[6] His "brow was of the sort phrenologically associated with more than average intellect"; he was "dominated by intellectuality"; and he was "intellectually capable of adequately appreciating the moral phenomenon" of Billy Budd. In fact, Claggart's perceptive intellectuality and Billy's simplicity combine to account fully for Claggart's malice towards Billy: "If askance he eyed the good looks, cheery health, and frank enjoyment of young life in Billy Budd, it was because these went along with a nature that, as Claggart magnetically felt, had in its simplicity never willed malice or experienced the reactionary bite of that serpent." Unlike the God-like Dansker, whose knowledge of good, evil, and innocence leaves him yet aloof or transcendent, Claggart's similar knowledge impels him to a "cynic disdain of innocence—to be nothing more than innocent!" Billy Budd is thus destroyed by a person who embodies an uncontrollable hatred for innocence and, by implication, an uncontrolled desire for the advance of prideful knowledge. The destruction of the politically virtuous "Handsome Sailor" by modern science, technology, and philosophy thus points ultimately to the destructiveness of prideful science or philosophy per se.

One may thus conclude that Melville saw the consequences of modernity—atheism, egalitarianism, utilitarianism, scientism, and so forth—as epiphenomena which merely made obvious the moral and political tragedy which was contained in the hubristic birth of philosophy itself. The attack on modern science and philosophy does not lead Melville back to ancient science and philosophy but leads him rather to an attack on philosophy as such. Claggart's intellectually-grounded hatred for simple Billy Budd thus symbolizes the destruction of real human heroism and virtue by the proud love of intellectuality. Moreover, it is impossible not to see Melville's own hand in the revengefulness made apparent in the narrator's exact description of Claggart's murder by Billy Budd; again:

The next instant, quick as the flame from a discharged cannon at night, [Billy's] right arm shot out, and Claggart dropped to the deck. Whether intentionally or but owing to the young athlete's superior height, *the blow had taken effect full upon the forehead, so shapely and intellectual-looking a feature in the master-at-arms*; so that the body fell over lengthwise, like a heavy plank tilted from erectness. A gasp or two, and he lay motionless. [P. 99, italics added]

Thus one witnesses not only the destruction of John Claggart —who is as pale as the Socrates of Aristophanes' *Clouds*, and who, like the Socrates of the *Symposium*, "never allows wine to get within [his] guard," and who, like the Socrates of the *Meno*, has a numbing effect on speech like a "torpedo fish"— but also another "poetic reproach," this time the reproach of the poet, Herman Melville, to philosophy, the purest source and the clearest manifestation of man's "phenomenal pride."[7]

The above should suggest why it is not adequate to describe Herman Melville, who thus reveals himself as an enemy of Socrates and Socratism, as a "romantic." While Melville certainly shared with the romantics such traits as the longing for the past, the lack of faith in progress through reason, and the advocacy of heart over mind, the past which he advocated and the "state of nature" of which he spoke were, in their hierarchical and politically constraining characteristics, the very antitheses of the Romantics' dreams.[8] More adequate for the comprehension of Melville is to locate him with Aristophanes on the side of the poets in the "old quarrel between philosophy and poetry." Or perhaps, it may be well to understand Melville as he agrees in part with his contemporary, Nietzsche, whose own rejection of modernity led him also to an attack on Socrates. Nietzsche certainly would have agreed with the marginal note of Herman Melville that reads: " 'You are undermining the laws, and are dangerous to the young,' said the judges to Socrates. They said the truth, and from this point of view were just in condemning him."[9]

What final judgment can be made of the author of *Billy Budd*? Two lines of thought suggest themselves. As a thinker or "diver" after the truth, Melville may be credited with a very perceptive critique of the modern age. Precisely because

[*177*]

this is a major intellectual achievement, it is imperative that Melville not be reduced to the status of a mere advocate of romanticism, or of modern conservatism or radicalism. As a thinker, the Melville of *Billy Budd* is far more a disinterested advocate of the truth than a partisan proponent of any modern ideological position.

Secondly, and more importantly, Melville reminds one of the older view of poetry which holds that the great poet's primary task is to teach and therefore to move men. In this older view, the poetic ability to please and delight is understood as the means by which the great poet may present his views of the true nature of good and evil, of justice and injustice, and of nobility and baseness, views upon which he would have his readers or audience direct their own lives.[10] So understood, poetry evidences a claim to knowledge of the nature of things, knowledge which is not the product of reason but of a far more comprehensive process whereby the poet claims to have been inspired by the cosmic dimensions of life. The poet thus faces the philosopher as a rival claimant to wisdom. But while the poet sees the philosopher's exclusive celebration of the power of reason as the quintessential human claim of superiority to nature and its truths, he sees his own openness to the fullness of nature as a celebration of nature itself. Thus poetry, as Aristotle tells us, is an essentially imitative activity.[11]

From this point of view, it is no wonder that Melville, as a poet, would develop a stand against the major representatives of modernity. He saw in the enlightened philosophy of his day an unabashed claim to human superiority to nature. Modern enlightened philosophy was marked by the "gaping flaw" Melville had discerned in the philosopher Emerson, namely, "the insinuation, that had he lived in those days when the world was made, he might have offered some valuable suggestions."[12] Secondly, Burke's conservatism, while opposed to enlightened politics, nevertheless also argued that man, his history and his practical reason, not nature, are the ultimate standards for right and wrong. Thus, Melville presents Burkean Vere as a reader of Montaigne, and he identifies "Montaignism" with the belief, as expressed by Hamlet, that "there is nothing either good or bad, but thinking makes it so."[13] Ironically, while Vere's education was aimed at achieving "a domestic heaven" under the disciplined Puritan rule of a Fairfax, Vere's "settled convictions" actually undermine political rule by severing rank from any ground in nature. And finally, the "return to Nature" advocated by romanticism masks the fact that the romantics' "Nature," following Rousseau, has been stripped of any fixed teleological principle, thus destroying the possibility of fixed natural *standards* for human action. Romanticism's celebration of the child*like* "baby bud," its natural man, results in an inability to distinguish the child*ish* from the manly. Where the romantics expected man's flowering toward perfectibility, Melville saw only an invitation to man's quiescent immaturity.

For Melville, the essential tragedy of modernity is that, in each of its variant forms, modernity denies nature and destroys man's opportunity for true glory. The perennial fact of human life is that nature is the source of both hostility and nobility. Nature's hostility is evidenced in the elemental and martial tempests which threaten man from without and in the intellectualized "natural depravity" which threatens him from within. Nature's nobility is witnessed in its production of natural kings and aristocrats, in whose active fronting of nature's hostility man learns, through the poets, what it means truly to be human. In effect, modern men have tried to turn their backs upon the human condition implied in nature's ambivalence: the enlightened suppose nature's hostility can be overcome, so they live lives of inglorious optimism; the romantic suppose nature is egalitarian and beneficent in the end, so they live lives of ignoble innocence; and the conservative suppose that nature cannot be trusted, so they live in support of authority without being able ultimately to defend any legitimate claim upon the ruled. In these lives lies the tragedy of the modern predicament. Modern man has lived out to its tragic end the hubris implied in the Socratic project; for Melville, modernity presents the full realization of the tragedy inherent in man's attempt to re-make his world, an attempt first celebrated in Socrates' "phe-nomenal pride" in his noetic capacities and first condemned by the biblical "doctrine of man's Fall."

Finally, thus, Melville belongs neither to the modern "left" nor to the modern "right," and neither is his artistic vision of the modern, "protoexistentialist" variety. Rather, he was a poet who imitated nature, and who advanced the "regality" of nature in opposition to modernity's advocacy of the regality of man, an advocacy ultimately derived from the birth of philoso-phy. Unlike Nietzsche, Melville did not seek to create "meas-ured forms"—he found them and defended them against philosophic destruction. He was a poetic conservative or a pes-simist because he believed that the abandonment of modernity would mean, not the achievement of perfection, but a return to an acceptance of the natural limitations of the human con-dition. He was a poetic radical because he believed that the abandonment of modernity would require man's abandonment of his deepest source of pride, that is, his rejection of the worth of western civilization's celebrated rationalism. In light of these facts, perhaps the most which can be said in incipient criticism of Melville is that *Billy Budd* seems to be the product not of philosophic wisdom, but of a poetic nature, akin to that of a prophet or a giver of oracles, which sees man's glory in heroic deeds, rather than in faith or thought.

Notes

¹ *Moby-Dick; or, The Whale*, ed. Harrison Hayford and Hershel Parker (New York: Norton, 1967), p. 20. See *H&S*, p. 11, on this point.

² Edmund Burke, *Reflections on the Revolution in France*, ed. Thomas H. D. Mahoney, (Indianapolis: Library of Liberal Arts, 1955), p. 68.

³ Thomas Paine, *The Rights of Man*, in *Complete Writings of Thomas Paine*, ed. Philip S. Foner, 2 vols. (New York: Citadel, 1945), 1:244.

⁴ For the connection between modernity and optimism, see Leo Strauss, *Socrates and Aristophanes* (New York: Basic Books, 1966), pp. 6–7. And for a study which locates Melville in modernity between "utopian optimism" and "unrelieved despair," see John B. Noone, Jr., "*Billy Budd*: Two Concepts of Nature," *American Literature* 29 (November 1957): 249–62.

⁵ Rousseau, *Discourse on the Origin and Foundations of Inequality Among Men*, in *The First and Second Discourses*, ed. Roger D. Masters and trans. Roger D. and Judith R. Masters (New York: St. Martin's, 1964), p. 110.

⁶ Compare *Redburn: His First Voyage*, and *White-Jacket: or, The World in a Man-of-War*, in *The Writings of Herman Melville*, ed. Harrison Hayford, Hershel Parker, and G. Thomas Tanselle, 15 vols. (Evanston and Chicago: Northwestern University Press and The Newberry Library, 1968–   ), 4:56–62 and 5:187–90, respectively.

⁷ Compare pp. 64, 76, 98 with Aristophanes *Clouds* 103, and Plato *Symposium* 214a and *Meno* 80a; note also *Symposium* 218a, where Alcibiades compares the "bite" of philosophy to the bite of a serpent.

⁸ For Melville's advocacy of the heart, see his letter to Nathaniel Hawthorne, 1? June 1851, in *The Letters of Herman Melville*, ed.

Merrell R. Davis and William H. Gilman (New Haven: Yale University Press, 1960), pp. 126–31. Again, on Melville's "state of nature," compare especially the description of the "Handsome Sailor" in chap. 1 of *Billy Budd* with the description of King Mehevi in *Typee: A Peep at Polynesian Life*, in *The Writings of Herman Melville*, ed. Harrison Hayford, Hershel Parker, and G. Thomas Tanselle, 15 vols. (Evanston and Chicago: Northwestern University Press and The Newberry Library, 1968–), 1:77–78, 90, 188–90; in turn, contrast these with the character of Billy Budd himself as a Rousseauean savage. (See the *Discourse on Inequality*, pp. 104–41.)

⁹ Cited in Herbert Spiegelberg, ed., *The Socratic Enigma* (Indianapolis: Library of Liberal Arts, 1964), p. 135.

¹⁰ See Allan Bloom (with Harry V. Jaffa), *Shakespeare's Politics* (New York: Basic Books, 1964), pp. 1–12; see also Howard B. White, *Copp'd Hills Towards Heaven: Shakespeare and the Classical Polity*, International Archives of the History of Ideas, no. 32 (The Hague: Martinus Nijhoff, 1970), pp. 1–24.

¹¹ Aristotle *Poetics* 1447a. On the *Poetics*, see Laurence Berns, "Aristotle's *Poetics*," in Joseph Cropsey, ed., *Ancients and Moderns* (New York: Basic Books, 1964), pp. 70–87.

¹² Letter to Evert A. Duyckinck, 3 March 1849, in *The Letters of Herman Melville*, p. 79.

¹³ Jay Leyda, *The Melville Log: A Documentary Life of Herman Melville, 1819–1891*, 2 vols. (New York: Harcourt, Brace, 1951), 1:291. See W. G. Kilbourne, Jr., "Montaigne and Captain Vere," *American Literature* 33 (January 1962): 514–17.

A Note on the Text

Twenty-two months before his death on 28 September 1891, Herman Melville wrote to a friendly critic and described his life in retirement:

> But you do not know, perhaps, that I have entered my eighth decade. After twenty years nearly, as an outdoor Custom House Officer, I have latterly come into possession of unobstructed leisure, but only just as, in the course of nature, my vigor sensibly declines. What little of it is left I husband for certain matters as yet incomplete, and which indeed may never be completed.[1]

One of those "matters as yet incomplete" in 1889 was *Billy Budd, Sailor*. Begun as a note to a short ballad Melville was writing in 1886 (the ballad which came to be "Billy in the Darbies" and the subject of the last chapter of *Billy Budd*), the story developed into a classic American short novel. Thus, Melville expanded the work into its final form during his last five years of life, a time of "unobstructed leisure" which permitted him to make one last and careful attempt to secure literary fame. He no doubt sought to insure that his last work would not follow the log book dropped overboard in *Mardi*: *that* book "met the fate of many other ponderous tomes; sinking quickly and profoundly."[2]

Melville did not submit his manuscript for publication before his death, and *Billy Budd* did not appear in public until 1924, when it was published in Volume 13 of the Standard Edition of *The Works of Herman Melville*. In effect, *Billy Budd* had a thirty-three year waiting period before it was cast upon the public waters and tested for its buoyancy, a test which, of course, it has admirably survived. While Melville, however, thus succeeded in writing a final novel which would endure and preserve his name, *Billy Budd* has been plagued by textual difficulties that have made its value as a commemorative work debatable.

The 1924 Standard Edition of the work, entitled *Billy Budd, Foretopman: What Befell Him in the Year of the Great Mutiny, Etc.*, supposedly was "so far as possible . . . printed verbatim from Melville's manuscript." Moreover, the editor of the volume, Raymond W. Weaver noted: "Here and there, . . . owing to the heavily corrected condition of many of the papers, *slight adjustments* in the interests of grammar or of style have been made in Melville's wording." Since only eleven of these "slight adjustments" were actually footnoted by Weaver, the impression was given that Weaver's editorial task was not a decisive one, consisting mostly of his working his way through Melville's many "heavily corrected" pages to eliminate "here and there" the author's abandoned "wording." For the rest, Weaver's 1924 edition presents the novel as consisting of the indicated title, a dedication, a preface, and twenty-six chapters of narrative.[3]

Weaver himself, however, went on to correct the impression left by the small number of his editorial notes. In the Introduction to his 1928 edition of the novel, Weaver said that his new text had "certain minor variations" from his 1924 text, and then he wrote:

> Such is the state of the *Billy Budd* manuscript that there can never appear a reprint that will be adequate to every ideal. In the first place (though this is not the worst difficulty) the script is in certain parts a miracle of crabbedness: misspellings in the grand manner; scraps of paragraphs cut out and pasted over disembowelled sentences; words ambiguously begun and dwindling into waves and dashes; variant readings, with no choice indicated among them. More disheartening than this even, is one floating chapter (Section IV in both this and the Constable Edition) with no numbering beyond the vague direction "To be inserted." The manuscript is evidently in a more or less tentative state as to details, and without some editing it would be in parts unintelligible. In such editing for intelligibility with the least possible departure from accuracy, I have only occasionally varied from the Constable text. In several cases, I have been persuaded to change a single word; less frequently, the order of words; and once, in Section XXV, I have shifted a paragraph.[4]

The situation caused by Weaver's two differing texts clearly called for an independent transcription of the "in parts unintelligible" *Billy Budd* manuscript, and in 1948 F. Barron Freeman ostensibly answered that call in his book, *Melville's Billy Budd*. Noting the need for "exact editing" and criticizing Weaver's first text as "markedly inaccurate" and second text as "even less accurate," Freeman promised "an effort to establish a definitive text, through the presentation of all variant readings." In Freeman's "transcription," Melville's final novel has a title, dedication, and preface substantively identical with those of Weaver's two texts, but the novel itself is divided into thirty-one chapters and differs in many particulars from Weaver's texts. Also, throughout his text, Freeman provided hundreds of footnotes indicating variant readings, and he published a separate short story, "Baby Budd, Sailor," which he had supposedly found "embedded in the manuscripts of the novel" and out of which he claimed the full novel had grown.[5]

Unfortunately, Freeman had not in fact lived up to his standard of "exact editing." In 1951, his book was withdrawn from sale after errors had been found in his transcription, and the book was reissued in 1953 with an affixed pamphlet of hundreds of *corrigenda*. The textual situation thus was, if anything, even more confused than in 1928 after Weaver published his second text. In 1962, however, Harrison Hayford and Merton M. Sealts, Jr., published a completely new study of the *Billy Budd* manuscript, in which for the first time the reader was given an exact transcription of the surviving manuscript, along with a "Reading Text" in which the editors deliberately set out to approximate Melville's final intentions in writing the story.[6]

Hayford and Sealts concluded that Weaver "had not studied the manuscript sufficiently" to produce a reliable reading text and that Freeman's execution of his intention to produce a literal transcription of the manuscript "was not satisfactory." Freeman also had apparently relied on Weaver's erroneous readings in many instances.[7] Since the Weaver and Freeman texts had been used in all subsequent collations with the *Billy Budd* manuscript, Hayford and Sealts could justly claim to have presented the first entirely independent transcription of Melville's final work since 1924.

In addition to criticism of Freeman's "literal" text on particular genetic grounds, including their rejection of "Baby Budd, Sailor" as a separate short story, Hayford and Sealts made three major substantive corrections in the "definitive" text which existed prior to their study. Freeman had mistaken Elizabeth Shaw Melville's handwriting for her husband's in three cases; according to Hayford and Sealts, Freeman thus had included as a "Preface" and as part of a chapter material which had been discarded by the author in the process of his revisions, and Freeman had given as the title of the work an earlier title erased by Melville and traced over by his wife. In addition to these three errors, Hayford and Sealts found that Melville had changed the name of Captain Vere's ship from the *Indomitable* to the *Bellipotent* in passages in a late copystage, and they therefore used the latter name throughout their Reading Text. And beyond these major corrections, they gave the closest reading of the manuscript throughout, with their genetic transcription serving as the defense for all their editorial judgments.[8] Whatever the importance of the corrections made by Hayford and Sealts in these minor cases, the fact remains that their work as a whole is indispensable for a study of *Billy Budd*, for they first established a text drawn with precision from the manuscript leaves which survived at Melville's death.

The only serious challenge to the text of Hayford and Sealts has been presented by Milton R. Stern, who published yet another edition of *Billy Budd* in 1975.[9] Stern, however, did not dispute what Hayford and Sealts had *presented* in their Reading Text as much as he questioned what they had *excluded*. According to Stern, Hayford and Sealts had followed the editorial principle of "correctness," a principle which led them to delete "loose ends" in the manuscript and to make changes in some passages, which would have given the real "flavor" of Melville, for the sake of "editorial propriety." Stern himself preferred to stay as close to the "actual Melville" as possible, and in problematic instances, he chose to present whatever Melville had written, rather than to delete.[10]

In addition to "smaller differences" between the texts of Stern and of Hayford and Sealts, the major textual differences concern the old "Preface" and a paragraph entitled "Lawyers, Experts, Clergy," both of which Hayford and Sealts had deleted from the Weaver and Freeman texts but which Stern includes in his final text.[11] Hayford and Sealts had deleted both portions of the manuscript after they discovered that it was *Mrs.* Melville who had written "Preface for Billy Budd?" and "For Billy Budd/Find proper place for insertion" on the manuscript leaves involved.

Stern argued, however, that an editor can neither absolutely trust nor absolutely dismiss Mrs. Melville's authority, and in light of the fact that the manuscript leaves involved had not been *clearly* superseded by Herman Melville, he chose to include the debated passages in his final text, placing the old "Preface" now within his Chapter 22 and making the "Lawyers, Experts, Clergy" paragraph a separate Chapter 12.[12]

It seems that Stern's arguments concerning these two "major differences" are the more persuasive editorially. In general, in a case like *Billy Budd*, the editor's duty is to present the reader, as far as is possible, with the author's final intentions in writing his manuscript. In those instances, then, where an editor is faced with an absolutely problematic question of inclusion or deletion, the better judgment would call for inclusion—deletion, after all, prevents the reader from seeing something that the author wrote and did not clearly discard. A little confusion or some repetition seems far more preferable than the substitution of an editorial judgment for an author's own words.

Nevertheless, no *critically* substantive differences between the texts of Hayford and Sealts and of Stern are evident. Indeed, Stern himself admits that the material of the old "Preface" is "echoed in . . . many ways in the story" and that the paragraph entitled "Lawyers, Experts, and Clergy" is "obviously applicable" to various other parts of the story.[13] In other words, the disputed segments may further *emphasize* elements in the rest of the manuscript, but they do not *add* substantively to it. While the scholarly dispute between Stern and Hayford and Sealts should not be belittled, this argument should not greatly concern the interpretive critic of *Billy Budd*. In *either* text, there exists a novel that one can confidently accept as Herman Melville's final prose work and with which one can confidently work. The text of Hayford and Sealts is used in this study only because Stern's is too recent to be generally used and available.

Even if, however, the textual problems in *Billy Budd* have now been adequately handled, there remain two related issues that still do greatly concern the interpretive critic of the novel. The chaotic state of the *Billy Budd* manuscript not only caused technical editorial difficulties but also has led to the notion that the novel is not a completed literary work, and the survival of the manuscript, with all its revised leaves, has led to the notion that one can discern in those revisions major alterations in Melville's intention as he wrote *Billy Budd*. If the old textual problems kept Melville's work hidden from the reader, these two notions combine to question the artistic integrity of that work now that the reader has obtained it.

In expanding his story, Melville apparently took it through three main phases, centering on Billy Budd, John Claggart, and Captain Vere, respectively. The phases developed during tidying-up stages in which he prepared fair copies of earlier leaves, discarding heavily corrected leaves and adding new ones as he went along. The surviving manuscript thus contains many revisions and was not as a whole put in fair-copy form for publication. Hayford and Sealts claimed that it is a matter of conjecture whether Melville would have entered into further revisions "had he lived to continue work on the manuscript," and they went on to conclude: "In short, the manuscript was in a heavily revised, still 'unfinished' state when he died, on September 28, 1891." Stern appears to take their conclusion for granted.[14]

Billy Budd was indeed "unfinished" in the sense that it was not finally prepared for publication; but in order to conclude that the work is not a completed work of art, one must disregard two salient facts. The first is that Melville wrote, "End of Book/April 19th 1891" on the manuscript's final leaf. He had carefully noted other dates on the surviving leaves: "Friday Nov. 16, 1888./Began" and "Revise—began/March 2d 1889." One should grant the author's deliberate notations paramount significance in determining the final state of his work. Hayford and Sealts point out that the "End" note was written in pencil, during a final series of revisions through the whole manuscript, but they go on to speculate that it is "more likely" that the other pencil corrections were made after the "End" note. They offer no defense of their conjecture.[15] In any case, it is unnecessary to argue that Melville made or would have made absolutely *no* further corrections after marking an "End" to his manuscript; the fact that the work was, in its author's eyes, substantially complete on 19 April 1891, is incontrovertible, conjecture as to the order of his late pencil revisions and "possible" later additions notwithstanding. Secondly, beyond these extra-textual notations, one who would argue that the story's internal "loose-ends" themselves indicate the substantively "incomplete" character of *Billy Budd*, must disregard the narrator's apology for his tale: "Truth uncompromisingly told will always have its ragged edges; hence the conclusion of such a narration is apt to be less finished than an architectural finial." [16] Hence, the hypotheses here have been that *Billy Budd* was completed by Melville five months before his death, that any actual or conjectural revisions after this time do not affect its essential character, and that the story's substantive "ragged edges" are artistically deliberate unless *proven* to be otherwise.

Secondly, there is the notion associated with the fact that the "history" of Melville's process of writing the story has been preserved in written record, that is, in the "Genetic Text" of the novel. Hayford and Sealts were able to show how the manuscript grew, and they could generally demonstrate "earlier" and "later" stages of inscription and composition. [17] The unfortunate effect of their demonstration is that the work can appear disjointed, and the accident of the manuscript's survival can thus threaten the novel's standing as a unified and whole work of art. Had Melville prepared the manuscript for a publisher and, as was his practice, had he then arranged for the manuscript's destruction, his future editors would have had only to face the ordinary textual problems that follow upon printers' errors, authorized and unauthorized revisions, and so on. The history of *Billy Budd*'s composition would then have been a mystery, but the work would unquestionably have been seen as a unified whole.

The point is that the presentation of the "Genetic Text" and its analysis by Hayford and Sealts is a mixed blessing. A thorough study of the manuscript was absolutely necessary to approximate Melville's intentions, and a literal transcription of the manuscript in its final state was indispensable to corroborate the editorial judgments necessitated by such an enterprise. But the resulting "inside story" of *Billy Budd*'s composition opens up a Pandora's box of conjecturing and analyzing which threatens to undermine the possibility of seeing the consistent whole which the novel emphatically is. The emphasis on the "stages and substages" in the analysis of the manuscript tends to weaken the critic's adherence to the work as an artistic unit, a unit that exists despite the questionable moments of a technically unfinished manuscript.

There is no question that Hayford and Sealts could use the details of the surviving manuscript—for example, the inks and paging schemes—to draw probable inferences as to the process of inscription of the surviving leaves. Moreover, further analysis could move from the order of inscription to the order of composition, in a still more general ordering scheme.[18] It is hazardous, however, to identify written revisions as *changes in Melville's intentions,* and it is impossible to determine from the written record whether or not Melville planned from the beginning the basic elements of those parts of the story that were written onto paper at later "stages."

As a matter of fact, Hayford and Sealts derived very few new critical perspectives from their genetic study of the manuscript. It is true that the manuscript draws the critic's attention to the details of wording, for example, by showing the alteration of *Indomitable* to *Bellipotent,* but *attention* to detail—in this case the ship's name—will also occur in a close reading of the Reading Text, independently of the fact that changes had been made. The Reading Text provided by Hayford and Sealts was their critically essential contribution, for that text was the first text that was really true to the details of Melville's final manuscript. In another particular, moreover, when the study of the story's genesis had a salutary effect, the result was accidental. Because the *Somers* affair is mentioned in the text of *Billy Budd* and because Melville's first-cousin, Guert Gansevoort, was involved in the episode, some critics have, again, read *Billy Budd* as Melville's "inside story" of the historical event. The case of the *Somers,* in which three sailors were hanged for plotting a mutiny on the American vessel in 1842, has some similarity to the events aboard H.M.S. *Bellipotent,* and that similarity led these critics to see the *Somers* affair as the hidden *subject* of *Billy Budd.* But, through their genetic study, Hayford and Sealts concluded that "the theory that Melville *began* with the *Somers* case [is] untenable. . . . That case . . . was not the primary and motivating source of *Billy Budd.*"[19] While this conclusion correctly reasserted *Billy Budd*'s standing as a work of art, rather than history, the same conclusion can and should be reached, as in the first chapter of the present study, without recourse to merely genetic "proof" of the work's status as art.

Hayford and Sealts suggested one crucial perspective on the novel in their remarks concerning the relationship between the genetic study of the manuscript and the standing of Captain Vere in the story. They claimed that in Melville's late additions and revisions of the manuscript, the tone of the story in regard to Vere was altered. In summary, they argued:

A Note on the Text

The cumulative effect—whatever the intention—of his subsequent deletions and insertions . . . was to throw into doubt not only the rightness of Vere's decision and the soundness of his mind but also the narrator's own position concerning him. As the revised sequence now stands, it is no longer as narrator but in terms of the surgeon's reflections that Melville introduces the reaction to Vere and his plan to place Billy on trial. [*H&S*, p. 34]

The revised scene in question involves the ship's surgeon's misgivings about Vere's mental state because of his intention to call a drumhead court immediately to try Billy Budd. The narrator then goes on to say, "Whether Captain Vere, as the surgeon professionally and privately surmised, was really the sudden victim of any degree of aberration, every one must determine for himself by such light as this narrative may afford" (pp. 101–2).

The claim made by Hayford and Sealts in this regard illustrates the pitfalls of the genetic study of the manuscript. The fact that the editors could observe changes in the written text served to isolate those changes from the work as a whole. When this result was coupled with the underlying premise that written textual changes, in themselves, indicate effective changes in tone or focus, the overall result was the conclusion that the changes in question threw "into doubt" important elements of the story. The narrator's suggestion, however, that one must judge the elements of the story "by such light as this narrative may afford" acts as a counterweight to the editors' conclusion; the narrator suggests, that is, that all the parts of the narrative must be judged in the light of the whole. And the editors themselves went on to hedge their own conclusions with these remarks, made precisely in the light of the work as a whole:

For one thing, there are retained, passages . . . in which the narrator's tone and comments are sympathetic to Vere. For another thing, given the near-caricature of the surgeon . . . , which emphasizes his unimaginative obtuseness—in line with Melville's usual treatment of doctors and other "men of science"—it is hardly justifiable to take his views of Vere as embodying Melville's own. And for a third thing, one obvious point of the revisions was to reemphasize the important theme . . . that to such ordinary minds as the surgeon's . . . truly "exceptional natures" . . . are in effect closed books.[20]

A Note on the Text

Whatever qualifications Hayford and Sealts admitted in this regard, the fact remains that their "perspectives for criticism" resulted in an emphasis on the "ambiguity" and "inconsistencies" of the story. This is not to suggest that "the lines of demarcation in the story" are "easy to determine" or that one must hold that "Melville's own attitude was altogether clear cut" (*H&S*, pp. 38, 39). The point is simply that the paramount critical need, once a usable text of *Billy Budd* was established, was to emphasize the artistic integrity and wholeness of the work. The work may, in the end, be "ambiguous," and in a certain sense the work itself asserts that fact explicitly, but it can only be seen as such and retain critical esteem when it is judged as an integral unit. Such "ambiguity" is the message of a particular artistic and intellectual point of view, rather than the mark of artistic incompleteness or fickleness. An unfinished manuscript is not necessarily an incomplete work of art, and the critic must *begin* with the assumption that there *may* be a deeper consistency beneath the surface raggedness first encountered. Indeed, one would have thought that the force of this critical rule of thumb would certainly not be challenged in the case of an author of Melville's stature.[21]

Notes

[1] Letter to Professor Archibald Macmechan, 5 December 1889, in *The Letters of Herman Melville*, ed. Merrell R. Davis and William H. Gilman (New Haven: Yale University Press, 1960), p. 291.

[2] *Mardi: and A Voyage Thither*, in *The Writings of Herman Melville*, ed. Harrison Hayford, Hershel Parker, and G. Thomas Tanselle, 15 vols. (Evanston and Chicago: Northwestern University Press and The Newberry Library, 1968–), 3:94.

[3] Raymond W. Weaver, ed., *Billy Budd and Other Prose Pieces*, in *The Works of Herman Melville*, 16 vols. (London: Constable, 1922–24), 13: v (italics added); Weaver's footnotes appear on pp. 3, 63, 64, 66, 93, 94, 100, 101, 109, 110, 112—five of these deal with the one problem of the name of Captain Vere's vessel; note especially *Billy Budd*'s Preface, pp. 3–4.

[4] Raymond Weaver, ed., *Shorter Novels of Herman Melville* (New York: Liveright, 1928), Introduction, p. xi.

[5] F. Barron Freeman, ed., *Melville's Billy Budd* (Cambridge, Mass.: Harvard University Press, 1948), pp. vii–ix, 129–32.

[6] Herman Melville, *Billy Budd, Sailor (An Inside Narrative)*, Reading Text and Genetic Text, Edited from the Manuscript with Introduction and Notes by Harrison Hayford and Merton M. Sealts, Jr. (Chicago: University of Chicago Press, 1962).

[7] *H&S*, pp. 15, 21, 23. Textual background may also be found in Milton R. Stern, ed., *Typee and Billy Budd* (New York: Dutton, 1958), pp. 269–74. For a perceptive review of Freeman's 1948 edition, see Quentin Anderson, "Second Trip to Byzantium," *Kenyon Review* 11 (Summer 1949): 516–20. The Hayford-Sealts edition is reviewed by William T. Stafford, "The New *Billy Budd* and the Novelistic Fallacy: An Essay-Review," *Modern Fiction Studies* 8 (Autumn 1962): 306–11.

[8] *H&S*, pp. 16–23. See also plate V, following p. 4.

⁹ Herman Melville, *Billy Budd, Sailor (An Inside Narrative)*, Edited, with an Introduction and Annotation by Milton R. Stern (Indianapolis: Bobbs-Merrill, 1975).

¹⁰ Ibid., p. 143.

¹¹ Ibid., pp. 149–60. See also pp. 161–84. Stern regards the title used by Hayford and Sealts as another "major" area of dispute, but he finally prints the same title himself, that is, *Billy Budd, Sailor (An Inside Narrative)*. See ibid., pp. 156–59.

¹² Ibid., pp. 152–56. See also ibid., pp. 62, 97–98.

¹³ Ibid., pp. 153–54, 170.

¹⁴ Compare ibid., pp. vii, 146, with *H&S*, pp. 1, 12. (On p. 33, Hayford and Sealts also indicate that the manuscript is incomplete, but they seem to hedge on this conclusion on p. 39.)

¹⁵ *H&S*, pp. 11–12. See also their "Genetic Text," pp. 281, 425, and plate VI, following p. 4. Melville's date notations were also reproduced by Weaver both in *Billy Budd and Other Prose Pieces* (pp. 1, 114) and in *Shorter Novels of Herman Melville* (pp. 227, 328), and by Freeman in *Melville's Billy Budd* (pp. 133, 281).

¹⁶ P. 128. See *H&S*, p. 200. The editors give great weight to Mrs. Melville's *undated* reference to *Billy Budd* as "unfinished" (see p. 144). Especially in light of their own corrections concerning Mrs. Melville's hand in *Billy Budd*, this kind of evidence hardly counterbalances Melville's own "End" notation.

¹⁷ *H&S*, pp. 1–12. The details of the editors' study of the manuscript's leaves, inks, and page numberings are given in the sections, "Analysis of the Manuscript" and "Table & Discussion of Foliations," pp. 223–69.

¹⁸ Ibid., pp. 223–40. Note the relevant criticism of Stern, ed., *Billy Budd, Sailor*, pp. 149–51.

¹⁹ *H&S*, pp. 29–30. The editors go on to cite alternate sources, pp. 30–33.

²⁰ *H&S*, p. 35. The editors argue that the surgeon episode resulted as part of Melville's revision process of dramatizing the story

and leaving the narrator more "noncommital," pp. 35–38. Compare, however, Stern, ed., *Billy Budd, Sailor*, pp. xxxiv–xl.

[21] The essential similarity of all the edited texts of *Billy Budd* and the consistency that I see in the novel's complex argument lead me respectfully to reject Hershel Parker's insistent complaint against "treating *Billy Budd* as a finished work of art." See Hershel Parker, "Melville," in *American Literary Scholarship: An Annual/1973*, ed. James Woodress (Durham, N.C.: Duke University Press, 1975), p. 83.

Selected Bibliography

I. PRIMARY SOURCES

A. Editions of *Billy Budd*

Weaver, Raymond W., ed. *Billy Budd and Other Prose Pieces. The Works of Herman Melville*, Vol. 13. London: Constable, 1924.

———, ed. *Shorter Novels of Herman Melville*. New York: Liveright, 1928.

Freeman, F. Barron, ed. *Melville's Billy Budd*. Cambridge, Mass.: Harvard University Press, 1948.

Melville, Herman. *Billy Budd, Sailor (An Inside Narrative)*. Reading Text and Genetic Text, Edited from the Manuscript with Introduction and Notes by Harrison Hayford and Merton M. Sealts, Jr. Chicago: University of Chicago Press, 1962.

———. *Billy Budd, Sailor (An Inside Narrative)*. Edited, with an Introduction and Annotation by Milton R. Stern. Indianapolis: Bobbs-Merrill, 1975.

B. Other Primary Sources

Melville, Herman. *The Confidence-Man: His Masquerade*. Edited by Elizabeth S. Foster. New York: Hendricks House, 1954.

———. *Israel Potter: His Fifty Years of Exile. The Works of Herman Melville*. Vol. 11. London: Constable, 1923.

———. *Journal of a Visit to Europe and the Levant, October 11, 1856–May 6, 1857, by Herman Melville*. Edited by Howard C. Horsford. Princeton: Princeton University Press, 1955.

————. *Journal of a Visit to London and the Continent by Herman Melville, 1849–50.* Edited by Eleanor Melville Metcalf. Cambridge, Mass.: Harvard University Press, 1948.

————. *The Letters of Herman Melville.* Edited by Merrell R. Davis and William H. Gilman. New Haven: Yale University Press, 1960.

————. *Mardi: and a Voyage Thither. The Writings of Herman Melville.* Edited by Harrison Hayford, Hershel Parker, and G. Thomas Tanselle. Vol. 3. Evanston and Chicago: Northwestern University Press and The Newberry Library, 1970.

————. *Moby-Dick; or, the Whale.* Edited by Harrison Hayford and Hershel Parker. New York: Norton, 1967.

————. *Omoo: A Narrative of Adventures in the South Seas. The Writings of Herman Melville.* Edited by Harrison Hayford, Hershel Parker, and G. Thomas Tanselle. Vol. 2. Evanston and Chicago: Northwestern University Press and The Newberry Library, 1968.

————. *Piazza Tales.* Edited by Egbert S. Oliver. New York: Hendricks House, 1962.

————. *Pierre: or, The Ambiguities. The Writings of Herman Melville.* Edited by Harrison Hayford, Hershel Parker, and G. Thomas Tanselle. Vol. 7. Evanston and Chicago: Northwestern University Press and The Newberry Library, 1971.

————. *Redburn: His First Voyage. The Writings of Herman Melville.* Edited by Harrison Hayford, Hershel Parker, and G. Thomas Tanselle. Vol. 4. Evanston and Chicago: Northwestern University Press and The Newberry Library, 1969.

————. *Typee: A Peep at Polynesian Life. The Writings of Herman Melville.* Edited by Harrison Hayford, Hershel Parker, and G. Thomas Tanselle. Vol. 1. Evanston and Chicago: Northwestern University Press and The Newberry Library, 1968.

————. *White-Jacket: or, The World in a Man-of-War. The Writings of Herman Melville.* Edited by Harrison Hayford, Hershel Parker, and G. Thomas Tanselle. Vol. 5. Evanston and Chicago: Northwestern University Press and The Newberry Library, 1970.

Selected Bibliography

II. SECONDARY SOURCES

Abel, Darrel. " 'Laurel Twined with Thorn': The Theme of Melville's *Timoleon.*" *The Personalist* 41 (Summer 1960): 330–40.

Adler, Joyce Sparer. "*Billy Budd* and Melville's Philosophy of War." *PMLA* 91 (March 1976): 266–78.

Anderson, Charles R. "The Genesis of *Billy Budd.*" *American Literature* 12 (November 1940): 329–46.

———. *Melville in the South Seas.* Columbia University Studies in English and Comparative Literature, no. 138. New York: Columbia University Press, 1949.

Anderson, Quentin. "Second Trip to Byzantium." *Kenyon Review* 11 (Summer 1949): 516–20.

Arendt, Hannah. *On Revolution.* New York: Viking Press, 1965.

Aristophanes. *Clouds.*

Aristotle. *Nicomachean Ethics.*

———. *Poetics.*

———. *Politics.*

Arvin, Newton. "A Note on the Background of *Billy Budd.*" *American Literature* 20 (March 1948): 51–55.

Auden, W. H. *Collected Poetry of W. H. Auden.* New York: Random House, 1945.

———. *The Enchafèd Flood: or the Romantic Iconography of the Sea.* New York: Random House, 1950.

Baird, James. *Ishmael.* Baltimore: Johns Hopkins University Press, 1956.

Barrett, Laurence. "The Differences in Melville's Poetry." *PMLA* 70 (September 1955): 606–23.

Berns, Laurence, "Aristotle's *Poetics.*" *Ancients and Moderns.* Edited by Joseph Cropsey. New York: Basic Books, 1964.

Berthoff, Warner. " 'Certain Phenomenal Men': The Example of *Billy Budd.*" *ELH* 27 (December 1960): 334–51.

———. *The Example of Melville.* Princeton: Princeton University Press, 1962.

Bickel, Alexander M. "Notes on the Constitution." *Commentary*, August 1975, pp. 53–57.

Bloom, Allan. "An Outline of *Gulliver's Travels.*" *Ancients and Moderns.* Edited by Joseph Cropsey. New York: Basic Books, 1964.

——— (with Jaffa, Harry V.). *Shakespeare's Politics.* New York: Basic Books, 1964.

Booth, Wayne C. *The Rhetoric of Fiction.* Chicago: University of Chicago Press, 1961.

Braswell, William. "Melville's *Billy Budd* as 'An Inside Narrative'." *American Literature* 29 (May 1957): 133–46.

Brodtkorb, Paul, Jr. "The Definitive *Billy Budd*: 'But aren't it all sham?'" *PMLA* 82 (December 1967): 602–12.

Brown, John Mason. "Hanged from the Yardarm." *As They Appear.* New York: McGraw-Hill, 1952.

Browne, Ray B. "*Billy Budd*: Gospel of Democracy." *Nineteenth-Century Fiction* 17 (March 1963): 321–37.

Burke, Edmund. *Reflections on the Revolution in France.* Edited by Thomas H. D. Mahoney. Indianapolis: Library of Liberal Arts, 1955.

———. *Thoughts on the Cause of the Present Discontents. The Works of the Right Honorable Edmund Burke.* Vol. 1. Boston: Little, Brown, 1865.

Campbell, Harry Modean. "The Hanging Scene in Melville's *Billy Budd, Foretopman.*" *Modern Language Notes* 66 (June 1951): 378–81.

———. "The Hanging Scene in Melville's *Billy Budd*: A Reply to Mr. Giovannini." *Modern Language Notes* 70 (November 1955: 497–500.

Camus, Albert. *The Rebel: An Essay on Man in Revolt.* Translated by Anthony Bower. New York: Random House, Vintage Books, 1956.

Canavan, Francis P., S.J. *The Political Reason of Edmund Burke.* Durham, N.C.: Duke University Press, 1960.

Carpenter, Frederic I. "Melville: The World in a Man-of-War." *University of Kansas City Review* 19 (Summer 1953): 257–64.

Casper, Leonard. "The Case against Captain Vere." *Perspective* 5 (Summer 1952): 146–52.

Chandler, Alice. "Captain Vere and the 'Tragedies of the Palace.' " *Modern Fiction Studies* 13 (Summer 1967): 259–61.

Chase, Richard. "Dissent on *Billy Budd.*" *Partisan Review* 15 (November 1948): 1212–18.

Conrad, Joseph. *The Nigger of the Narcissus: A Tale of the Forecastle.* Garden City, N.Y.: Doubleday, Page, 1922.

Donahue, Jane. "Melville's Classicism: Law and Order in His Poetry." *Papers on Language and Literature* 5 (Winter 1969): 63–72.

E——, T. T. "Melville's *Billy Budd.*" *Explicator* 2 (December 1943), Query 14.

Fogle, Richard Harter. "*Billy Budd*—Acceptance or Irony." *Tulane Studies in English* 8 (1958): 107–13.

————. "*Billy Budd*: The Order of the Fall." *Nineteenth-Century Fiction* 15 (December 1960): 189–205.

Freeman, John. *Herman Melville.* New York: Macmillan, 1926.

Gildin, Hilail, ed. *Political Philosophy: Six Essays by Leo Strauss.* Indianapolis: Bobbs-Merrill, 1975.

Giovannini, G. "The Hanging Scene in Melville's *Billy Budd.*" *Modern Language Notes* 70 (November 1955): 491–97.

Glick, Wendell. "Expediency and Absolute Morality in *Billy Budd.*" *PMLA* 68 (March 1953): 103–10.

Hawthorne, Nathaniel. "The Birthmark." *The Celestial Railroad and Other Stories.* New York: New American Library, 1963.

SELECTED BIBLIOGRAPHY

Howard, Leon. *Herman Melville: A Biography.* Berkeley: University of California Press, 1951.

Ives, C. B. "*Billy Budd* and the Articles of War." *American Literature* 34 (March 1962): 31–39.

Jaffa, Harry V. *Thomism and Aristotelianism.* Chicago: University of Chicago Press, 1952.

Kaplan, Sidney. "Explication." *Melville Society Newsletter* 13, no. 2 (Summer 1957): [3].

Kilbourne, W. G., Jr. "Montaigne and Captain Vere." *American Literature* 33 (January 1962): 514–17.

Ledbetter, Jack W. "The Trial of Billy Budd, Foretopman." *American Bar Association Journal* 58 (June 1972): 614–19.

Ledbetter, Kenneth. "The Ambiguity of *Billy Budd.*" *Texas Studies in Literature and Language* 4 (Spring 1962): 130–34.

Leyda, Jay. *The Melville Log: A Documentary Life of Herman Melville, 1819–1891.* 2 vols. New York: Harcourt, Brace, 1951.

Matthiessen, F. O. *American Renaissance: Art and Expression in the Age of Emerson and Whitman.* New York: Oxford University Press, 1941.

May, Rollo. *Power and Innocence: A Search for the Sources of Violence.* New York: Norton, 1972.

Montale, Eugenio. "An Introduction to *Billy Budd* (1942)." *Sewanee Review* 68 (Summer 1960): 419–22.

Montesquieu, Baron De. *The Spirit of the Laws.* Translated by Thomas Nugent. Hafner Library of Classics, no. 9. New York: Hafner, 1949.

Mumford, Lewis. *Herman Melville.* New York: Harcourt, Brace, 1929.

Murdoch, Iris. *The Fire and the Sun: Why Plato Banished the Artists.* Oxford: Clarendon Press, 1977.

Murry, John Middleton. "Herman Melville's Silence." *Times Literary Supplement,* no. 1173 (10 July 1924), p. 433.

Selected Bibliography

Nathanson, Leonard. "Melville's *Billy Budd*, Chapter 1." *Explicator* 22 (May 1964), Item 75.

Noone, John B., Jr. "*Billy Budd*: Two Concepts of Nature." *American Literature* 29 (November 1957): 249–62.

Paine, Thomas. *The Rights of Man. Complete Writings of Thomas Paine.* Edited by Philip S. Foner. 2 vols. New York: Citadel, 1945.

Palmer, R. R. "Herman Melville et la Révolution Française." *Annales Historiques de la Révolution Française* 26 (1954): 254–56.

Parker, Hershel. "Melville." *American Literary Scholarship: An Annual/1973.* Edited by James Woodress. Durham, N.C.: Duke University Press, 1975.

Plato, *Euthyphro.*

———. *Meno.*

———. *Phaedrus.*

———. *Republic.*

———. *Symposium.*

Plutarch. *The Lives of the Noble Grecians and Romans.* Translated by John Dryden and revised by Arthur Hugh Clough. New York: Random House, Modern Library, n.d.

Reich, Charles A. "The Tragedy of Justice in *Billy Budd*." *Yale Review* 56, New Series (Spring 1967): 368–89.

Rosenberry, Edward H. "The Problem of *Billy Budd*." *PMLA* 80 (December 1965): 489–98.

Rousseau, Jean-Jacques. *The First and Second Discourses.* Edited by Roger D. Masters. Translated by Roger D. and Judith R. Masters. New York: St. Martin's, 1964.

Sale, Arthur. "Captain Vere's Reasons." *Cambridge Journal* 5 (October 1951): 3–18.

Schiffman, Joseph. "Melville's Final Stage, Irony: A Re-examination of *Billy Budd* Criticism." *American Literature* 22 (May 1950): 128–36.

Scorza, Thomas J. "Tragedy in the State of Nature: Melville's *Typee*." *Interpretation* 8 (January 1979): forthcoming.

Sedgwick, William Ellery. *Herman Melville: The Tragedy of Mind*. Cambridge, Mass.: Harvard University Press, 1944.

Sherwood, John C. "Vere as Collingwood: A Key to *Billy Budd*." *American Literature* 35 (January 1964): 476–84.

Sidney, Sir Phillip. *An Apology for Poetry*. Edited by Forrest G. Robinson. Indianapolis: Bobbs-Merrill, 1970.

Smylie, James H. "Billy Budd: The Work of Christ in Melville." *Religion in Life: A Christian Quarterly* 33 (Spring 1964): 286–96.

Spiegelberg, Herbert, ed. *The Socratic Enigma*. Indianapolis: Library of Liberal Arts, 1964.

Stafford, William T. "The New *Billy Budd* and the Novelistic Fallacy: An Essay-Review." *Modern Fiction Studies* 8 (Autumn 1962): 306–11.

Sten, Christopher W. "Vere's Use of the 'Forms': Means and Ends in *Billy Budd*." *American Literature* 47 (March 1975): 37–51.

Stern, Milton R. *The Fine Hammered Steel of Herman Melville*. Urbana, Ill.: University of Illinois Press, 1957.

————, ed. *Typee and Billy Budd*. New York: Dutton, 1958.

Stone, Geoffrey. *Melville*. New York: Sheed & Ward, 1949.

Stout, Janis. "Melville's Use of the Book of Job." *Nineteenth-Century Fiction* 25 (June 1970): 69–83.

Strauss, Leo. *Natural Right and History*. Chicago: University of Chicago Press, 1953.

————. *Persecution and the Art of Writing*. Glencoe, Ill.: Free Press, 1952.

————. *Socrates and Aristophanes*. New York: Basic Books, 1966.

————. *Thoughts on Machiavelli*. Glencoe, Ill.: Free Press, 1958.

Swift, Jonathan. *A Full and True Account of the Battel Fought Last Friday Between the Antient and the Modern Books in St.*

Selected Bibliography

James's Library. The Prose Works of Jonathan Swift. Edited by Herbert Davis. Vol. 1. Oxford: Basil Blackwell, 1939.

Thompson, Lawrance. *Melville's Quarrel with God.* Princeton: Princeton University Press, 1952.

Tindall, William York. "The Ceremony of Innocence." *Great Moral Dilemmas in Literature, Past and Present.* Edited by R. M. MacIver. New York: Harper and Brothers, 1956.

Trimpi, Helen, P. "Conventions of Romance in *Moby-Dick.*" *Southern Review* 7, New Series (January 1971): 115–29.

Watson, E. L. Grant. "Melville's Testament of Acceptance." *New England Quarterly* 6 (June 1933): 319–27.

Weir, Charles, Jr. "Malice Reconciled: A Note on Melville's *Billy Budd.*" *University of Toronto Quarterly* 13 (April 1944): 276–85.

West, Ray B. Jr. "The Unity of 'Billy Budd'." *Hudson Review* 5 (Spring 1952): 120–27.

White, Howard B. *Copp'd Hills Towards Heaven: Shakespeare and the Classical Polity.* International Archives of the History of Ideas, no. 32. The Hague: Martinus Nijhoff, 1970.

Widmer, Kingsley. "The Perplexed Myths of Melville: *Billy Budd.*" *Novel* 2 (Fall 1968): 25–35.

Withim, Phil. "*Billy Budd*: Testament of Resistance." *Modern Language Quarterly* 20 (June 1959): 115–27.

Wright, Nathalia. "Biblical Allusion in Melville's Prose." *American Literature* 12 (May 1940): 185–99.

———. *Melville's Use of the Bible.* Durham, N.C.: Duke University Press, 1949.

Zink, Karl E. "Herman Melville and the Forms—Irony and Social Criticism in 'Billy Budd'." *Accent* 12 (Summer 1952): 131–39.

Index

Afterguardsman, 92–93, 94
An Apology for Poetry
  (Sidney), xxxv
Anderson, Charles R., 6
Aquinas, Saint Thomas,
  xxx, xxxiii
Aristophanes, xxxv, 177
Aristotle: on magnanimous man,
  51, 59; on nature, xxx
Athée, 157
Atheism, 22, 23–24, 58, 172, 176
Authorized journal: relates
  Bellipotent affair, 3–4;
  and truth, 4–10, 14

Babbalanja, 9, 12
Battel of the Books (Swift),
  xxxiii–xxxiv
Bellipotent: detached service
  of, 42, 98; sailing qualities of,
  98; significance of name, 173
Bentham, Jeremy, 47–48,
  58, 173, 176
Berthoff, Warner, 128
Bible: doctrine of the Fall in,
  27, 77–78, 151; truth of,
  78–80, 162–63; unpopularity of,
  27, 78–79, 151–52, 172
Billy Budd: ambiguity of, xxi,
  192; Christian interpretation of,
  xxi–xxii, 152–53; composition
  of, 189–92; conservative
  interpretation of, xxi–xxiii;
  conservative tone of, xxiii,
  xxvi, xxvii; critical dispute

about, xxi–xxv; definitive
  edition of, xxi, 185–87;
  historical sources of, 6, 141, 190;
  as "Inside Narrative," 3–14;
  irony in, xxiii–xxiv, 7,
  127–28, 130; nihilism of, xxi; as
  political fiction, xxiv; social
  repercussions of, xxiii;
  Stern's interpretation of,
  xxiv–xxxvi; as testament of
  acceptance, xxii–xxiii, 7, 84,
  128–29, 170; as testament of
  resistance, xxiii–xxiv; as
  unfinished work, 15 n.1,
  187–89, 194 n.16, 195 n.21;
  unity of, xxi, 189–92, 195 n.21
Black Handsome Sailor, 20–21
Blackstone, Sir William, 77,
  173–74
Britain. *See* England
Budd, Billy: as animal, 25–26; as
  barbarian, 29–35, 153;
  benediction of, 162–63; as
  child, 96–97; as Christ,
  xxii–xxiii, 28, 152–53; compared
  to "Handsome Sailor," 25–35,
  51–52; 175; conviction of, 148;
  execution of, 115, 148–63;
  and fear of death, 153; and
  gangway punishment, 73–74;
  kills Claggart, 107; magnanimity
  of, 95, 150; as noble savage,
  28–35; as peacemaker, 51–52,
  107–8; perjury of, 132; reacts to
  Claggart's accusation, 104–5;

Index

Mehevi, King, 29–30, 55

Melville, Herman: and ancients, xxxiv–xxxvi; aristocratic views of, 172; and Billy Budd, 173; and Burke, 178–79; Christian resignation of, xxi–xxiii, xxxvi, 163; conservatism of, xxi–xxiii, xxv–xxxvi, xl n.22 as cosmic; rebel, xxiii–xxiv; and critics, 10–14; defends England, 158, 160–61, 172; and Enlightenment, 31–32, 178; and intellectuality, 81, 88 n.17, 176–77; intentions of, in *Billy Budd*, 5, 14, 35, 45, 68–69, 89–90, 115–16, 130, 147, 170; and modernity, xxxii–xxxvi, 59, 108, 128–29, 173–74, 177–80; mood of, while writing *Billy Budd*, xxv, 9–10, 19, 183; and nature of "people," 160–61; and Nietzsche, 177, 180; as poet of nature, 178, 180; and poetry-philosophy dispute, xxxiv–xxxvi, 177–78; and recorded history, 6, 8–9; and revolution, 170–72; and romanticism, 177, 179; and science and technology, 173–74; and Vere, 141–42, 173, 178–79; as Whig, xxii–xxiii. Works: *Mardi*, 5, 8–9, 12, 129, 183; *Moby-Dick*, xxii, 13–14, 170; *Omoo*, 5, 11–12; *Redburn*, 5, 7–8, 13; *Typee*, 5, 10–11, 29–31, 55, 66–68; *White-Jacket*, 5, 13, 53, 54, 59–60, 175

Modernity, xxxii–xxxvi, 89–90, 174

Mohi, 9

Montaigne, Michel, 179

Murray, John, 10

Mystery of iniquity, 79, 133

Narratives: and fiction, 4–14; and truth, 4–14, 16–17 n.11

Narrator: completes narrative,

169; defends Vere, 126–27; distinguished from author, xxvii–xxix, 5–8, 36 n.1; English bias of, 43–45, 89, 171

Natural depravity, 65–67, 78–80, 81, 151

Natural regality. *See* "Handsome Sailor"

Nelson, Lord Horatio, 41, 42, 45–46; death of, 47–49; as Great Sailor, 45–46, 49, 65

Nietzsche, Friedrich, 177, 180

Noble savage, 28–31, 34–35. *See also* Rousseau, Jean-Jacques

Nore Mutiny. *See* Great Mutiny

Paine, Thomas: and *Billy Budd*, xxiv; and human nature, 79–80, 83; and Melville, 170–74; and *Rights of Man*, 31–33, 171

"People": as Calvinists, 150–51; insist upon usage, 158–61; understand Billy Budd as Christ, 152–53

Philosophes, 68, 83

Philosophy: attacked by Melville, 81, 174–80; and poetry, xxxiv–xxxv, 178–80; and right rule, 23–24

Plato, 78–79, 81, 151

Poetry: and exaltations of sentiment, xxxv, 48–49, 166–67 n.11; and philosophy, xxxiv–xxxv, 178–80

Protoexistentialism, xxxi–xxxvi, XI n.22. *See also* Nietzsche, Friedrich

Ratcliffe, Lieutenant, 102, 107

Red Whiskers, 26, 107, 108

Republic (Plato), xxxv, 81

Revolution, French, 41–44, 170–71

Romanticism, xxvi, xxix–xxxiii, 177, 179

Rousseau, Jean-Jacques: and Billy Budd, 28–35; 59, 73–74, 108–9, 175; and compassion,

[*209*]